Hotel Asset Management

Principles & Practices

Educational Institute Books

UNIFORM SYSTEM OF ACCOUNTS FOR THE LODGING INDUSTRY
Ninth Revised Edition

RESORT DEVELOPMENT AND MANAGEMENT
Second Edition
Chuck Y. Gee

PLANNING AND CONTROL FOR FOOD AND BEVERAGE OPERATIONS
Fifth Edition
Jack D. Ninemeier

TRAINING FOR THE HOSPITALITY INDUSTRY
Second Edition
Lewis C. Forrest, Jr.

UNDERSTANDING HOSPITALITY LAW
Fourth Edition
Jack P. Jefferies/Banks Brown

SUPERVISION IN THE HOSPITALITY INDUSTRY
Third Edition
Raphael R. Kavanaugh/Jack D. Ninemeier

MANAGEMENT OF FOOD AND BEVERAGE OPERATIONS
Third Edition
Jack D. Ninemeier

MANAGING FRONT OFFICE OPERATIONS
Sixth Edition
Michael L. Kasavana/Richard M. Brooks

MANAGING SERVICE IN FOOD AND BEVERAGE OPERATIONS
Second Edition
Ronald F. Cichy/Paul E. Wise

THE LODGING AND FOOD SERVICE INDUSTRY
Fifth Edition
Gerald W. Lattin

SECURITY AND LOSS PREVENTION MANAGEMENT
Second Edition
Raymond C. Ellis, Jr./David M. Stipanuk

HOSPITALITY INDUSTRY MANAGERIAL ACCOUNTING
Fifth Edition
Raymond S. Schmidgall

PURCHASING FOR HOSPITALITY OPERATIONS
William B. Virts

THE ART AND SCIENCE OF HOSPITALITY MANAGEMENT
Jerome J. Vallen/James R. Abbey

MANAGING TECHNOLOGY IN THE HOSPITALITY INDUSTRY
Fourth Edition
Michael L. Kasavana/John J. Cahill

MANAGING HOSPITALITY ENGINEERING SYSTEMS
Michael H. Redlin/David M. Stipanuk

BASIC HOTEL AND RESTAURANT ACCOUNTING
Fifth Edition
Raymond Cote

ACCOUNTING FOR HOSPITALITY MANAGERS
Fourth Edition
Raymond Cote

CONVENTION MANAGEMENT AND SERVICE
Sixth Edition
Milton T. Astroff/James R. Abbey

HOSPITALITY SALES AND MARKETING
Fourth Edition
James R. Abbey

MANAGING HOUSEKEEPING OPERATIONS
Second Edition
Margaret M. Kappa/Aleta Nitschke/Patricia B. Schappert

DIMENSIONS OF TOURISM
Joseph D. Fridgen

HOSPITALITY TODAY: AN INTRODUCTION
Fourth Edition
Rocco M. Angelo/Andrew N. Vladimir

MANAGING BAR AND BEVERAGE OPERATIONS
Lendal H. Kotschevar/Mary L. Tanke

ETHICS IN HOSPITALITY MANAGEMENT: A BOOK OF READINGS
Edited by Stephen S. J. Hall

HOSPITALITY FACILITIES MANAGEMENT AND DESIGN
Second Edition
David M. Stipanuk

MANAGING HOSPITALITY HUMAN RESOURCES
Third Edition
Robert H. Woods

FINANCIAL MANAGEMENT FOR THE HOSPITALITY INDUSTRY
William P. Andrew/Raymond S. Schmidgall

HOSPITALITY INDUSTRY FINANCIAL ACCOUNTING
Second Edition
Raymond S. Schmidgall/James W. Damitio

INTERNATIONAL HOTEL MANAGEMENT
Chuck Y. Gee

QUALITY SANITATION MANAGEMENT
Ronald F. Cichy

HOTEL INVESTMENTS: ISSUES & PERSPECTIVES
Third Edition
Edited by Lori E. Raleigh and Rachel J. Roginsky

LEADERSHIP AND MANAGEMENT IN THE HOSPITALITY INDUSTRY
Second Edition
Robert H. Woods/Judy Z. King

MARKETING IN THE HOSPITALITY INDUSTRY
Fourth Edition
Ronald A. Nykiel

CONTEMPORARY HOSPITALITY MARKETING
William Lazer/Roger Layton

UNIFORM SYSTEM OF ACCOUNTS FOR THE HEALTH, RACQUET AND SPORTSCLUB INDUSTRY

CONTEMPORARY CLUB MANAGEMENT
Edited by Joe Perdue for the Club Managers Association of America

RESORT CONDOMINIUM AND VACATION OWNERSHIP MANAGEMENT: A HOSPITALITY PERSPECTIVE
Robert A. Gentry/Pedro Mandoki/Jack Rush

ACCOUNTING FOR CLUB OPERATIONS
Raymond S. Schmidgall/James W. Damitio

TRAINING AND DEVELOPMENT FOR THE HOSPITALITY INDUSTRY
Debra F. Cannon/Catherine M. Gustafson

HOTEL ASSET MANAGEMENT: PRINCIPLES & PRACTICES
Edited by Paul Beals and Greg Denton

Hotel Asset Management

Principles & Practices

Edited by

Paul Beals, Ph.D.

Greg Denton, MAI

EDUCATIONAL INSTITUTE

American Hotel & Lodging Association

Disclaimer

This publication is designed to provide accurate and authoritative information in regard to the subject matter covered. It is sold with the understanding that the publisher is not engaged in rendering legal, accounting, or other professional service. If legal advice or other expert assistance is required, the services of a competent professional person should be sought.

—From the Declaration of Principles jointly adopted by the American Bar Association and a Committee of Publishers and Associations

The author or authors of each chapter are solely responsible for its content. All views expressed herein are solely those of the authors and do not necessarily reflect the views of the Educational Institute of the American Hotel & Lodging Association (the Institute) or the American Hotel & Lodging Association (AH&LA).

Nothing contained in this publication shall constitute a standard, an endorsement, or a recommendation of the Institute or AH&LA. The Institute and AH&LA disclaim any liability with respect to the use of any information, procedure, or product, or reliance thereon by any member of the hospitality industry.

The Educational Institute of the American Hotel & Lodging Association is a nonprofit educational foundation.

Printed in the United States of America
1 2 3 4 5 6 7 8 9 10 09 08 07 06 05 04

ISBN 0-86612-259-1

Editors: Timothy Eaton
Donald Peterson

Contents

Acknowledgements

THIS BOOK WAS MADE POSSIBLE by the enthusiasm and hard work of numerous contributors. Special thanks go to those HAMA members who took time from their duties to write so thoroughly and knowledgeably about their profession. Their passion for their work is evident in the pages that follow.

The members of the board of HAMA also deserve my gratitude for their vision and their support throughout the long process of producing this book. They demonstrated flexibility and understanding as we worked to arrive at a conception of this book satisfactory both to HAMA and the University of Denver. As my boss points out in the Introduction, this work represents industry-academe collaboration at its best.

Greg Denton, co-editor of this book and my *compagnon de route* throughout the journey, deserves special credit as the individual who made this book happen. We started out with a simple model for our work together, but that our roles blurred, merged, and reemerged is proof of how easy it was to work with Greg. Nights, weekends, and in the middle of his busy workday, Greg was always ready to pitch in, never flagging in his determination to get this book into the reader's hands.

Many other persons contributed to this book in various, often time-critical, ways (in addition, in some cases, to writing chapters). At the risk of omitting some, I will nevertheless cite: Steve Rushmore, Dick Williams, Laurence Geller, Jim Burba, Dave Johnstone, Deb Steele, Allen Toman, Lori Raleigh, Ken Geist, and Allen Ostroff.

I also want to acknowledge the cheerful assistance of three staff members at University of Denver's School of Hotel, Restaurant, and Tourism Management—Shari Zerobnick, Hermine Kallman, and Nicci Crowley. While each of the three contributed in her own way, special mention is owed to Hermine Kallman, who has never met a balky exhibit or a piece of messed-up formatting she cannot best.

Finally, and as always, thanks to my wife Audrey and son Alex for planes met, dinners missed, and weekends forgone.

Paul Beals
Denver, Colorado
November 2003

CLEARLY, THIS BOOK WOULD NOT have come to fruition without the efforts of the individual authors. However, as Paul points out above, the price paid by the authors included not only the tolls of organizing thoughts and putting them to paper, but a considerable amount of personal sacrifice as well. None of our "day jobs" gives us the flexibility to lock our doors and write, so much (if not all) of this book was written over weekends, evenings, holidays, and other times "stolen" from our personal schedules and paid for by our loved ones. To that end, I would like to acknowledge the sacrifices made by the spouses, children, and companions of the authors, and I sincerely hope that they feel the effort was worthwhile.

Thanks are in order, too, for George Glazer and his professional staff at the Educational Institute, including especially Tim Eaton, who was most patient and helpful throughout the production process.

Finally, I'd like to acknowledge Stephanie Roy, who is HAMA's most valuable resource, Paul Beals, who by his efforts has come closer than anyone in history to making me look like I have something intelligent to say, and my wife Silvana and daughter Cristina for making it all worth doing.

Greg Denton
Miami, Florida
November 2003

Introduction

Peter Rainsford, Ph.D., is a professor and the director of the School of Hotel, Restaurant, and Tourism Management in the Daniels College of Business at the University of Denver. Before assuming his current position, he was the J. Thomas Clark Professor of Entrepreneurship and Personal Enterprise in the School of Hotel Administration at Cornell University, where he taught courses in strategic management and entrepreneurship. He received his bachelor's degree from the same college and received his M.S. and Ph.D. degrees from the Graduate School at Cornell University.

Dr. Rainsford joined the Cornell faculty in 1968. During his tenure there he taught a variety of courses, including food and beverage management, food and beverage production, food science, accounting and financial management, food and beverage control, principles of management, strategic management, and entrepreneurship and small business management. In addition to his teaching responsibilities, he served for three years as the school's assistant dean. In that role, he initiated a major review of the school's curriculum and established the faculty annual review process. As assistant dean, he also had responsibility for administering the school's overseas academic programs located in San Juan, Puerto Rico; São Paulo, Brazil; Paris, France; Santo Domingo, Dominican Republic; and Mexico City, Mexico.

He has served on the editorial boards of Upstart Publishing Company and The Journal of Small Business Strategy *and held the post of National Vice President—Publications for the Small Business Institute's Directors Association. He received a Hatfield Award for the Enhancement of Undergraduate Education for the Fall 1992 semester and again for the 1998–1999 academic year. His book,* The Restaurant Planning Guide, *was published in 1992 and the second edition appeared in 1996. He is also the author of* The Restaurant Start Up Guide*—originally published in 1997, followed by the second edition published in 2001—and* The Club Operational Review.

I WAS BOTH HONORED AND PLEASED when Paul Beals and Greg Denton asked me to write this introduction because it represented the resumption of two teacher-student relationships, albeit with a twist. A number of years ago, I served as the chairperson of Paul's Ph.D. committee and, more recently, I served as a member of Greg's M.S. committee. The rewards of being a faculty member are numerous—although salary is not one of them—and I have always taken pleasure in the reflection that I learn more from my students than they learn from me. Reading this book to prepare this introduction has clearly shown me that I have been right—although in the present situation, it is former students rather than current charges who are instructing me. Greg's and Paul's efforts with this manuscript have taught me a great deal, and I trust you, too, will benefit from their hard work.

The Role of HAMA

During approximately the last fifteen years, the asset management of hotel properties has become a staple of the lodging real estate industry. The increasingly important role of hotel asset managers has coincided with the transformation of traditional hotel owner-operators into service companies and brand purveyors. As hotel companies have ceded ownership of lodging properties to real estate entities of all stripes—from public C-corps and REITs to private companies, institutional owners, overseas investors, and investment funds—the asset manager has developed an arsenal of skills to serve the needs of these sophisticated investors. Owners and investors have come to value the asset management function, relying on it to coax the maximum operating and investment performance from properties that are both management-intensive businesses and real estate holdings.

One of the significant developments in the short but vital history of hotel asset management was the creation, in 1992, of the Hospitality Asset Managers Association (HAMA). By the time the University of Denver was contemplating the first MBA in hotel asset management some five years ago, HAMA was established as *the* organization that spoke for the emerging profession. When we asked the advice and counsel of HAMA's board and its members, they were readily given. Our MBA in hospitality asset management was created as a result of HAMA's encouragement, and it continues to thrive, thanks in large part to the ongoing classroom participation of HAMA members.

The present book—the first full-scale treatment of hotel asset management ever published—is the result of the continuing partnership between the University of Denver and HAMA. Above all, this book owes its content to the energy and dedication of the individual HAMA members who have contributed their knowledge and their (often hard won) wisdom, developing with us a much needed resource to serve hotel owners, real estate professionals, hotel company executives, faculty members teaching real estate, and students. HAMA and the University of Denver are proud of the industry-academe cooperation evident in the pages of *Hotel Asset Management: Principles and Practices*, and trust that the work will serve the lodging industry while advancing the interests of the asset management profession.

The task of deciding what to put in any book is daunting, but doubly so when the work is the first treatment of a new discipline or phenomenon. We trust, however, that users of this book will find a wide range of information, not only on the specifics of the asset management function, but also on the contemporary hospitality real estate and investment scene. In the space afforded in this introduction, let me anticipate the contents of the pages that follow, indicating the significance of the contributions to the profession and the lodging industry.

Part I: Context

Paul and Greg have done an excellent job of organizing the material they received from 18 different authors into a logical treatise on the subject, presenting the contributions in three interrelated but sequential parts.

Part I of the text provides a broad overview of the context of hotel asset management. In Chapter 1, "A History of Hotel Asset Management," Paul Beals offers a historical perspective on the growth and development of—as well as the need for—asset management in the hotel industry. Paul's attempt to develop a metaphor to define asset management is particularly well conceived and prepares the reader for the rest of the chapter and the rest of the book.

Greg Denton provides a comprehensive overview of asset management as a process rather than as a single function or series of tasks in Chapter 2, "The Asset Management Process." Greg's graphic representation of the process sets the stage well for both the specific issues he introduces and for concepts that other authors discuss in subsequent chapters. His discussion of the four-step process of monitoring ongoing operations provides a preview of the complex, painstaking nature of the asset manager's role and responsibilities.

Defining a process for asset management is important. However, if it is not implemented, the process remains no more than an interesting academic exercise. In Chapter 3, "Creating the Asset Management Plan," John Boettger details the steps necessary—and the detail needed—to take Greg Denton's process and turn it into a "well crafted plan to assist the asset manager in the oversight of a lodging property." I particularly enjoyed John's discussion of what asset managers must do to evaluate a property's performance and to estimate capital expenditures.

Part I concludes with Chapter 4, "Investing in a Global Economy," by David Johnstone. I strongly believe that all business executives—and particularly hospitality industry executives—must have a global perspective. To that end, the faculty of our hospitality program here at the University of Denver has made study abroad for a minimum of one term a requirement for graduation, and our current junior class is the first cohort held to the requirement. David's experience in both Europe and the Asia-Pacific region makes him extremely well qualified to write this chapter. Not only does David contrast doing business in both of these regions with conducting business in the United States, but he also provides detailed analysis of such items as legal systems, currency risk, local business practices and conditions, tax and financial considerations, political stability, and communication.

Part II: Contracts

Part II of the book focuses on management contracts and franchising. Chapter 5, "Management Contract Terms and Trends," by Paul Beals and Greg Denton, sets the stage—and provides the background—for the rest of Part II. The authors move quickly to the heart of the matter in their opening paragraph, citing the importance of the owner-operator relationship and noting that "[i]n some respects, the relationship can be likened to a mixture of nitroglycerin—benign, with many useful applications under normal conditions, but capable of exploding if disturbed by outside forces." They go on to detail many of the new considerations that owners have developed as they have become more sophisticated and provide an excellent analysis of the current balance of power between hotel operators and owners.

While it might be easy to draft a management agreement, it is virtually worthless unless the parties agree to the terms and execute the contract. Chad Crandell, Kristie Dickinson, and Fern Kanter do a superb job describing just how to get to a signed contract in Chapter 6, "Negotiating the Hotel Management Contract." The chapter "outlines the key steps in the process of negotiating the management agreement, beginning with the selection of the operator and setting the stage for negotiations through the introduction of the owner-operator bill of rights, which establishes the desired posture of the owner with respect to the salient terms of the agreement." I found the details in the authors' bill of rights—for both parties—

especially insightful, and the section dealing with requests for proposals provides a good description of the key items that should be included.

The rubber meets the road once the management contract has been signed, and Bruce Stemerman provides advice on how to move forward in Chapter 7, "Managing the Manager: The Owner—Management Company Relationship." As Bruce points out, once a contract has been negotiated, "the goals and objectives of a hotel owner and a hotel manager are relatively well aligned from the start. Both parties want the hotel to be a commercial success." However, the relationship must still be nurtured to be effective, and the management of the relationship begins with the selection of a general manager. The section describing the characteristics of the ideal general manager provides an excellent framework for commencing the selection process.

Part II concludes with Chapter 8, "Evaluating Franchise and Chain Affiliation Programs," by John McCarthy and Lori Raleigh. As they aptly point out, "the decision to be a franchise or chain-affiliated property is one of the most critical decisions affecting the value of a hotel investment. With the cost of a typical franchise or chain affiliation program representing seven to nine percent of revenue, and given that the hotel industry in general is bringing approximately 18 to 20 cents of the average revenue dollar to the net operating income line, franchise and affiliation fees can potentially account for the equivalent of 35 to 40 percent of a hotel's bottom line." They continue not only with a discussion of what to look for in franchise agreements, but they also provide a comprehensive explanation of the alternatives. Fees, other cost considerations, and the outlook for the future are some of the additional topics they tackle.

Part III: Tools

While Part I sets the context of hotel asset management and Part II provides the background details of management contracts and franchising, this information is not sufficient to permit the asset manager to function effectively. The asset manager must do the analysis necessary to determine a multitude of relationships and facts to evaluate properly the asset's performance. Part III, *The Asset Manager's Analytical Tool Box*, provides the reader with a variety of techniques needed to conduct the necessary analysis.

The opening chapter of Part III, Chapter 9, "Benchmarking and Financial Analysis," by Michelle Russo and Tracy Cooper, provides the reader with the fundamental techniques for conducting the necessary analysis. The authors not only discuss the benchmarking of revenues, but they also provide an excellent section on the benchmarking of expenses. With respect to revenues, Michelle and Tracy make the point that the key is to determine accurately the competitive set, since the wrong competitive set may have the asset manager comparing apples with oranges. Throughout the chapter, the authors provide valuable information about where and how to obtain and interpret comparative data.

In Chapter 10, "The Hotel Investment Decision: Buy, Hold, and Sell Analyses," Craig Mason and Richard Musgrove begin with a case study that reveals some of the dilemmas facing asset managers. The authors caution the reader that "[t]he first step in making any investment decision is establishing goals and objectives for that investment." They explain the additional complications of hotel investments caused by the many factors involved with operating the business. The sections on identifying upside potential and downside risk include checklists that should be extremely helpful.

As I noted at the outset of this introduction, I had the pleasure of serving on Greg Denton's M.S. committee. For his master's thesis, Greg developed a model and a hypothetical plan for dealing with capital expenditures. That model and plan have been refined and expanded by Greg and Deno Yiankes in Chapter 11, "Planning and Managing Capital Expenditures." The authors begin with a description of capital expenditures and the asset manager's role in both near-term and long-term CapEx planning. They then use the CapEx Planning Model to demonstrate how it can and should be used as a management tool.

Dan Connolly and Rick Swig address three aspects of information technology (IT) in Chapter 12, "The Hotel Asset Manager's Guide to Information Technology." Specifically, they discuss (1) the importance of IT as a core competency for asset managers; (2) the key IT-related issues and decisions facing asset managers; and (3) the development of a structured, disciplined approach to IT decision-making, thus equipping asset managers with the key questions to ask. As the authors point out, "[u]nfortunately, IT is one of the least understood aspects of the lodging business and one of the issues that causes consternation at all levels, from ownership through property management to operations." This chapter should eliminate much of that consternation.

Chapter 13, "Quantitative Risk Analysis for Hotel Investors," by Ross Woods, concludes both Part III and the book itself. As Ross appropriately points out: "Despite the importance of risk to the success of most hotel investment decisions, it is undoubtedly one of the most difficult of the decision variables to define and quantify." The author provides a broad overview of the nature of risk and then compares the risk-return tradeoff of hotels to those of other real estate asset classes. Finally, he provides an excellent description—and a lodging industry illustration—of the Monte Carlo Simulation, a "powerful and comprehensive risk analysis technique suitable to the inherent complexity of hotel investments and the range of risk factors likely to affect an investor's return." Users of this technique will likely have a leg up on asset managers who do not employ it.

Conclusion

Over the years I have continually strived to be a better teacher to my students, and I have attempted to learn from my students and colleagues the characteristics that distinguish a good teacher from an inadequate teacher. My unscientific research has led me to the conclusion that excellent teachers are able to combine the theoretical underpinnings of their academic discipline with the practical applications. Paul Beals and Greg Denton have certainly succeeded in doing so with their efforts. As a professor, I am plagued by the ingrained habit of assigning grades to students. Thus, I feel the necessity to assign a grade to my former students, Paul and Greg. Unfortunately, the highest grade available is A+! I would sorely like to award a higher grade—they certainly deserve it.

I hope you enjoy—and learn as much—reading this book as I have.

Peter Rainsford
Denver, Colorado
November 2003

Part I

The Context of Hotel Asset Management

1

A History of Hotel Asset Management

By Paul Beals

Paul Beals, Ph.D., *is a professor at the University of Denver's School of Hotel, Restaurant, and Tourism Management, where he is responsible for the MBA in hospitality property development and asset management. Dr. Beals has served as executive editor of* The Cornell Quarterly *and as director of the Institut de Management Hôtelier International (IMHI), a joint MBA program between the Cornell Hotel School and L'Ecole Supérieure des Sciences Economiques et Commerciales (ESSEC), one of France' s most prestigious business schools.*

For more than 20 years, Dr. Beals's academic research and consulting have been concentrated in hotel industry development and financing, asset management, and management contracts. He has taught hospitality financial management and real estate finance at Cornell University, IMHI, Boston University, and Switzerland's Glion Hotel School.

Dr. Beals's writings, primarily in the area of hotel finance and investments, have appeared in The Cornell Quarterly, Journal of Real Estate Finance, Real Estate Review, Journal of Hospitality Financial Management, L'Hôtel Revue, *and* Le Monde. *A member of Phi Beta Kappa, the Cornell Hotel Society, and the Association of Hospitality Financial Management Education, Dr. Beals earned master's and doctorate degrees from Cornell University.*

IN THE CHAPTERS THAT FOLLOW, several contributors will offer definitions of asset management, some more comprehensive than others, but none complete enough to give the reader a full understanding of the asset management function. To some extent, this entire book is required by way of definition because it is very difficult to corral all of what asset management is into a few words. In the case of *hotel* asset management, the complexity of the definition reflects the evolution of the profession as well as the nature of lodging, which combines both real estate and an operating business.

This chapter begins by charting selected definitions of asset management over the last two decades, using these definitions to sketch a rudimentary history of asset management, with emphasis on hotel asset management. Expanding on this historical groundwork, a full-scale definition of hotel asset management is offered, followed by a discussion of the factors contributing to the emergence of the profession. The role of the Hospitality Asset Managers Association (HAMA) and its contribution to the evolution of the profession will also be treated. These four intertwined strands will, it is hoped, provide the reader with a comprehensive introduction to hotel asset management, including not only its *raison d'être* but also its multifarious parts.

Parsing Two Simple Words: What Is Asset Management?

The first definition of asset management, both for hotels and other real estate asset classes, was the simplest and most literal interpretation of the term. Asset management meant (1) oversight of the day-to-day management of the real estate property and (2) responsibility for husbanding and preserving the physical asset. Thus, one early (1990) discussion of the role of asset managers for office buildings published in the *Journal of Property Management* emphasizes that asset managers must "effectively monitor the performance of property managers by establishing guidelines and reporting requirements for operational, financial, and marketing/leasing aspects of property management."[1] Although the writer is emphasizing that more intense oversight of business aspects of property management represents an expanded role for the asset managers, she concludes by reminding asset managers of their hands-on responsibility to monitor all aspects of the asset's physical plant, from the condition of bathroom tiling and fixtures and exterior landscaping to checks of elevators, life-safety systems, and structural integrity.[2]

The late Stephen Brener, who appears to hold the distinction of having introduced the term asset management to the lodging industry in a 1987 article,[3] described hotel asset management in a 1991 article in similar terms, observing: "The goal of asset managers is to make recommendations about the operating performance, physical plant, market position, and management [of a hotel]."[4]

The Strategic Element

As the real estate industry practiced asset management in the fashion suggested in the preceding paragraphs, another definition of asset management was lurking. Although it is impossible to know what the real estate industry had in mind when it settled on the term asset management to describe a still amorphous activity, it is reasonable to speculate that the term was borrowed, consciously or subliminally, from the financial services industry.

In the financial services industry, asset management is the process of managing investments for clients. Asset managers in the financial services industry are fiduciaries who listen to investors, contributing to and refining their clients' financial objectives. They make allocations among different types of investments according to their clients' risk tolerance, investment horizon, and tax situation. Competent asset managers "read" investment cycles, surveying the broader marketplace to find performing investments that contribute to the client's long-term financial goals, while disposing of those declining, or likely to decline, in productivity. Asset managers of this stripe are responsible for decisions of a strategic nature; they may read analysts' reports that explain the operating fundamentals of their clients' investments, but they do not have the skills to oversee the repair or replacement of the moving parts when a business breaks down.

The real estate asset management profession began with an orientation toward managing the asset, both in terms of overseeing the execution of the rental activity occupying the property and in terms of preserving the physical plant. This set of fundamental activities continues as the mainstay of the profession, although the addition of a strategic role for the asset manager undoubtedly fostered the expansion and increasing acceptance of the profession. Hotel asset managers—like asset managers for other classes of real estate—enjoyed greater credibility as a result of the addition of a strategic role, but the role does not seem to have originated in the hotel industry.

In the same issue of the *Journal of Property Management* that contains the more limited definition of asset management cited above, another asset manager for offices and retail observes that "[t]he increase in pension fund and institutional ownership has given rise to a new segment of the real estate industry—the asset manager." The author, then a vice president at Equitable Real Estate, elaborates on the function of the asset manager, describing a role that goes far beyond property oversight, as follows:

> A successful asset manager is a catalyst for change. He or she makes positive things happen, creating value and solving problems.
>
> Today's asset manager will have a thorough understanding of the owner's objectives and of the property and its market.
>
> The best asset managers can perceive, express, and balance owners' and tenants' views.
>
> Nor should the asset manager's knowledge stop with the property and its immediate market. To successfully guide the financial future of a building, the asset manager must have an understanding of world issues and of technical innovation. [5]

Less than a year later, again in the pages of the *Journal of Property Management*, a similar description of asset management is offered by another real estate generalist, who also alludes to the emergence of institutional owners as a force in the development of asset management:

> As property managers became separate entities from property owners, and as managers' duties became more general, the need arose for an intermediary professional—one who would serve as the owner's coordinator of activities beyond property management, including financing, construction, and disposition. Thus the asset manager was born.[6]

The same evolution in the definition of asset management to an oversight *and* strategic function appears to have occurred more slowly for lodging than it did for other real estate property types.[7] For example, the first definition of the bipartite asset management practiced in the lodging industry did not appear until 1994. Writing in *Lodging Hospitality*, Stephen Rushmore captured succinctly the essence of asset management as it had evolved in the lodging industry:

> In general terms, hotel asset management is the service of assisting hotel owners in realizing their investment goals. Asset managers act as an

> owner's agent or representative to insure that a hotel is acquired for a reasonable price; is then operated properly during the period of ownership; and ultimately is disposed of at an appropriate time and price.[8]

As is pointed out in Chapters 2 and 3, the asset manager is involved not merely in operational oversight but also in strategic-level investment decisions affecting the asset throughout its lifecycle. As best as this researcher can establish, Rushmore was the first to describe the hotel asset management function with the thoroughness of the definition above, and the first to include explicit mention of the asset manager's role as a strategist and investment manager.

Asset Management: A Metaphor

As indicated at the outset of the chapter, it is difficult to define hotel asset management fully in a few words. There have been several succinct definitions of hotel asset management[9] since Rushmore promulgated the apparently seminal definition of hotel asset management quoted above, but this writer has found no attempt to describe asset management metaphorically. In the hope that a metaphor can provide the "picture worth a thousand words"—and orient the reader to the twelve chapters to come—the following definition of hotel asset management is offered.

The hotel asset manager is simultaneously the chief engineer and the navigator of a ship that must arrive at its destination with the greatest economy of resources yet at the highest speed possible. In the role of chief engineer, the hotel asset manager must possess the requisite technical and interpersonal skills to descend to the bowels of the ship and coach the engine-room crew, working harmoniously to coax the maximum speed from the diesels while consuming as little fuel as possible. Back on the bridge, the hotel asset manager confers constantly with the master of the ship, confirming the captain's intended landfall, continually evaluating and communicating an estimate of the horsepower that can be winkled out of the engine room, and charting for the captain a course that exploits the swiftest current, picking up speed by riding the cusp of rough seas where necessary but always conserving enough fuel to bring the ship to an alternative port of call.

For this writer, the single most distinctive aspect of the profession is that effective asset managers must be *both* robust, engaging personalities down in the engine room and flinty, steely-eyed strategists as they work side-by-side with the ship's captain. There are individuals (and firms) that hold themselves out as asset managers but whose talents extend only to the role of *gaillard* exhorting the boys in the engine room. Hotel asset managers of this ilk may provide some value added as a redundant system to the property's general manager and executive committee, but they are not truly asset managers. Navigators who read the financial waters competently have value as portfolio managers, but unless they know their way around the engine room and rightfully enjoy the respect of its denizens, they cannot aspire to the role of asset manager. Only individuals able to perform the chief engineer's role, protecting the ship's integrity and extracting the maximum from its economic engine, and the navigator's strategic role, reading the financial waters and charting the most risk-efficient course to the ship's destination, prove effective hotel asset managers.

Functions of the Asset Manager

While metaphors are an effective means to encapsulate a profession, it is also useful to deconstruct the hotel asset manager's job, displaying the parts making up the whole. Presented in Exhibit 1 is a table derived from Greg Denton's work on hotel asset management.[10] Denton described the work of hotel asset managers by enumerating their tasks in a somewhat different order from the presentation in Exhibit 1, where the left-hand panel, "Oversight of Operations and the Physical Asset," contains the asset manager's responsibilities in the role of the ship's chief engineer, and the right-hand panel, "Managing the Investment," displays the responsibilities of the asset manager in the role of navigator. Note further that the responsibilities in the right-hand panel are ordered to emphasize the asset manager's more strategic role as the fiduciary of ownership who verifies the investor's objectives and measures the performance of the owner's lodging properties against these objectives, as well as serving as the investor's interpreter of the property market and the market for financing.

Finally, note that choosing and monitoring the management company and brand affiliation, as well as approving and monitoring capital expenditures, are listed as strategic activities. Although these activities—especially, for example, the administration of contracts—may seem quotidian tasks more appropriately categorized as part of the asset manager's oversight role, they are in fact decisions and activities of significant importance in determining the hotel's value and therefore the achievement of the investor's objectives. For example, the decision to embark on the renovation of a property is ostensibly one that falls under the role of oversight of the physical asset. From the asset manager's perspective, however, it is above all a strategic decision—an investment that, like the initial acquisition of the property, must add value, earning returns that exceed the investor's cost of capital.

Factors Contributing to the Emergence of Asset Management

Although the first mention of hotel asset management appeared in 1987, the function existed more than a decade before Brener's sighting. As Lori Raleigh has pointed out, the tax-driven limited partnerships of the 1970s employed asset managers, who in some cases were general partners charged with making all of the partnership's important investment decisions to preserve the limited partners' status as passive investors.[11] In other cases, the asset manager's role was more akin to that of an auditor and analyst.[12] For example, Matthews opens his discussion of the expanded role of asset managers cited earlier with a disclaimer, reassuring the reader that "today's asset manager is the antithesis of [the] unflattering image [of] blue suits, computer printouts, financial reports, and offices far removed from the daily operation of real estate."[13]

Although asset managers practicing at various levels existed before the 1980s, it is not surprising that, in the minds of most real estate veterans, the function originated in the 1980s and 1990s. Indeed, the wider emergence of asset management can be attributed to a number of factors, some common to all real estate asset classes, others specific to hotels.

Exhibit 1 The Hotel Asset Manager's Roles and Responsibilities

Role: Oversight of Operations and the Physical Asset

Monitor ongoing financial performance:

- Review actual performance compared to budget and prior years.
- Compare performance to comparable properties.

Monitor the competitive market:

- Track occupancy and average rate trends.
- Track new properties being considered for development.
- Monitor demand generators for significant increases/decreases.

Monitor the asset:

- Evaluate physical condition and anticipated capital requirements.
- Evaluate major systems (HVAC, phone, PMS, etc.) for appropriateness and competitiveness.
- Ensure legal compliance (health codes, life-safety, access for disabled).

Support and review the budgeting processes:

- Benchmark operations against comparable properties.
- Communicate ownership expectations to property management.
- Review proposed budgets, marketing plans, and operating plans for compliance with ownership's expectations.
- Facilitate approval of budgets, marketing plans, and operating plans by ownership.

Advise ownership as to management issues:

- Evaluate operator strengths and weaknesses.
- Review industry trends that may affect the property.

Role: Managing the Investment

Advise ownership as to optimum investment strategies:

- Perform annual strategic review, comparing properties' expected performance to ownership's investment objectives.
- Determine market value of properties and project future increments in market value from holding, renovating, expansion, or other strategic alternatives.

Monitor the investment community:

- Track sales prices for comparable properties.
- Track capitalization rates for hotel purchases.
- Remain apprised of financing terms available.

Select and oversee operators, franchise affiliations, and consultants:

- Determine appropriate franchise affiliation for property.
- Determine appropriate management for property.
- Retain appraisers, environmental consultants, engineering consultants as appropriate.

Negotiate and administer contracts:

- Ensure franchise services are provided and billed properly.
- Ensure management contract compliance.
- Negotiate outside contracts (vendors, retail leases, service contracts) for optimal returns to ownership.

Approve/monitor capital expenditures:

- Create long-term capital expenditure plan.
- Review annual budget proposals for consistency with capital plan.
- Evaluate impact on profitability/value from discretionary expenditures.
- Approve capital budgets for presentation to ownership.
- Review spending requests for compliance with capital budget.

Source: Gregory A. Denton, *Hotel Asset Management at a Crossroads: Identifying Challenges and Developing New Methodologies to Improve the Effectiveness of Hotel Asset Managers.*

Increasing Investor Sophistication

As Raleigh has noted, the late 1980s and early 1990s saw the emergence of a more sophisticated and more demanding real estate investor.[14] A summary of the 1990 asset management symposium of the Institute of Real Estate Management (IREM) notes that "performance measures have increased in importance for several reasons" and identifies the following factors as pushing investors to demand greater accountability:

1. Significant growth in institutional investment in real estate, including closed-end funds
2. An increase in the number of designated pools investing in specific types of real estate assets
3. A corresponding increase in institutions' interest in understanding the economics and operating characteristics of the properties they invest in
4. Increasing concentration of real estate investments in the hands of a limited number of registered investment advisors and pension funds[15]

The mentality of the sophisticated real estate investor that was ineluctably replacing the individual owner-operator is summed up by the remarks of William Ramseyer of JMB Realty, at the time a significant investor in hotel real estate: "We no longer have the luxury of selling blind pools on good faith and management.... We have to express to institutional investors the essence of properties and portfolios, a big change in the business."[16]

The hotel asset management function took root at institutional investors with significant portfolios of lodging real estate in the late 1980s and early 1990s. At Prudential Insurance, for example, Allen Ostroff led a team of asset managers overseeing more than $3 billion of hotel assets. At Equitable Real Estate, Thomas Engel headed a separate hospitality asset management group that oversaw Equitable's in-house lodging investments and also contracted to provide third-party services to investor-clients holding hotel assets. Starting in 1989, Geller and Associates expanded a small practice in asset management services to individual hotels into a portfolio approach, earning fees as a percentage of the value enhancement or taking equity stakes in client hotels, ultimately parlaying the value created into today's Strategic Hotel Capital.[17]

Owner-Operator Misalignment

As the ownership of lodging real estate became more and more concentrated in the hands of institutional owners, real estate investment trusts (REITs), and investment pools, these entities' need for property-management expertise fostered the growth of hotel operating companies. For a significant period of time, however, hotel owners paid dearly for the expertise of the operating companies they helped create. As noted elsewhere in this book (see especially Chapter 5), hotel management contracts heavily favored the operator, often leaving the hotel investor with no return on investment and no exit from long-term contracts.

To enhance their franchise with consumers, hotel property companies were driven to expand the number of rooms they operated. The fee structure of management contracts in the 1980s and early 1990s provided substantial earnings from base fees and left little incentive for operators to drive the profitability of the assets they managed for owners. In fact, operators' incentive was to *over*spend, to create ever more lavish hotels offering more services and amenities, thus ensuring the brand's continuing acceptance in the consumer marketplace. Owners of course financed the operators' brand-building binge—only to be told, if they questioned the cost of the improved product, that their management contract did not permit them to question budgets or brand standards.

As is noted in the sidebar about HAMA, the principal impetus behind the creation of the organization was the founding members' frustration with management companies and the hegemony they enjoyed through contracts that heavily favored the operator. "We wanted to create an association that would be a voice for ownership," reports David Johnstone, HAMA's first president. "It was time to turn the tide, to gain some say over the operators and the brands instead of their telling us how to spend our money."[18]

The Lodging Industry Shakeout

In the late 1980s and the early 1990s, the U.S. lodging industry struggled through the worst period of its history since the Great Depression. As the excessive tax-driven overbuilding of the early 1980s collided with a declining economy and the travel slowdown resulting from the Gulf War, equity investors, lenders, and the Resolution Trust Corporation turned to workout specialists to regain some fraction of the value they had lost. This "disaster control" activity was arguably the single most important factor in increasing the prominence of the hotel asset management function.

Like all stereotypes, the image of the asset manager as a "troubleshooter" contained some risks because it suggested that the asset manager could safely be retired when the lodging industry returned to prosperity. As Denton points out, the earliest literature of asset management typically described the work of the asset manager during the lodging industry shakeout and emphasized the role of the asset manager as workout specialist.[19] The perception of the asset manager as an emergency worker only was probably an inevitable result of the times and asset managers' day-to-day duties as they attempted to salvage value from distressed properties. It was also inevitable that the perception would linger for a certain period, but today real estate professionals and lodging industry executives understand better the role of the asset manager. Above all, thoughtful observers understand that asset managers are equal parts overseers of lodging properties and long-term strategists charged with maximizing value for the investors they serve. The effort to position the asset manager correctly among the players working toward the achievement of the owner's investment objectives must continue, however. Certainly one of the most important objectives of the present book is to communicate accurately and fully the hotel asset manager's duties and to enunciate the multiple ways that the profession adds value.

HAMA and the Asset Management Profession

The Hospitality Asset Managers Association, or HAMA as it is more often known, had its origins in a hotel room at Los Angeles International Airport. Six men assembled there to devise a means to address their frustration with their lack of influence over the management companies operating their hotels. The meeting was the brainchild of David Johnstone, then an asset manager with a significant third-party practice as well as in-house responsibilities at Denver-based Sage Hospitality Resources. Johnstone had concluded that, by combining their forces, he and other asset managers could share information and work in consort to present a united front to both operators and brands.

Although the participants' recollections are conflicting, it seems certain that the formative meeting occurred in late 1991. In addition to Johnstone, the participants were Kenneth J. Geist, then with Metric Realty, Robert Kline of the Yarmouth Group, Gary M. Driggers of USAA Insurance, C. Barry Robinson, then with Prudential Insurance, and Anthony C. Dimond, an independent third-party asset manager. In effect, the small contingent agreed to form what would today be called a support group. The intended purpose of the group, which would eventually be formally organized as an association, was above all to counter the strength of the large operators, but other activities also became logical extensions of the original purpose. HAMA grew quickly into a networking and information exchange role, whereby members traded recommendations on resources that all members used regularly, from engineers and project managers through designers and consultants to attorneys. Eventually, some members used their contacts within the group when they sought to purchase or dispose of assets, but this remains an informal function of HAMA.

Johnstone returned to Denver, where he saw to the formation of the association, registering it in Colorado. The initial association members included the original group of six, plus an additional nine asset managers, bringing the total of charter members to 15. Johnstone was elected the association's first president. He served as president for two years, notwithstanding the one-year term limit specified by the association's by-laws, because the group was relatively small and members were very much occupied with their day-to-day professional activities as the U.S. lodging market emerged from the debacle of the early 1990s.

Broadening HAMA's Base

In late 1994 or early1995, Johnstone turned the reins of the organization over to Lori Raleigh of the Travers Group. The HAMA membership remained small in numbers, and the constant employment changes among members that accompanied the rebound in the lodging industry occurring in the mid-1990s made it difficult to accomplish the organization's objectives. Raleigh reports that a decision was taken to become more systematic in recruiting members. A core group of board members met and assembled a list of the types of hotel-investment entities they concluded were critical to HAMA's continued viability. To broaden HAMA's membership, the

(continued)

group resolved to invite asset managers to join the association from real estate investment trusts, large institutions, opportunity funds, private real estate companies, and overseas investment entities. This effort was successful, allowing HAMA to broaden its membership base, gain greater credibility within the lodging industry, and grow into a viable organization by the late 1990s.

HAMA Today

The purpose of HAMA, according to by-laws revised in 1995, is quite simple: "The Association is founded as an association of professional individuals who are fiduciaries dedicated to the enhancement of hotel asset values." The requirements for membership are similarly spare: members must be practicing asset managers, pay their dues, and attend a minimum of three membership meetings in three years.

Currently, HAMA's efforts are focused on four fundamental activities: improving the practice of asset management through the education of its members; communicating to the hotel industry the concerns of ownership; serving as a networking opportunity for its members; and promoting ethical standards of conduct and mutual respect among members and the hospitality industry. The principal vehicle for fulfilling these objectives is HAMA's semiannual forums—highly efficient meetings that last one and a half days and feature numerous educational sessions on various asset management topics and industry trends. The meetings are held at locations across the U.S.; participation is not limited to HAMA members, but in fact includes invited guests as both speakers and attendees.

HAMA's Members and Their Companies

Today, HAMA's membership numbers approximately 90 practicing asset managers from a wide variety of contexts. HAMA's current members are employed at the largest and most well-known public and private hotel ownership groups, including Host Marriott, CNL Hospitality, Cornerstone Real Estate Advisers, Strategic Hotel Capital, FelCor Lodging, and Interstate Hotels and Resorts. Members oversee properties representing every major domestic and international brand in the lodging industry. Several companies employing HAMA's members hold the distinction of being the largest owners of several major lodging industry brands, including Marriott full- and select-service brands, Renaissance, Hilton full- and select-service brands, and Ritz-Carlton.

The companies represented among HAMA's members own approximately 375,000 guestrooms worldwide. Approximately 65 percent of these rooms are in the upper-upscale or luxury tier as defined by Smith Travel Research, while the remainder are in the upscale or mid-priced segment.

The Changing Character of Lodging

The rapid proliferation of lodging products provided a final spur to the development of the hotel asset management function. The increased complexity of the lodging industry's structure, with its gamut of products ranging from budget through mid-scale to boutique and luxury properties, requires a perspective that hotel asset managers, unlike traditional operators, can and do provide. As one asset manager with multiple lodging property types in his portfolio noted, "My job is to move the chess pieces around, to put the right product in the right place at the right time so that my side [ownership] wins."

Conclusion

Although the asset management function has gained wider acceptance in the lodging industry, there remain detractors—often, but not universally, hotel operators—who maintain that asset managers are unnecessary. Too often, this opinion results from the speaker's ignorance of the full role of asset managers and their importance in today's investment environment. As demonstrated in the preceding pages, the growing need for asset managers resulted from the greater sophistication of the real estate industry and an increasing emphasis on achieving superior investment returns. As the real estate sector was transformed from an entrepreneurial industry dominated by individual owner-operators into centralized, professionally managed entities pooling the funds of investors large and small, the emergence of a fiduciary role like the asset manager's was inevitable.

The author wishes to thank Professor Allen Toman of the Ecole Hôtelière de Lausanne and Greg Denton for sharing bibliographies that reduced considerably the research effort necessary to prepare this chapter.

Endnotes

1. M. K. Brooks-Liberator, "Analyzing Property Management Performance," *Journal of Property Management*, Vol. 55, No. 4 (1990): 38–42.
2. Brooks-Liberator, p.42.
3. Stephen W. Brener, "Asset Management: An Overview," *Lodging Hospitality*, Vol. 43, No. 4 (1987): 28.
4. Stephen W. Brener, "Fielding Distress Calls," *Lodging Hospitality*, Vol. 47, No. 4 (1991): 21.
5. C. Matthews, "The Asset Manager: More than a Bureaucrat," *Journal of Property Management*, Vol. 55, No. 4 (1990): 8–10.
6. W. Norwell, "The Real Estate Decision Process," *Journal of Property Management*, Vol. 56, No. 2 (1991): 58.
7. In both his 1987 (fn. 3) and his 1991 (fn. 4) articles, Brener confines his definitions of asset management to the operational aspect of the function. However, in a 1993 article titled "It's Time for Definitions," Brener describes the role of the asset manager: "Asset managers are critical to the hospitality industry. They review operating results and work with owners during preparation of the annual business and marketing plans. They are also involved in various approval processes and preparation of short- and long-term capital improvement plans. Most asset managers advise on the correct time to sell and help owners and lenders during a workout." Although Brener did not articulate the role of the asset manager as fully as Rushmore did a year later, it is clear he construed several strategic activities (capital improvement, disposition, refinancing) as lying in the purview of the asset manager. See Stephen W. Brener, "It's Time for Definitions," *Lodging Hospitality*, Vol. 49, No. 10 (1993): 16. In a 1991 article, Rushmore also confines his definition of asset management to the operational aspect of profession. See Stephen Rushmore, "No Time for Passivity," *Lodging Hospitality*, Vol. 47, No. 10 (1991): 28.
8. Stephen Rushmore, "Who Needs an Asset Manager?" *Lodging Hospitality*, Vol. 50, No. 1 (1994): 20.

9. See, for example, Greg Denton's excellent definition at the opening of Chapter 2 of this text. David Johnstone and Jeffrey Duni offered one of the earliest: "Asset management for hotels is the fiduciary responsibility of managing a hotel investment to accomplish stated financial objectives on behalf of ownership." See David T. Johnstone and Jeffrey A. Duni, "Asset Management Issues" in *Hotel Investments: Issues and Perspectives*, edited by Lori E. Raleigh and Rachel J. Roginsky (East Lansing, Mich.: The Educational Institute of the American Hotel & Motel Association, 1995), p. 109.

   Lori Raleigh and John McCarthy offer a similar definition: "Asset management is the managing of a hotel investment from the investor or ownership perspective." See Lori E. Raleigh and John McCarthy, "Managing the Investment: An Introduction to Hospitality Asset Management" in *Hotel Investments: Issues and Perspectives*, 3rd ed., edited by Lori E. Raleigh and Rachel J. Roginsky (Lansing, Mich: The Educational Institute of the American Hotel & Lodging Association, 2003), p. 52.

10. Gregory A. Denton, *Hotel Asset Management at a Crossroads: Identifying Challenges and Developing New Methodologies to Improve the Effectiveness of Hotel Asset Managers.* Unpublished master's thesis (Ithaca, N.Y.: Cornell University, 1999), pp. 20–21.

11. Lori E. Raleigh, "Asset Management," in *Hotel Investments: Issues and Perspectives*, edited by Lori E. Raleigh and Rachel J. Roginsky (East Lansing, Mich.: Educational Institute of the American Hotel & Motel Association, 1995), p. 93.

12. Paul Beals, "Hotel Asset Management: A Valued Function with a Problematic Future," *Real Estate Review*, Vol. 25, No. 4 (1996): 42–47. Some of the explanations for the emergence of the asset management function are drawn from this earlier article.

13. Matthews, p. 8.

14. Raleigh, pp. 93–94.

15. N. Pekala, "Short-Term Measures, Long-Term Markets: A Summary from the 1990 IREM Asset Management Symposium, *Journal of Property Management*, Vol. 55, No. 4 (1990): 26.

16. Pekala, p. 26.

17. Personal communication with Laurence Geller, CEO of Strategic Hotel Capital, 15 November 2003.

18. Personal communication with David Johnstone, Senior Vice President, Miller Global Properties, 12 November 2003.

19. Denton, pp. 24–25.

2

The Asset Management Process

By Greg Denton

Greg Denton, MAI, is Vice President of Finance and Asset Management for The Gencom Group, with responsibilities for asset management and financial and acquisition analysis for various hospitality-related investments of The Gencom Group and its affiliates. Gencom is a private developer and owner of hotels and luxury resorts throughout the United States, Canada, and Mexico. Gencom's owned and asset-managed portfolio currently includes properties operated under the Ritz-Carlton, Renaissance, Wyndham, Radisson, and Holiday Inn affiliations.

Before joining The Gencom Group, Mr. Denton served as Director of Portfolio Management for CNL Hospitality Group, a real estate investment trust located in Orlando, Florida. In this capacity, he oversaw aspects of acquisition and asset management for a $600 million portfolio of owned hotels throughout the United States. From 1996 to 1999, Mr. Denton served as Vice President of Asset Management for White Lodging Services Corporation, a private developer, owner, and operator of hotel properties.

He has lectured frequently and published several articles on hotel real estate finance and asset management and serves as an adjunct professor in the Hospitality Management program at Florida International University. Mr. Denton earned his bachelor's and master's degrees from the Cornell University School of Hotel Administration. In addition, he has earned the MAI designation from the Appraisal Institute. He currently serves as a member of the board of directors of the Hospitality Asset Managers Association (HAMA).

IN ITS BASIC FORM, asset management is defined as *the process of providing the information tools to ownership to make appropriate decisions and ensuring that the property is managed and maintained as an investment in accordance with ownership's expectations regarding financial returns, value creation and maintenance, and financial risk mitigation.*[1] A key component of this definition is the characterization of asset management as a process rather than as a single function or series of discrete tasks. In meeting their fiduciary responsibility to owners, asset managers must reflect each owner's particular investment parameters and create a process for overseeing the property in the manner most appropriate to realizing ownership's objectives.

A second key element in this definition of asset management is the statement that the process is accomplished "in accordance with ownership's expectations." To succeed, an asset manager must understand and reflect the owner's investment philosophy, return expectations, investment horizon, risk tolerance levels, etc. and manage the investment consistently with those specific expectations. Understanding and meeting these expectations have become increasingly important aspects of the asset manager's duties in recent years because of the high level of diversification of hotel ownership and the vast disparities in investment philosophies, risk tolerance levels, and investment return objectives among different categories of owners.

As is detailed in this book's opening chapter, the ownership of hotels and resorts in the United States has changed considerably over the past twenty years, with multi-unit and institutional ownership supplanting the traditional "mom-and-pop" motel owner and family proprietorship of a hotel or resort passed down through generations. This evolution in ownership was enabled by the creation of hotel management companies, permitting the separation of the operational responsibilities of managing the hotel from the financial commitment of real estate ownership. This separation has allowed each to develop at a greater pace than would have been possible if management and ownership had remained wedded.

Concurrent with the development and rapid growth of hotel operators and brands (often as public companies), there has been a corresponding segmentation in real estate ownership in the United States. This multiplication in the types of real estate entities has been facilitated by an advanced and relatively stable financial and legal system that has fostered the creation of a variety of investment platforms, including limited partnerships, joint ventures, real estate opportunity funds, real estate investment trusts, and publicly-held taxable C corporations. These platforms have created an environment that permits individual investors to acquire interests in professionally managed real estate assets and to diversify their investments among a variety of property types and locations. The aggregation of investment dollars into larger pools of capital fits well with the separation of management from ownership, creating larger investment entities capable of owning multiple properties managed by large hotel operators that have been able to grow to meet the demand for their services because they have been freed from the requirement to raise investment capital to expand their earnings base.

Today's hotel ownership landscape contains a much higher proportion of ownership by large, sophisticated entities, and a large number of branded and independent hotel management companies that are not in the business of owning real estate. This separation of responsibilities has worked well on a number of fronts (e.g., access to capital, tax efficiency, efficient division of labor), but has also created challenges in aligning the interests of ownership and management. Above all, the separation of the management of lodging assets from ownership has reduced owners' ability to provide the input and oversight needed to ensure the optimization of their real estate investments. Out of this phenomenon has grown the need for asset managers with specific expertise in the hospitality industry.

Disparate Roles Performed by Different Asset Managers —

The progressive separation of hotel ownership from operations has created the need for a new and more advanced type of asset manager to act as a liaison between the two entities. Whereas the majority of asset managers twenty years ago were "troubleshooters" and "turnaround specialists" hired by lenders to salvage problem properties that the lenders came to own through foreclosure, today's asset manager typically fills a more long-term, calculated role in planning and managing the owner's hospitality real estate investments. Similarly, the tools of the trade employed by asset managers have evolved, and the traditional approach to bank-owned properties—"fix it up and unload it as quickly as possible"—has given way to the more proactive and strategic counsel that today's hotel asset manager provides to ownership.

There is still considerable variation in the tasks performed by today's hotel asset managers, and continuing confusion over their role in the lodging industry. This is partly attributable to the fact that there are at least three different types of asset managers in existence: (1) *investment managers*, (2) *troubleshooters*, and (3) *owner-operators*. A number of factors—e.g., the owner's size and level of sophistication, the complexity of the property, the owner's motivations and investment objectives, etc.—often determine the type of asset management services and consequently the type of asset manager that is most appropriate for a particular owner or a specific investment.

Asset managers in the *investment managers* category tend to perform more strategic functions and long-range planning, and are often not tied to the oversight of a particular property or type of property. They provide input on when to buy or sell assets, what performance levels should be expected in the near term and long term, and what capital structures would be appropriate or feasible to pursue. Once assets in investment managers' portfolios are sold, these managers are typically charged with reinvesting the proceeds of that sale into other assets to continue the process of increasing ownership's equity. Asset managers in this category often have extensive experience in the finance and financial consulting fields, but they may or may not have significant operational experience.

Asset managers in the *troubleshooters* category carry on the tradition of the earliest asset managers, typically focusing their efforts on resolving the problems of underperforming properties. They direct much of their attention to maximizing current revenues, controlling expenditures, and positioning their underperforming properties for a transaction. Troubleshooters are often more directly tied to the oversight of particular assets, and their role may end when the asset disposition is accomplished. This type of asset manager is more often an independent, third-party agent who is hired on retainer and discharged once the underperforming property's problems are resolved. Asset managers who serve as troubleshooters often have extensive experience in hotel operations, but less depth in the finance and real estate investment arenas.

Asset managers in the *owner-operator* category are less common, but are often the most strategic of the three categories. These individuals are employed by owners that manage their own hotels, or by companies that own some of the hotels they manage but also manage hotels on behalf of other owners. In these cases, the companies often have two divisions with competing objectives—the ownership side of the company pursues investment returns, whereas the operator or management side of the company focuses on building the infrastructure and systems that will ensure that both owned and operated properties are managed optimally. Each side of the company is simultaneously charged with maximizing profitability—and this, of course, is where the divergence of objectives originates. These companies use asset managers to bridge the gap and increase the level of internal alignment between the two divisions, making the entire company function more effectively.

The Asset Management Cycle

Because asset managers are charged with achieving the investment objectives of their owners, no single schematic can reflect the tasks and processes undertaken by all asset managers. Those representing long-term institutional owners tend to employ more strategic, long-range planning tools and focus less on near-term performance. By contrast, those representing short-term entrepreneurial owners may forgo long-range planning in favor of maximizing current returns and near-term sales prices.

The majority of asset management assignments incorporate the following four components, albeit to varying degrees:

- Determine ownership's objectives
- Acquire the asset and absorb it into the ownership entity or portfolio
- Monitor ongoing operations
- Dispose of the asset

Exhibit 1 illustrates the sequencing and interrelationship of the four components of the asset management process.

Determine Ownership's Objectives

In this initial phase of the asset management process, the asset manager works to identify ownership's investment objectives. Gaining an understanding of the owner's financial return expectations, tolerance for risk, and investment horizon enables the asset manager to assess the compatibility of a particular asset or strategy with the owner's investment needs.

For example, an institutional owner seeking steady annual cash flows and a high level of protection against losses will view investment opportunities in a different way from an entrepreneurial investor striving for a spot on the Forbes 400 list. The former will likely gravitate toward stabilized, upscale hotels in top-tier markets, and will be inclined to hold assets for a longer period of time. The latter will tend to have a shorter investment holding period and will be more likely to pursue distressed properties offering higher levels of financial risk but commensurately higher potential returns. The former wants to sleep well at night, whereas the latter prefers to eat well and is willing to suffer an occasional sleepless night.

An additional objective of this phase of the asset management process is to establish channels of communication among the owner, the asset manager, and the operator, as well as defining the desired frequency, format, and distribution of data on the investment and its performance. Depending upon the owner's preferences, reporting of property information to ownership may be voluminous and frequent,

Exhibit 1 The Asset Management Process

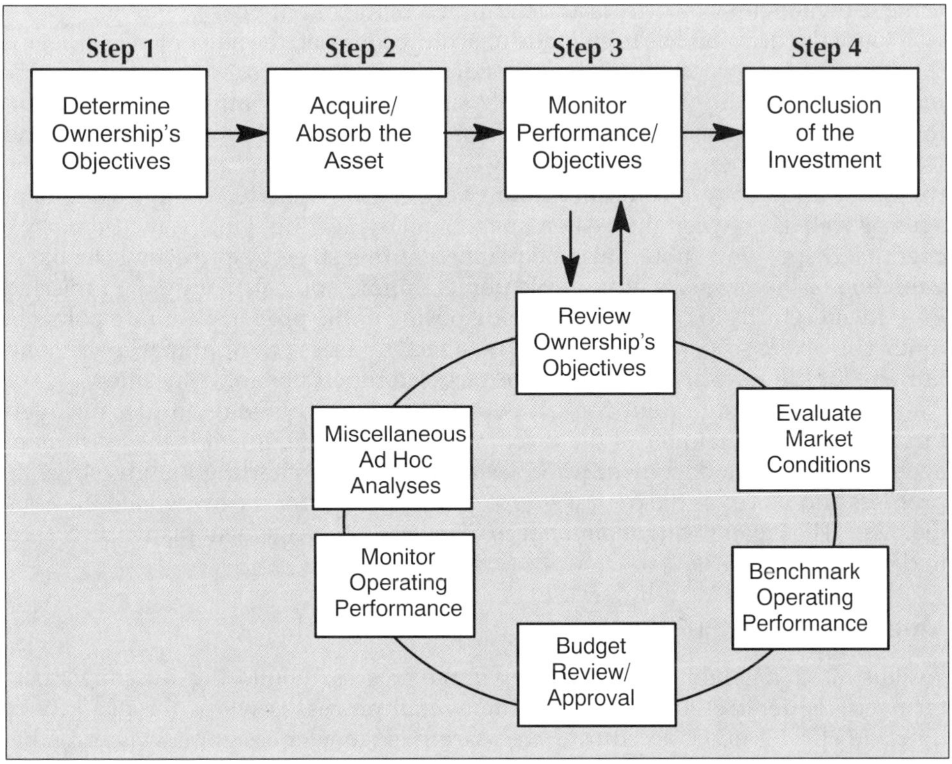

or reports may be sporadic, delivered on a management-by-exception basis whereby the owner receives reports only when there are problems or decisions that must be reached.

Acquire and Absorb the Asset

Once ownership's objectives are established, the asset manager assesses the compatibility of a particular property with these objectives to determine if acquisition of the asset is appropriate. Areas of evaluation include the property's physical plant, competitive market, current (where applicable) operations and financial performance, contracts for management, franchise, reservations, and other services, and the asset's existing capital structure.

Using these data—supplemented by the work product of third-party consultants, including feasibility reports, appraisals, property-condition reports, environmental studies, etc.—the asset manager can determine the property's appropriate positioning within the competitive market and gain a general idea of likely future trends in operating performance. In addition, opinions can be formed regarding the highest and best use of the property, as well as any appropriate management or franchise affiliations. In instances where ownership is considering an acquisition, the asset manager can recommend whether the property is likely to achieve ownership's objectives as determined in the initial phase.

Once the decision has been made to acquire an asset, the asset manager begins the "absorption" process. This involves developing and processing more specific information regarding the property's physical condition, identifying and negotiating appropriate agreements or affiliations, preparing operating pro formas and forecasted investment returns, planning capital expenditures, and establishing the frequency and depth of communications between the operator and the asset manager, as well as between the asset manager and ownership. Finally, the property's eventual disposition should also be planned at this stage by projecting the likely valuation of the property at multiple points in time and calculating the projected investment returns to ownership from disposing of the property at those points in time. This exercise permits the asset manager to assess the optimal investment horizon for the asset and determine the targeted timeframe for disposition.

The key management tool developed during this stage and employed throughout the remainder of the asset management assignment is the asset management plan. This document provides a roadmap for charting the investment's progress and serves as the central source of information for the owner and the asset manager. The creation and maintenance of the asset management plan is discussed in detail in Chapter 3.

Monitor Investment Performance

As illustrated in Exhibit 1, the third step in the process, monitoring investment performance, is iterative. This phase of the overall process is where the majority of time and effort is expended during the asset management assignment. During this stage, the asset manager is primarily responsible for property oversight, ensuring that the hotel is being managed in accordance with the owner's expectations. In addition, the asset manager must continually evaluate market conditions and the investment climate to determine when to undertake renovations, refinance the property's debt, recapitalize the investment structure, or divest of the asset.

The following discussion illustrates a number of the key areas of investigation and the aspects that the asset manager constantly evaluates in the process of monitoring the investment. The data collected in this phase of the asset management assignment come from a combination of sources discussed across the various chapters of this book, including discussions with ownership, regular meetings and exchanges of information with the operator, and research conducted with independent sources on market conditions, property performance levels, and the financing and investment climate.

Review Ownership's Objectives.

- Historically, has the property met ownership's investment objectives?
- Have the owner's investment objectives changed, or are they likely to change in the near term due to current market conditions, alternative investment opportunities, the availability of capital, personal considerations, or other factors?

- Based upon projected performance and any anticipated changes in the owner's investment objectives, is the property expected to continue to be a successful investment of owner's capital?
- Is the level of financial and operating risk that the property entails appropriate for ownership?
- Are there other investment opportunities that would be more appropriate for ownership, and what would be the incremental impact to ownership of divesting of this asset and acquiring an alternative investment?
- Is it time to dispose of the property because market conditions are appropriate, ownership's investment objectives have changed, or the level of risk that the property entails has become incompatible with ownership's objectives?

Evaluate Market Conditions.

- What is the operating performance of area hotels and specifically of the properties most competitive with the subject hotel?
- Are there current and anticipated changes in demand for hotel rooms (e.g., new development, expansion of nearby businesses, population increases)?
- Are there current and anticipated changes in the supply of hotel rooms or the competitiveness of other area hotels? For example, are there new properties being developed or renovations or conversions at existing properties that may affect the competitive landscape?
- Is the property's physical condition appropriate for its targeted operating performance, or are renovations and upgrades needed to improve the hotel's competitiveness?
- What financing terms are available for the property?
- What sales price would the property command in the current environment?

Benchmark Operating Performance.

- How are other properties performing that are similar to the subject property in size, location, and market positioning?
- What occupancy and average rate levels should this property be generating based on the performance of competitive or comparable properties?
- What trends are being experienced in the hotel industry or local market area that will affect the property's future performance? (For a detailed discussion of benchmarking and financial analysis, please refer to Chapter 9.)

Budget Review and Approval.

- Meet with ownership to discuss market conditions and benchmarking data obtained and to establish ownership's general expectations of property performance, budget submission materials and timeline, etc.
- Communicate ownership's expectations to the operator, along with the budget submission schedule and support information required.

- Receive a preliminary budget submission from the operator and review it for consistency with benchmarking data and the owner's expectations.
- Discuss issues and recommended changes with the operator.
- If the proposed budget is acceptable, present the budget to the owner, along with supporting information, and obtain approval.
- Communicate the approved budget to the operator, along with any required modifications and implementation guidelines.

Monitor Operating Performance.

- Create a schedule of reporting from the property to the asset manager and from the asset manager to the owner. This schedule usually combines items that are monitored on daily, weekly, and monthly cycles, with the level of detail typically inversely related to the frequency of reporting—i.e., daily reports typically contain much less depth than monthly reports. This enables the asset manager to track high impact items without being overwhelmed by data.
- Review occupancy and average daily rate (ADR) levels and top-line departmental revenues on a daily or weekly basis. Compare to budget and prior year performance, taking into consideration current market conditions or any unanticipated events.
- Review group booking pace, room rates, demand levels generated from various booking channels, and yield management practices to react to current conditions.
- Compare property occupancy and ADR performance to the market, using Smith Travel Research (STR) reporting or data generated from in-house sources.
- Review monthly financial statements, comparing line-item performance with the budget and the prior year's results. Generate abbreviated or exception reports for ownership to highlight areas of superior or poor performance.
- Monitor capital expenditure (CapEx) spending levels and adherence to timetables to ensure that ownership's CapEx dollars are being spent according to budget and that renovations are occurring at times designed to minimize guest inconvenience. (For a complete discussion of CapEx planning and monitoring, see Chapter 11.)
- Prepare updates to annual performance expectations, communicating to ownership areas where performance is anticipated to exceed or fall short of budgeted levels.
- Evaluate the property's balance sheet and ensure that receivables are properly collected, payables are administered according to ownership's instructions, and that the property maintains sufficient operating capital to manage effectively.

- Evaluate the property's cash flow position to enable ownership to make appropriate decisions regarding equity distributions or funding requirements.
- Review guest scores, franchisor inspection reports, employee turnover rates, and other qualitative data to ensure that non-financial performance indicators are being addressed.
- Review management contract, franchise agreement, and mortgage documentation to ensure that the property is in compliance with major covenants.

Miscellaneous Ad Hoc Analyses. In addition to routine performance monitoring efforts, the asset manager is often called upon to review ad hoc items or special requests made by ownership or the operator. These analyses span a wide range of topics and may demand specialized knowledge, requiring the asset manager to seek outside assistance. Some examples of these analyses include the following:

- Reviewing the property's real estate tax assessment and making an appeal to taxation authorities for a lower assessment
- Reviewing the property's insurance policies, coverage levels, and covenants to ensure that the asset is appropriately covered and premium costs are contained
- Evaluating requests from the operator for non-budgeted capital or operating items and determining whether the potential benefits (e.g., increased profitability, improved guest satisfaction) justify the expenditure
- Evaluating possible franchise affiliations for the property to determine if converting to an alternative affiliation would be cost-effective
- Comparing various computer, phone, and high-speed Internet access systems to determine those that would be most appropriate for the property
- Evaluating franchisor initiatives (e.g., collective marketing programs, purchasing programs, technology upgrades, etc.) to determine if participation is appropriate
- Tracking areas of guest-service failures to assist the operator in diagnosing the source of the problem
- Negotiating management contracts, retail lease agreements, service contracts with vendors, or new financing terms with lenders

In short, any question or request that would typically make its way to the owner's desk should first be evaluated by the asset manager. The asset manager thus lends his or her expertise to the issue at hand and acts as a filter, limiting the amount of time and effort ownership dedicates to the day-to-day oversight of the property.

Conclusion of the Investment

Eventually, ownership makes the decision to terminate the investment and dispose of the asset. It is important to point out that, although an assumed sale was incorporated into the investment decision and reflected in the asset management plan, property dispositions frequently do not occur on these original schedules for a number of reasons. The decision to sell may be based upon a predetermined timetable and a plan to recapture invested capital, or it may be predicated upon an opportunity that was not foreseen but is compelling enough to induce the owner to sell. As Craig Mason and Richard Musgrove discuss in Chapter 10, sophisticated owners are constantly assessing whether to hold or sell an asset, weighing the future cash flows—and risks—the property will produce against other investment opportunities.

Asset managers are charged with assisting owners in the hold-versus-sell decision, providing them with the appropriate information to make informed decisions that maximize their investment returns. Having continually updated information on the hotel's current valuation, projected investment returns, and projected capital needs will enable ownership to assess readily the relative benefits of owning the property versus other investment opportunities. In addition, knowing when critical junctures (e.g., franchise expiration, loan maturity) are on the horizon or when major changes are occurring in the market permits ownership to assess the relative risk of the property's projected income stream and plan capital events accordingly.

Depending upon the scope of the assignment, in this phase the asset manager may also be involved in the following processes:

1. Preparing the asset for sale by completing renovations and working to maximize current profitability levels, thus enhancing the value to the buyer
2. Communicating ownership's intentions to the operator to minimize miscommunication and allay employee apprehension
3. Marketing the property or working with a broker to show the property to prospective buyers and solicit offers
4. Negotiating the purchase-and-sale agreement on behalf of the owner
5. Facilitating the buyer's due-diligence research
6. Managing the sale and the transition of ownership and, if applicable, the transition of management

Once the property has been sold, the asset manager is able to prepare a final reconciliation of the investment to determine whether the owner's financial objectives were met. This analysis may also take into consideration any changes in market conditions, interest rates, or other investment factors that may not have corresponded to the initial investment assumptions. The asset manager may elaborate on these factors, providing commentary on the assumptions that proved true, those that failed to materialize, and the actions that might have been taken or approached differently to improve upon the owner's investment returns. The purpose of this type of reconciliation is to assess the overall quality of the asset management function, as well as to improve upon the investment-planning process for future benefit. Finally, the asset manager may then be charged with reinvesting the sale proceeds and acquiring new properties on the owner's behalf, thus beginning the asset management process anew.

Conclusion

The role of this chapter is to introduce a number of the principles and practices employed by contemporary hotel asset managers and to highlight some aspects of the asset management function that are explained in greater detail in the balance of this book. Because the asset management function is highly owner specific, the tasks undertaken and the depth and frequency of analysis will vary dramatically from property to property and from owner to owner, in accordance with ownership's expectations. In the future, as the ownership of hotels continues to evolve, the processes employed by hotel asset managers will likewise advance to meet owners' information needs, to optimize investment performance, and to continue to bridge the gap between hotel owners and operators.

Endnotes

1. Gregory A. Denton, *Hotel Asset Management at a Crossroads: Identifying Challenges and Developing New Methodologies to Improve the Effectiveness of Hotel Asset Managers.* Unpublished master's thesis (Ithaca, N.Y.: Cornell University, 1999), pp. 19–20.

3

Creating the Asset Management Plan

By John C. Boettger

***John C. Boettger** is Vice President of Asset Management at Host Marriott Corporation, where he directs a team of professionals responsible for actively overseeing a geographically diverse portfolio of more than 120 select- and full-service hotels with a value in excess of $1.5 billion. Host Marriott Corporation is the largest lodging real estate investment trust (REIT) in the United States, with assets valued at over $8 billion. Prior to assuming his current responsibilities, Mr. Boettger was responsible for the active oversight of a portfolio of full-service hotels that included the Marriott, Ritz-Carlton, and Swissôtel brands.*

Prior to joining Host Marriott, Mr. Boettger served as a principal with a hospitality advisory firm that specialized in asset management and value enhancement strategies for hotel assets. He also served as associate director of operations at a hotel management company specializing in distressed hotels, where, in addition to serving as an asset manager, he completed operational reviews of stabilized and under-performing hotels. Mr. Boettger began his career in the hospitality advisory practice of Laventhol & Horwath.

A past president and board member of the Hospitality Asset Managers Association (HAMA), Mr. Boettger is also a full member of the Urban Land Institute. He holds an associate's degree in culinary arts from Johnson and Wales University, a bachelor of science degree in hospitality management from Florida International University, and an MBA in finance from The George Washington University.

So you're an asset manager who has just inherited a new hotel property to oversee. What to do? This chapter will focus on the processes necessary to develop one of the most important tools used in the oversight of a lodging asset—the asset management plan. The asset management plan is an effective tool for communicating how the asset manager plans to achieve ownership's objectives, as well as a roadmap to arriving at ownership's desired outcomes. Like the role of the hotel asset manager, asset management plans have evolved over time and must be adapted to the specific needs of the owner, the asset manager, and the asset. The principal objective of this chapter is to identify the need for and value of a well-crafted plan to assist the asset manager in the oversight of a lodging property. In addition, this chapter will explore the goals and objectives of ownership. Topics treated in the remainder of the chapter include the origins of the plan; how it is utilized and by whom; the value of developing a plan before taking ownership of the asset; the components of an effective asset management plan; methods of implementing the plan; and how use of the plan makes the asset manager more efficient and productive.

A few points of clarification are appropriate at the outset. First, the term "asset manager" is used to describe the person engaged in the fiduciary role of overseeing a hospitality asset, regardless of the relationship between the asset's owner and the asset manager. Second, asset management plans come in all shapes and sizes and may be referred to by a number of different names. For our purposes, however, the two most commonly used names—*asset management plan* and *strategic plan*—will be employed interchangeably throughout the chapter. Finally, the underlying assumption of the chapter is that the asset manager is assuming responsibility for a newly acquired asset, thus permitting the reader to follow the development of a strategic plan from the beginning.

Origin of the Plan: Owners and Their Objectives

Before the asset manager commences the hands-on work of the profession—i.e., seeking ways to drive value and protect the asset—he or she must understand the objectives of ownership. In fact, the asset management plan must be driven primarily by an understanding of ownership's objectives for the asset. To that end, the development of an asset management plan should begin well before the first monthly operating statement, STR (Smith Travel Research) report, or capital budget arrives at the asset manager's desk.

Owners come in many forms and include those companies, either public or private, whose primary objective is the ownership (and sometimes operation) of multiple lodging assets; individual investors who desire the ownership of only one or two trophy assets; lending institutions who find themselves the unwilling owners of one or more hotels; portfolio managers who find hotels among the components of a diversified commercial real estate portfolio; and opportunistic investors. What characterizes each of these ownership entities is that they all have differing objectives for their ownership of a hotel. The asset manager's task is to understand those objectives, develop a plan to meet them, and then implement the plan effectively.

Since understanding the objectives of ownership is the first step in developing an asset management plan, it is appropriate to begin by reviewing how hotel owners' objectives vary. Public companies are typically focused on owning a sometimes large portfolio of lodging assets with clearly defined, conservative, and typically long-term investment objectives. These objectives usually include focusing on a single class or a limited set of asset classes (e.g., luxury, select service, extended-stay hotels, etc.), achieving a specific geographic distribution of properties, and adhering to defined strategies for the holding period of assets. Public-company owners typically have the most clearly defined strategies, seeking to add value by increasing profitability over the long term through sustainable initiatives, as well as through the opportunistic investment of capital periodically over the investment horizon.

Private companies may have the same objectives as publicly traded owners, although their investment horizons may be somewhat shorter and their focus may be on realizing improved profitability more quickly, while making only selective capital investments in the asset. Private companies may also employ a strategy of making a significant investment at acquisition to reposition an asset, then minimizing future investment while focusing on improving profitability until disposition.

Private investors may be wealthy individuals who desire ownership of a few high-profile, distinctive lodging assets. These so-called trophy assets are hotels in unique locations with high barriers to entry or with facilities, amenities, and services that are not easily (i.e., at a reasonable cost) duplicated. At the outset, the investment objectives of the wealthy owners of trophy properties may not extend beyond a desire to possess a particular asset and the gratification that comes with having the wherewithal to afford it. However, once they become owners, their objectives are likely to evolve over time, possibly changing without notice. These owners are typically the most challenging to work with because even the most well-developed asset management plan may change dramatically due to changes in the owners' investment objectives.

Lending institutions are typically unwilling owners, not because they fear ownership (their officers often exhibit a sophisticated command of the lodging business) but because they are in the complementary business of lending money to hotel owners and investors. Usually lenders find themselves in the role of owner only if things have gone terribly wrong. A lender may own a hotel because the business plan was flawed (an asset poorly positioned in the market), too high a price was paid for the asset using too much borrowed money (an over-leveraged capital structure), market conditions have experienced a severe and sustained downturn (a protracted recession), or simply because the asset was poorly managed.

Because of increased equity requirements and more conservative underwriting, in today's environment there are fewer occasions when a lender becomes an owner. Nevertheless, it is not uncommon for a lending institution to find itself the owner of multiple hotel assets. The universe of hotel lenders is relatively limited, and lodging is generally regarded as a risky investment compared with, say, an apartment complex. Consequently, regardless of their reluctance to play the role, hotel lenders must sometimes assume the position of hotel owner. Lenders' objectives are usually straightforward—recover as much loan value as possible in the least amount of time, moving the asset and the loan off their books.

Institutional portfolio managers who hold many real estate asset classes are still in evidence, although not to the degree they once were. In the past, portfolio managers at insurance companies (which have largely exited the ownership of real estate) and pension funds were typical clients of hotel asset managers. Today, portfolio managers who have a portion of their real estate investments in lodging assets have very well-defined criteria regarding acceptable types of hotel assets, return objectives, and holding periods. Hotel asset managers working on behalf of institutional owners are doing so under clearly defined expectations and investment criteria.

The opportunistic investor typically has an overriding, compelling objective: increase asset value as much as possible in the shortest time using the least possible amount of invested capital. Opportunistic investors know their mission (or think they do); they are banking on improving market conditions, combined with short-term profit enhancement, to maximize value so that the property is positioned for disposition. Their appetite for risking their own capital is quite limited, and they invest equity only when absolutely necessary or when the returns are lucrative.

The above descriptions of ownership's objectives are of course very broad characterizations that do not represent how every investor or entity in an individual ownership category views its assets. In fact, hotel owners may have many objectives based on the type of asset, lodging market conditions, and general economic conditions. An opportunistic investor or lender may find itself in for the long haul if market conditions take a prolonged turn for the worse. Similarly, a publicly traded company may deviate from its fundamental buy-and-hold strategy, leaping at the chance to sell a trophy property if a private investor willing to pay a hefty premium comes along. The importance of understanding ownership's objectives cannot be overstated. Every owner has objectives; although those objectives may change, the role of the asset manager is to tailor a plan that fits the owner's prevailing objectives.

Where necessary, the asset manager should be making the recommendations to ownership, altering the course established for the asset based on developments at the hotel or in the market. The asset manager must not be so focused on achieving a previously established objective that he or she fails to see changes on the horizon that argue for altering the plan to achieve the same objective, a comparable objective, or to avoid a complete failure.

Approach to the Preparation of the Asset Management Plan

The asset management plan should read like the *CliffsNotes* version of a good book—only shorter. Understanding the objectives of ownership should help the asset manager focus on the primary components of the plan—what steps are needed to achieve the objectives, when should they occur, what is the cost, and what impediments exist to achieving the objectives? The asset management plan should be informative and present a comprehensive view of the asset. Knowing who will be reading the plan is as important as understanding the owner's objectives. The length of the document and the elements included in the plan will differ, depending on whether or not the end user is knowledgeable about the lodging industry and focused on specific topics or if the end user is skilled in real estate and finance but knows little about the complexities of the lodging industry.

As with all cogent strategic plans, regardless of the industry or economic sector, the asset manager should be able to summarize the vision for the hotel in a few sentences, supporting it with several pages of information. Concisely articulating the vision for a hotel is the end result of the asset management plan. It is also the foundation of the asset manager's job. Moreover, almost everyone in today's business environment prefers brevity and content to volume. The length of a plan has little to do with its value.

Developing an effective asset management plan requires the accumulation of a significant amount of data, even if only a fraction of that information will find its way into the final product. The plan enumerates the action steps necessary to achieve the owner's objectives. The asset manager, however, must know and be able to explain the rationale that led to the conclusions. The asset management plan and the asset manager's role are far more art than science. Knowing where to start the task is relatively easy; arriving at the exercise's conclusions, however, will require considerable time and effort.

Start With the Basics—Information Gathering

As the first step in the information gathering process, the asset manager needs to begin to understand the key aspects of the hotel, summarizing the most basic information: property name, address, number of rooms, meeting space, opening date, facilities, outlets, unique characteristics, ownership structure, and acquisition cost, among numerous other pieces of data. When accumulated, most of this information will be relegated to a table that takes up three or four pages of the final document. However, the effort necessary to obtain the information is significant.

The asset manager also needs to seek out and review a number of documents, including acquisition due-diligence reports, recent appraisals, the property's management and franchise agreements, ground leases (if any), loan agreement(s), operating budgets, capital budgets, marketing plans, feasibility analyses, STR reports, and engineering reports, all of which constitute just a portion of the information the asset manager must assemble. It often requires ingenuity to discern the information needed and to access it efficiently. After it is collected, the information must be read. Finally, much of the data and insight the asset manager needs can only come from spending time at the subject hotel, investigating the local market, and touring the competitive supply. This is a hands-on effort that cannot be accomplished at a desk.

There is no doubt the asset manager will spend a significant amount of time digesting documents that are, for lack of a more euphemistic term, boring. The asset manager must, however, view the efforts to understand the asset and its market as both an opportunity and a challenge. The more diligent the asset manager is at this stage of the process, the more compelling the resulting asset management plan will be.

Components of the Asset Management Plan

At this point, the asset manager has a lot of information, but still has no plan. The asset manager must begin the development of the asset management plan by reviewing the owner's objectives and determining if the property will be able to meet those objectives. If the answer is yes, then the next questions the asset manager must address are how long will it take and what needs to be accomplished to meet the owner's objectives. If the asset and its position in the market are not well suited to the owner's objectives, the asset manager must determine what, if anything, can be done to change that conclusion.

To develop an effective, compelling strategic plan, the asset manager must understand the intended audience and what the users of the document need and want to know. Although the emphasis and length of individual asset management plans are customized to the particular audience, there are fundamental components that must be included in the document:

- A property summary
- An executive summary
- A SWOT (Strengths, Weaknesses, Opportunities and Threats) analysis
- Plans and actions
- An exit strategy
- A market overview
- A competitive supply overview
- A performance overview
- A capital overview
- A key data summary

Although the asset manager will present the plan in the order indicated above, the steps required to develop the analysis are performed in a quite different sequence. Moreover, each component of the plan requires many parallel tasks that contribute to other aspects of the plan. The complexity of the process, however, must not be apparent in the final product, which must be a concise summary of the actions necessary to achieve the owner's objectives.

The Property Summary

Summarizing all of the facilities, amenities, and services contained in the hotel forces the asset manager to review the condition of the guestrooms, public areas, food-and-beverage outlets, and other areas of the hotel. Although this review necessarily uncovers information pertinent to both the subject hotel's capital plan and operating performance review, the asset manager should not be diverted, but rather stick to the task of understanding the asset and what it has to offer. At this stage of the analysis, the asset manager should be immersed in the property, spending time with the appropriate department heads, engineering staff, marketing staff, as well as soliciting guest reaction. It is important for the asset manager to gain an understanding of how both the members of the hotel's executive committee and the line staff view the property, paying special attention to any dissonance between the two perceptions of the asset and its operation.

As part of this phase of the analysis, the asset manager will necessarily make value judgments regarding the quality of management at the hotel, especially if management's view of the property does not align with the asset manager's. At the conclusion of this phase, the asset manager should have developed an objective but narrow view of the asset—narrow because he or she has yet to comprehend the subject hotel's market and competitive environment. The asset manager must gain a broader perspective on the hotel's positioning and its competitors before developing a coherent, objective view of the subject's strengths, weaknesses, opportunities, and threats.

The Market

Gaining an understanding of the market the hotel operates in is sometimes easier said than done—for example, when analyzing the market for a major resort that competes on a national basis. However, as appealing as it may be to travel the country visiting upscale resorts, most hotels compete against local or regional competitors for local or regional business, and the task is typically far less glamorous.

The asset manager's analysis of the market begins with the subject hotel's marketing plan. This document will present property management's view of where its business comes from and against whom the hotel competes for that business. During this phase, the asset manager must attempt to understand the segments from which the hotel draws its demand and the depth, or robustness, of the markets served. This effort includes not only reviewing the marketing plan, but interviewing the sales and marketing staff and the general manager to drill down into the production from important accounts and gain an understanding of the key markets that drive group and transient demand. Ultimately, the asset manager must come to an understanding of the hotel's positioning, and then determine if that positioning is appropriate for achieving ownership's objectives.

Since the marketing plan typically includes a summary of direct competitors and their advantages and disadvantages compared with the subject property, the asset manager is also beginning to assemble elements of the strategic plan's SWOT analysis. The asset manager should be focused on both understanding the information provided by the property and validating it independently. Accordingly, the asset manager should also conduct primary research, surveying such local sources as the chamber of commerce and the convention and visitors bureau, as well as gleaning data on the market from local and regional publications.

Typically, a significant percentage of a hotel's occupancy will be driven by a number of local demand generators. The asset manager may need to gather information on commercial office space absorption and vacancy rates to determine if any changes in demand should be anticipated, including businesses entering or leaving the area. If convention demand is a component of the property's occupancy, the asset manager will need to research citywide convention data for the current and future years and establish if there are any anticipated changes to the local convention venues (e.g., a significant expansion in the amount of exhibit space) that may influence convention demand. Trends in enplanements and deplanements at the local airport are typically a key indicator of traveler demand into the market. Airport traffic information is particularly important if the property is located near a major domestic or international airport. The asset manager's objective is to develop a comprehensive knowledge of the factors driving demand in the market and then to assess the impact of the trends in demand on the subject hotel. A further focus should be to establish if the subject hotel has any point(s) of privilege, permitting it to capture the primary drivers of demand more readily than other competitors in the market. Ultimately, the asset manager is assembling key information to determine if the hotel's positioning is appropriate, given the sources of demand in the market.

Surveying the Competition

By this stage of the analysis, the asset manager has developed a view of how the hotel is positioned in the market. Now the asset manager must begin to validate this view and the view of property management by researching the competition. There is no better way to gain an appreciation of the competitive advantages and disadvantages of the subject hotel than by looking at the competition. If the asset manager is new to the market, he or she will have an unbiased view of the competition, looking at the subject's competitors in much the same way as guests do.

Once again, the asset manager will gain some insight into the subject hotel's managers based on their views of the competitors. Does the asset manager's view match that of the property management team? If not, where are the differences and what do these differences indicate about the operator's culture, competence, and motivation? This is also an opportunity for the asset manager to determine if the competitive set identified by the subject hotel's management team is the appropriate set. Are there other hotels that should rightfully be included in the subject's competitive set but are currently omitted? Why does the property management team not view these hotels as competitors?

Researching the competition can be an enjoyable part of the process, but it is also likely to be quite time-consuming. Unless the asset manager already has a very thorough understanding of the market, much time will be spent walking through lobbies, public areas, meeting space, guestrooms, corridors, food-and-beverage outlets, and fitness centers. In addition to gathering qualitative information about each hotel, the asset manager should be gathering property-specific information that will be useful in determining the competitive advantages and disadvantages of the subject property, as well as supporting other conclusions contained in the strategic plan. The asset manager must pay particular attention to the condition of competitors' facilities and the amenities they offer, while also identifying any unique attributes the competitive properties enjoy. Throughout this phase of the research, the asset manager must be constantly on the lookout for opportunities to differentiate the subject property from the competition, even if it requires capital investment to improve the hotel's offerings.

The physical product offered by the competitive hotels is only one of the areas the asset manager must consider. Competitors' levels of service must also be an area of focus, since this aspect of the lodging product may be as effective as the physical plant in distinguishing a hotel from its competition. Moreover, if the level of service at the subject property is below that of the competitive set, the asset manager has automatically established one aspect of the strategic plan he or she will propose to the subject's owner. Just as one of the asset manager's objectives is to identify the subject hotel's point(s) of privilege, he or she must also recognize those enjoyed by the subject's competitive set. Are competitor hotels located closer to key demand generators or do they offer facilities, amenities, and services that may be more appealing to some or all of the guests derived from the market's demand generators? Once again, the asset manager is in search of opportunities to enhance the competitive position of the subject hotel, improving operating performance to meet ownership's objectives.

Data provided by reports available from Smith Travel Research, commonly referred to as STAR reports, typically contribute significantly to the asset manager's competitive property review. (For a full discussion of the various reports available from STR and their use, see Chapter 9.) The asset manager must first ensure that the hotels comprising the subject's competitive set correspond to the sample of properties whose data are captured in the STAR reports utilized by the subject hotel. Once this fundamental comparability is established, the asset manager is reassured that the STAR report provides key operating information that is objective and pertinent. From the STAR reports, the asset manager and property manager may determine how effectively the subject hotel is competing among its competitors on such important metrics as occupancy percentage, average room rate, and revenue per available room (RevPAR).

The relationship between property performance and competitive set performance is typically referred to as the penetration, or yield, ratio. To the extent that the subject property is operating at a significant premium or discount to the competitive set in one or more metrics, it is the asset manager's responsibility to understand how the property's positioning yields those results. By closely analyzing the occupancy, average room rate, and RevPAR indices, the asset manager may be able to identify areas of opportunity in the pricing structure and marketing of the subject property.

Property Performance

Whether the asset manager's task is the development of a strategic plan or more routine ongoing oversight of a property, a thorough understanding of the subject's operating performance is critical. Typically, this step begins with a review of the operator's annual business plan for the hotel and concludes with a review of current and past operating statements.

Reviewing the business plan and operating statement will give the asset manager significant insight into the hotel's relative degree of success and reveal if any opportunities exist to improve operating performance through cost-containment strategies, alternate marketing strategies, or through programs that may be implemented, or at least influenced, by the owner. The asset manager draws on his or her experience to evaluate the profitability of the hotel's departments, based on the size and type of hotel and its level of operating performance. If the cost and profit metrics are out of alignment, the asset manager has very likely identified opportunities for improving operating performance and adding value. The asset manager should also ascertain if the marketing efforts are appropriately focused and if the deployment of the sales team is likely to achieve the desired results. It is not unusual to find, for example, that the addition of one or more sales managers to concentrate on selected markets or segments materially influences demand for the hotel.

This step also includes an analysis of areas such as property insurance, real estate taxes, and energy expenditures. Although market conditions influence the cost of insurance coverage (as witnessed by the steep rise in premiums after 9/11), the asset manager can exercise some control over insurance costs by evaluating the appropriateness of the insurance coverage, the level of deductibles, and the premiums paid for that coverage. The asset manager should also determine if the property-tax assessment for the subject hotel is reasonable based on its operating performance and its asset valuation in comparison with other properties in the same tax jurisdiction. Opportunities to control energy costs may be uncovered if the asset manager evaluates the efficiency of the systems within the property and researches the cost of various sources of energy. For example, in the current environment of increased deregulation, the asset manager may identify opportunities to enter into new agreements that materially reduce the cost of certain utilities, improving the hotel's profitability at no detriment to the guest experience.

The financial analysis of the property's performance is one that evolves as the process unfolds and the asset manager's comprehension of the hotel and its position in the market deepens. It is likely to take some time for the asset manager to mine all of the available opportunities. The answers do not come solely from plumbing the subject hotel's operating statements, but from a variety of sources, including the asset manager's increasing knowledge of the demand generators and the competitive market. However, the asset management plan is designed to evolve as the asset manager's knowledge grows and as events yield changes both at the property and within the market.

Capital Analysis

For owners, the analysis of the property's capital needs is one of the most important components of the strategic plan. For the asset manager, it determines not only how the owner's capital will be spent but also how the asset manager's time will be allocated during his or her stewardship of the asset. A thorough review of all of the physical plant systems must be accomplished, along with an assessment of the renovation needs of the guestrooms and public areas. In a well-maintained hotel, most of this information will be available to the asset manager. For a newly acquired property, a great deal of the information the asset manager needs will have been compiled during the acquisition due-diligence process. If an asset has been held in the owner's portfolio for a period of time, a review of the most current reports and surveys provides the asset manager with a good starting point for the capital-needs analysis.

As in prior steps, gaining an understanding of the capital needs of the asset also provides the asset manager with a great deal of insight into the capabilities of the property management team. One of the asset manager's primary responsibilities is the protection of the asset. Failure of the manager or prior owner to maintain the physical plant of the hotel adequately may—and most likely *will*—result in the need to replace key systems and components well before the end of the assets' normal lifespan. Even in the smallest hotel, HVAC (heating, ventilating, and air conditioning) units and fire alarm systems are very costly items. It is the asset manager's responsibility to understand the condition of the critical systems in the hotel and to know which systems will require repair or replacement and the cost to do so.

A hotel's physical plant systems are typically the most complex and costly to maintain, repair, and replace. The asset manager needs to gain a thorough understanding of the age, condition, and maintenance history of such all-important systems as HVAC, plumbing, electrical, life-safety, telecommunications, etc. Unless the lodging asset is new, the asset manager will need to know the expected useful lives of the primary systems and anticipate the need to complete major refurbishments or replacement. This may require engaging technical consultants to complete additional surveys or update existing reports to ensure that physical plant assessments are current.

An evaluation of the condition of the guestrooms and public areas is one that requires a higher degree of subjective judgment than the assessment of the hotel's physical plant systems. Although the asset manager will want to consider how recently a given area was renovated, some decisions are not entirely based on the date of the last renovation. If the hotel was renovated in stages or only selected components have been replaced or updated, the required work may be accomplished incrementally, with the cost of the next full renovation spread over a number of years. Moreover, if the operating performance of the hotel has been weak and the normal wear and tear on the asset has therefore been moderate, future investments may be spread over a longer period than indicated by typical renovation cycles. Similarly, if the hotel has been exceptionally well maintained or is in a condition the asset manager deems adequate to the current market conditions, renovation may be spread over a longer period, thus deferring capital infusions and improving returns.

If the asset manager determines that capital investment is needed to improve operating performance or reposition the asset, the timing of the expenditure is less subjective. However, the asset manager must still determine the cost of the necessary work and establish a reasonable, practical timeframe for its completion. The product of this analysis is a summary of the timing and cost of the capital investments necessary to preserve the asset, address any regulatory requirements, reposition the asset, or take advantage of other opportunities to create additional value.

The horizon of the asset manager's capital plan must be based on the holding period identified by ownership. It is usually prudent, however, for the asset manager to extend the horizon for the capital plan by an additional two to three years beyond the anticipated holding period. If the operating environment or ownership's objectives change, the anticipated holding period may be extended, and looming capital requirements may significantly affect the timing of the disposition. Moreover, when ownership is contemplating the sale of the property, the better the asset manager understands the property's eventual capital needs, the better positioned he or she will to be to set an appropriate sale price and anticipate the negotiating points prospective buyers might identify during the due-diligence process.

Preparing the Asset Management Plan

After completing the preceding steps, the asset manager has in hand all the quantitative and qualitative information necessary to begin preparing the asset management plan. Although the asset manager has an encyclopedic knowledge of the subject property, the strategic plan is not the vehicle for demonstrating this all-encompassing command. The document must be a concise statement of the asset manager's conclusions and recommendations, not a voluminous report replete with so much detail that the pertinent information ownership seeks is lost in the data. Ownership, upon reading the asset management plan, should have no questions regarding such key aspects as the subject hotel's positioning in the market, the state of the market and any anticipated changes, and the opportunities to be capitalized upon and their timing and cost. The reader may, however, have questions regarding selected elements of the plan or the reasoning leading to certain conclusions and recommendations. It is at this juncture that the asset manager is called upon to demonstrate his or her command of all the issues surrounding the asset, responding to ownership's questions in detail.

The opening section of the document should be straightforward, providing a summary of key property facts, including: name of the hotel, address, opening date, acquisition date and cost, number of rooms, square feet of meeting space, type of asset (e.g., resort, convention hotel, airport property), management company, and, if applicable, the franchisor.

Most of the first page of the plan should present an executive summary that concisely presents the current state of the property and enumerates the steps necessary to optimize the asset's value during the holding period. As part of the executive summary, the asset manager should clearly identify any major risks that are known as well as any factors that may influence the holding period or investment strategy, especially if the strategy promulgated by the asset manager differs from what may have been envisioned at the time of acquisition. A sample opening paragraph in the executive summary might read in part as follows:

> As one of the top performing properties in ownership's portfolio, this hotel should be viewed as a long-term hold, and consideration should be given to protecting this asset's ability to generate significant cash flow. This hotel does face challenges, including the age of the facility compared to several new competitors that are under construction in the market. Existing competitors have undergone significant upgrades to their physical product, and these will underscore the deficiencies of the hotel. The asset's competitive disadvantages will be magnified in the current economic environment, as increased supply competes for stable demand. Accordingly, over the last year a master capital investment plan has been developed that, if implemented, will convert current deficiencies into strengths and position the hotel for the long term. However, a significant investment will be necessary to fulfill the master plan over the next few years, and that investment must be balanced with the needs of the remainder of the portfolio.

The asset manager may also include selected points specifying the nature of the capital investments needed, along with the proposed timing. In addition, the asset manager may want to summarize briefly any other actions needed to either protect the asset or enhance its value over the holding period.

The executive summary should also include a positioning statement for the hotel. As noted earlier, one of the asset manager's analytical tasks is to identify the hotel's point(s) of privilege. The positioning statement is the opportunity for the asset manager to clarify the point(s) of privilege that the hotel enjoys compared with its competitors. In addition, the positioning statement should validate the objectives that were identified when the asset was acquired. A positioning statement might read in part as follows:

> This property should be viewed as a core asset with a location that cannot be duplicated and a niche that is unlikely to be challenged by any new or existing properties—i.e., a family-friendly oceanfront resort. While significant capital expenditures are needed to address pre-existing and emerging needs, that investment will yield favorable returns over the mid to long term and sustain the quality of the asset. This property should be viewed as a significant and strategic asset.

The amount of detail included in the executive summary should be driven by both the number of action steps necessary to implement the strategic plan and the needs of ownership. It is the asset manager's responsibility to understand how much detail will be needed to explain the salient points of the plan. Again, the objective is to be concise; however, the needs and expectations of ownership are likely to vary. As suggested at the outset of this chapter, owners have different motivations and objectives, and they are also likely to have varying degrees of industry knowledge. The content of the plan must be customized to ensure that the user's needs are met.

Once the asset manager has summarized the goals and objectives for the asset and prepared its positioning statement, the next step in the plan is to develop the SWOT analysis. It is unlikely that all of the information that has been uncovered during the plan-development process will be favorable. The SWOT analysis should identify only the most salient points for each category of the analysis. For example, cogently identifying the weaknesses and threats serves a twofold purpose. First, both the asset manager and the owner are fully alerted to the weaknesses and threats currently affecting the asset, as well as those that can be expected to affect it in the future. Second, it should be obvious how the asset manager's announced strategy to add value or, if necessary, reposition the hotel mitigates or eliminates the property's weaknesses and threats. Bullet points rather than narratives are a concise means to summarize the SWOT analysis. A sample SWOT analysis is presented in Exhibit 1.

Having presented a thumbnail sketch of the hotel, a positioning statement, and a SWOT analysis, the asset manager must next detail the plans and actions necessary to optimize the value of the asset. This section is likely to be the lengthiest of the plan and should consist of treatments of two fundamental components—the business model and capital issues. Hotels almost always have opportunities to drive additional value through both improvements to the property's business model and through capital investment; this upside potential was probably ownership's principal motivation for acquiring the asset. However, if the asset manager anticipates a comprehensive repositioning of the property, there are typically many more capital issues than operating issues. As always, the discussion must be concise, yet the asset manager must ensure that this section of the plan identifies all actions necessary to drive value, the timing of the actions, their costs if material, and the benefits to be derived from each action. Clarifying the timing of the implementation of an action is important, since the plan must

Exhibit 1 Sample SWOT Analysis

STRENGTHS	OPPORTUNITIES
➢ Relaxed and unpretentious resort environment ➢ Outstanding oceanfront location ➢ Outstanding service and total guest experience	➢ More aggressive regional and national marketing, public relations, and sales efforts ➢ Forge additional relationships with area golf courses ➢ Greater focus on asset preservation
WEAKNESSES	**THREATS**
➢ Lack of market/general public knowledge of destination and its appeal ➢ Inadequate facilities: lack of spa, insufficient function space, and under-sized pool deck ➢ Lack of ownership/control of adjacent golf course	➢ Six new competitive properties to open in the next two years. Potential loss of staff and clients ➢ Significant capital investment has occurred at most of the existing competitive properties ➢ Weak economy will suppress the recovery of group and leisure demand

explicitly acknowledge that, as a practical matter, not all actions can be accomplished at once.

If the owner's objective is to hold the asset for three or fewer years, it is likely that a number of the action steps will be occurring concurrently. If the action steps required are significant and likely to result in some measure of business disruption, the plan should consider that not all of the value enhancement may be realized before disposition. Conversely, an asset that is considered a long-term hold may have action steps that are scheduled to commence as far as two or three years into the future. Of course, the asset management plan is a living document. The asset manager can readily alter the timing of action steps and add or delete components as conditions change.

This section of the asset management plan will also detail the need for the individual projects comprising the overall capital spending plan, including their timing, costs, and, where appropriate, their return on investment. The asset manager may also need to specify the source of funding for the individual projects if there are limitations on how the hotel's reserves for replacement of FF&E (furniture, fixtures, and equipment) may be spent, or if it is clear that the reserve will be insufficient to fund all of the proposed work. A schedule that identifies the impact of the projects on the FF&E reserve is of significant value. If, for example, the intent is to fund all the proposed capital projects from the FF&E reserve, this

Exhibit 2 Value Enhancement Opportunities

- Reinvest in the core asset by renovating the guestrooms and corridors. Estimated cost \$8.5 million; escrow shortfall of \$4.0 million to be funded by owner. Renovation to begin in Q4.
- Investigate opportunities in paid parking, including improved service and reduction of operating costs. May reduce demand, avoiding need for development of additional on-site parking facilities. To begin immediately. Minimal investment is anticipated. Cost reduction of \$100,000 per year possible.
- Pursue negotiating preferential use agreements with area golf courses. To begin immediately. No investment is anticipated.
- Pursue reduction in real estate taxes based on most recent operating performance and assessment. Outside consultant to be retained. To begin immediately. Annual operating cost reduction of \$100,000 is possible.
- Replace roof. To occur in 2006 at an estimated cost of \$250,000. Project to be funded through the escrow.

will influence the timing of the projects, sometimes deferring their accomplishment by a number of years. A sample of the value enhancement opportunities that might be contained in the plans and actions section of the asset manager's strategic plan appears in Exhibit 2.

Exit Strategy

The final component in the asset management plan is the exit strategy for the property. Depending upon the owner's objectives, this section of the document will be either the most critical component of the strategic plan or an incidental aspect. Opportunistic or unwilling owners of a hotel will often be seeking the earliest exit possible, while for long-term owners, disposition may not be paramount. Nevertheless, the asset manager should clearly define the exit criteria, specifying the strategic and financial conditions necessary for a disposition to be contemplated.

Like the other elements of the plan, the exit criteria are likely to change over time. But the objective remains the same— to identify the appropriate timing for a disposition based on the completion of the action steps put forth in the strategic plan or because the property has achieved its optimal financial return. Should those criteria be met sooner than anticipated, it is the asset manager's responsibility to make ownership aware that the value has been optimized and a disposition should be considered. There is the possibility that no exit will be recommended for the foreseeable future. However, the criteria for an exit should nevertheless be identified, since market conditions may change. If changing market conditions affect the value of the asset, the opportunity to optimize the return to ownership should not be missed merely because the asset was initially considered a candidate for a long-term hold. Depending on the criteria for achieving ownership's objectives, the exit strategy may be very specific and opportunistic—for example, a

Exhibit 3 Sample Summary of Hotel Amenities

Type	Size	Operator	Last Redo	Scope
Health Club	3500 sq. ft	Managed	1996	Added new fitness center
Retail	2356 sq. ft	Managed	2002	Consolidate outlets
Spa	1900 sq. ft	Managed	N/A	
Real Estate Sales Office	450 sq. ft	Leased	N/A	

recommendation to ownership to consider disposition immediately preceding a significant, non-recurring event such as the Olympic Games.

Key Data Summary

At this point, the asset management plan is essentially complete. The asset manager has summarized all of the key criteria for ownership; developed a listing of plans and actions that will, when completed, yield an increase in value; and promulgated the criteria for and timing of an exit strategy. The addition of further information is driven by the owner's needs. High-net-worth individuals holding only one trophy asset may have no desire to know the number of parking spaces or the number of seats in the hotel's restaurant(s). Institutional owners may want to know these and similar details, although not necessarily in the context of the asset management plan's key recommendations and conclusions. The challenge to the asset manager is to perceive correctly the owner's needs, providing the necessary information to ensure that ownership is fully informed but not overwhelmed.

This challenge often can be met by developing a key data summary as an addendum to the strategic plan. This addendum may be provided as part of the plan or held in reserve for use when needed. For example, if oversight of the asset is being passed from one asset manager to another within the same firm, the key data summary permits the new asset manager to gain an understanding of the property quickly and efficiently. Some firms have found it useful to compile the information contained in the key data summary for all of the assets in their portfolios. These databases can then be used to benchmark operating performance or evaluate the best practices of like assets. The key data summary can be quite detailed; however, it too should be concise. Thus, this addendum is likely to be a combination of tables and bullet-point lists addressing a variety of topics.

To expand upon the property summary contained in the body of the document, the asset manager may want to list the key management staff at the property along with their respective tenures as part of the key data summary. Similarly, a summary of all of the hotel's food-and-beverage outlets and other amenities is valuable. For example, the asset manager may prepare a table similar to the one that appears in Exhibit 3 to explain the pertinent details of the hotel's amenities.

Exhibit 4 Sample Competitive Set Summary

Hotel Name	Year Open	Room Count	Meeting Space SF	Meeting SF/Room	Comp. Set Rank
Subject Hotel	1991	440	25,000	57	1
Comp 1	1984	360	49,000	136	2
Comp 2	1985	410	25,000	61	3
Comp 3	1986	440	22,000	50	4
Comp 4	1999	400	20,000	50	5
Comp 5	1987	500	46,000	92	6
TOTALS		2,550	187,000	73.3*	

* Weighted average

If the hotel is situated on leased land, a brief abstract of the key terms of the ground lease may be included in the data summary. Similarly, an abstract displaying key management agreement terms is particularly valuable when the asset manager's portfolio includes hotels operated under a variety of brands and management companies. If the management contract contains performance clauses that provide for termination of the operator, the asset manager should explain the contractual thresholds and conditions that permit termination of the contract. If the property's performance has been sufficiently inadequate to trigger termination, the asset manager should note this, whether or not ownership has acted to remove the operator.

Since some management agreements use comparative RevPAR metrics as a mechanism for measuring the operator's performance, it is useful to provide a summary of the hotel's competitive set in a tabular form, as shown in Exhibit 4. A separate summary of the anticipated changes in the competitive supply, prepared in the same format as shown in Exhibit 4, provides a snapshot of future supply conditions in the subject hotel's market. Finally, the addition of a brief summary of the subject's demand generators and market segments rounds out the overview, providing the user of the strategic plan with a concise picture of the hotel's market.

Additional sections of the key data summary include an overview of operating results and a capital overview. The operating results overview should include a summary of selected historical performance data, including occupancy percentage, average daily rate (ADR), RevPAR, RevPAR penetration, total revenue, house profit, house profit-margin percentage, net operating income, EBITDA (earnings before interest, taxes, depreciation, and amortization), and return on investment. The objective is to provide a profile of the hotel's operating performance and to illustrate the trends in that performance. This section is a complement to the asset management plan and is designed for the user who is unfamiliar with the asset.

Like the operating results summary, the capital overview is designed to provide supplemental information that supports the discussion contained in the body of the asset management plan. Capital expenditures are readily placed into three categories of projects: physical plant, renovation, and return on investment. For the physical plant summary, the objective is to identify the hotel's major systems, their age and operating condition, and the timing and estimated cost of the next major refurbishment or replacement. Similar details are provided for renovation projects, including a brief discussion of the scope of work in both prior and anticipated renovations. For return-on-investment projects, such as retrofits that reduce costs, the summary should include mention of both recently completed and future projects, specifying the date, cost, and anticipated return.

Conclusion

After wading through all of the operating data, technical reports, and legal documents, as well as touring the property and its competitors, the asset manager typically feels that he or she knows the hotel better than the entire executive team, the architect who designed it, and the general contractor who built it. The asset management plan that is developed from this encyclopedic knowledge is a concise distillation of the asset manager's research and analysis. The document must be streamlined but thorough, clearly defining the asset manager's vision for the hotel based on ownership's objectives.

Like the hotel's environment and market, the asset management plan evolves over time. By completing a plan and regularly reviewing it, the asset manager develops a powerful tool for planning and implementing the steps necessary to optimize the value of the operating business while protecting the physical asset. The document also serves as a single source of information that is shared with representatives of ownership, conveying the path to the achievement of their goals.

4

Investing in a Global Economy

By David T. Johnstone

__David T. Johnstone__ is a Senior Vice President of Miller Global Properties, a multi-asset-class investor in real estate, with holdings in the United States and Europe valued in excess of $2 billion. Mr. Johnstone has primary responsibility for coordinating and managing Miller Global's hotel acquisitions, development, and operations.

Mr. Johnstone began his career in hospitality real estate with Laventhol & Horwath, eventually managing the consulting firm's Denver office. He also served as an asset manager with Prudential Property Company, where he was responsible for a $600 million portfolio of upscale hotels. For seven years, Mr. Johnstone was a principal of Sage Hospitality Resources, where he was responsible for acquisitions and for developing and maintaining investor and partner relations.

In 1996, Mr. Johnstone joined the Ritz-Carlton Hotel Company as Vice President of Development for the Asia-Pacific region. During his tenure in Asia, he concluded or initiated negotiations for management contracts and technical service agreements in Manila, Jakarta, Bangkok, Shanghai, Tokyo, Beijing, and Cavite City, Philippines. Mr. Johnstone is a member of the Hospitality Asset Managers Association (HAMA) and served as HAMA's founding president. A frequent lecturer at hospitality management schools, he holds a BSBA degree in hotel, restaurant, and institutional management from Michigan State University and an MBA in real estate and construction management from the University of Denver.

OVER THE PAST TWENTY YEARS, much has been written about the globalization of business and the appetite of American corporations, institutions, and opportunity funds for investments outside of the United States. Although offshore investment has definitely occurred in the securities and durable goods industries, in comparison, investment of institutional and private equity capital in commercial real estate outside of America has been substantially less. Although no specific data are available, the proportion of investment in hotels as opposed to other forms of commercial real estate is likely even smaller. However, this may be changing because significant sums of money have been raised since the late 1990s for the purpose of investing in commercial real estate.

International Real Estate Investment Flows

According to a recent survey conducted by Ernst & Young, there are now more than one hundred real estate fund general partners that have raised more than $90

Exhibit 1 Cumulative Fund Equity Raised

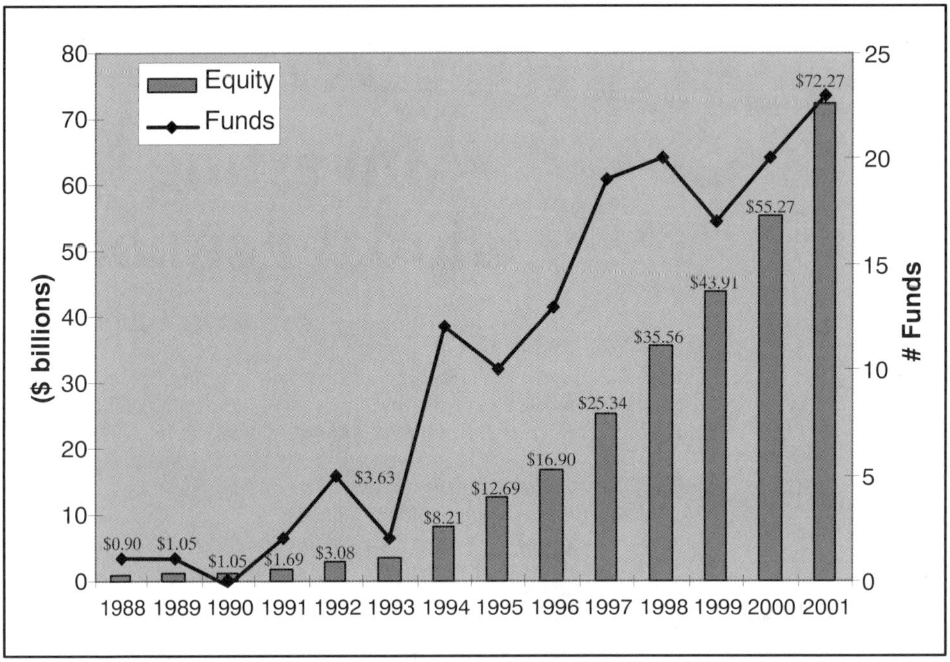

Source: *Opportunistic Investing: Real Estate Private Equity Funds,* p. 1.

billion in equity since 1991, with more than $20 billion of that sum left to deploy.[1] Since the early 1990s, the amount of capital eligible or specifically earmarked for investment outside the United States has gradually increased. According to the same Ernst & Young study, more than 60 percent[2] of the capital currently outstanding or committed is available for non-U.S. investment. Exhibit 1 shows the number of funds and the cumulative private fund equity raised in the 1988–2001 period, while Exhibit 2 shows the incremental amounts raised each year during the same period. As the exhibits demonstrate, a decade-long bull run on Wall Street and the enormous wealth created in the United States during the 1990s resulted in an increasing amount of capital being allocated to real estate private equity funds, especially in the 1997–2001 time frame.

Foreign Investment in U.S. Real Estate

In contrast to the relatively constrained level of U.S. investment in overseas real estate, foreign direct investment in commercial real estate in the United States has been very strong over a long period. According to a recent study by the National Association of Realtors (NAR), foreign investment in U.S. real estate increased to $42 billion in 2001, up from $38 billion in 1997.[3] In a statement accompanying the release of the study, David Lereah, the NAR's chief economist observed, "United States real estate offers foreign investors diversification of their investment portfolio so that their assets are not fully tied to the health of their domestic economy."

Exhibit 2 Total Fund Equity Raised

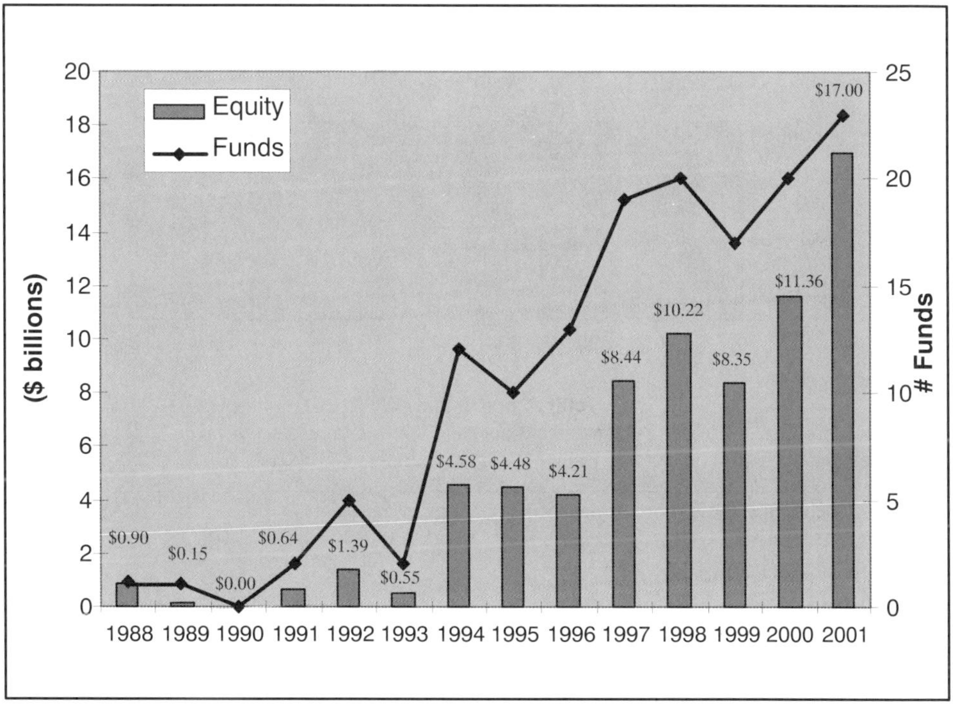

Source: *Opportunistic Investing: Real Estate Private Equity Funds,* p.2.

Lereah also noted that income-producing properties in the United States generally offer higher yields than similar investments abroad, as well as serving as an inflation hedge. Gail Lyons, chairman of NAR's International Affairs Committee, summed up the appeal of investments in the United States, saying, "For international investors looking for a stable investment with good earnings potential, U.S. real estate and financial markets both remain the global standard."

The Association of Foreign Investors in Real Estate (AFIRE) regularly tracks investor sentiment regarding the attractiveness of various real estate sectors and markets around the world. Collectively, AFIRE's membership has more than $226 billion invested globally, including $70 billion in the United States. In an AFIRE survey released in early 2003, the United States was ranked first in terms of offering the most stable and secure real estate investments as well as the best opportunity for capital appreciation and the best risk-adjusted potential return.[4]

As shown in Exhibit 3, according to AFIRE's membership, the best global cities for real estate investment in 2002 included two American cities, and the first-place city by a significant margin is Washington, D.C.

The relative attractiveness of U.S. real estate by product type for the years 2001 and 2002 is charted in Exhibit 4. It is interesting to note that hotel and leisure investments were rated as more attractive in 2002 than in 2001. This counterintuitive ranking is probably explained by hotels' greater sensitivity to swings in

Exhibit 3 Best Global Cities for Real Estate Investment—2002

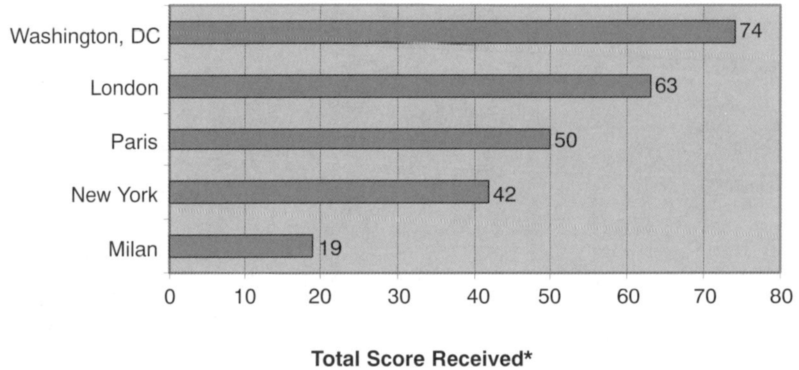

*Total score was calculated by assigning 3 points to the respondent's 1st choice, 2 points to the respondent's 2nd choice, and 1 point to the respondent's 3rd choice.

Source: 2002 AFIRE Foreign Investment Survey; Kingsley Associates.

Exhibit 4 Attractiveness of U.S. Real Estate Investment Product Types

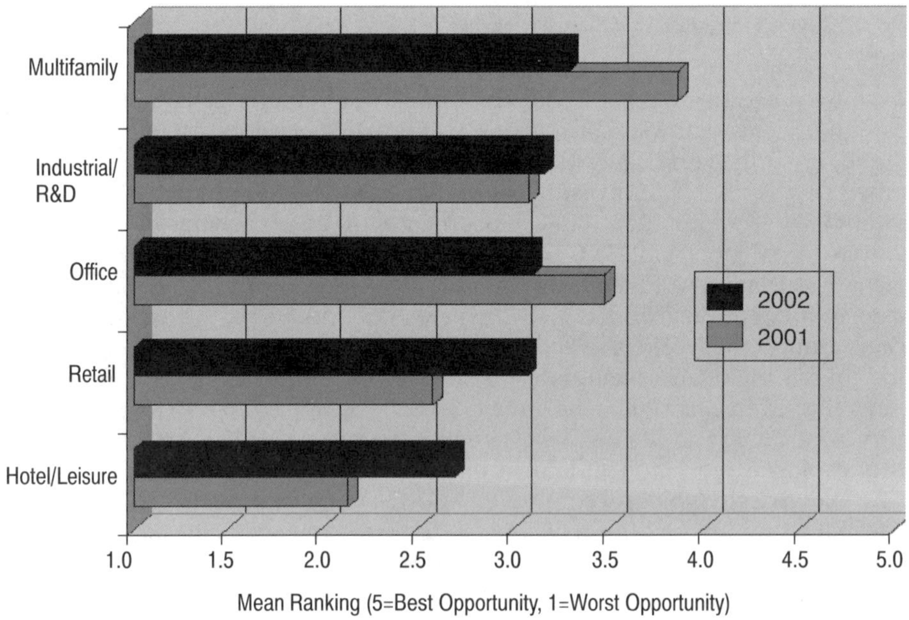

Source: 2002 AFIRE Foreign Investment Survey; Kingsley Associates.

Exhibit 5 Measurements of Power

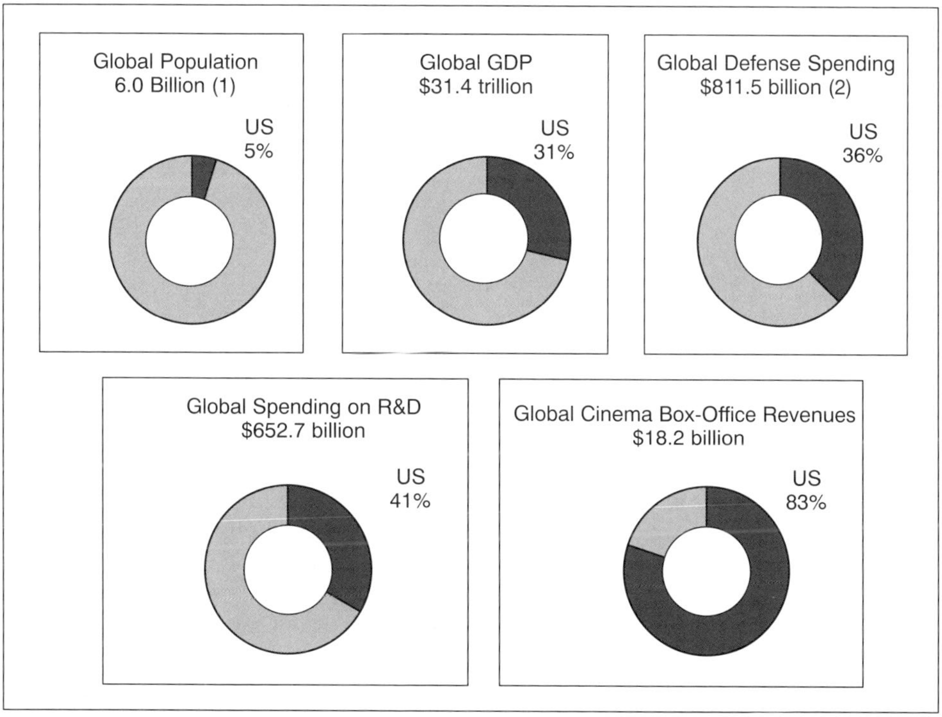

Source: *The Economist*, June 29, 2002, p. 4.

market value; apparently foreign investors anticipated more opportunities for bargains in the lodging sector in a post-9/11 environment.

America is the fourth largest country in the world with respect to area. It is also the largest democracy in the world. As discussed in a special issue of *The Economist* subtitled "America's Role in the World," the United States leads the world in all dimensions of power—military, economic, cultural, and scientific—by a margin way out of proportion to its population (see Exhibit 5).

It is not surprising that the United States is perceived as a much larger, safer, and generally more profitable real estate market. This explains why, in general, few U.S. real estate equity investors have ventured outside of America. It also helps to explain why so many foreign investors have been attracted to U.S. real estate. More money comes into the United States for real estate than flows out because foreign investors perceive an investment in America to be relatively safe, whereas domestic investors do not share the same sense of security when investing outside their national borders.

Impediments to International Real Estate Investment

A primary reason for investing in international real estate is to reduce the volatility of a domestic real estate portfolio—or, stated differently, to be counter-cyclical.

Real estate is inherently a cyclical business; however, since regions, nations, markets, and asset classes are not synchronized in their swings in value, logic suggests that when one region is down there is opportunity in another. The counter cyclicality of macro markets is a phenomenon that we can observe to a certain degree. However, at least as it pertains to hotel real estate, the world comprises a collection of independent real estate markets and submarkets, each one different from the other but predominantly affected by the economic condition of the local area.

In addition to knowing the local markets, an American organization investing overseas must consider a variety of additional factors not common to domestic investments. The normal decision making criteria used in the United States are also used to evaluate foreign property and investment opportunities, but the rules and customs of the real estate game vary from country to country and continent to continent. Americans are generally unfamiliar with these rules and customs, which places them at a decided disadvantage. When investing in the United States, certain elements of a real estate transaction are all but automatic, and the investor takes them for granted. When investing outside of the United States, many of these aspects are not automatic and will exert significant influence on the risk-return profile of an international hotel or other type of real estate investment.

This writer cannot claim omniscient knowledge of the impact of local rules and customs on lodging real estate transactions. Nonetheless, based on my experience in Europe, Asia, Australia, and North America, a pattern of issues can be seen that provides a useful framework for explaining at least some of the complexities of global investing. In the writer's experience, the major issues to consider in a foreign hotel investment include the following:

- Legal system
- Currency risk
- Local business practices and conditions
- Tax and financial considerations
- Political stability
- Communication

These factors can add substantial risk, time, and costs over and above the normal decision-making, organizational, and managerial challenges faced when investing in domestic hotel or other real estate. For the additional risk inherent in international transactions, additional return is usually required. When a development opportunity (as opposed to an acquisition) is being considered, the additional time and cost factors alone will usually prevent a U.S. investor from proceeding unless the entity partners (via a joint venture) with an experienced local developer who can deal with the complexities in a cost-efficient manner.

Legal System

The legal systems in the United States, most western European countries, Australia, Japan, Singapore, and the territory of Hong Kong are considered to be equitable, permitting an investor, if needed, to pursue recourse or a remedy to correct an injustice. In many countries, however, the practical reality is that the legal system heavily favors the local party against the foreigner, regardless of what contracts or other evidence indicates.

For example, while working in Asia for a major U.S. hotel company, this writer attempted to enforce contracts for the development and management of a luxury hotel in Jakarta, Indonesia. When the local Indonesian owner willfully abrogated the contracts, the hotel company initially pursued enforcement of the contact, then a remedy for the breach through the Indonesian court system. After contacting many law firms, the hotel management company's executives were advised to settle the company's claim and informed that no foreigner had ever won a lawsuit against an Indonesian local in the history of the country! Ultimately the hotel company settled with the local owner, receiving a small fraction of its original investment and of course forgoing all potential profits, despite having worked several years on the project.

The ability to pursue recourse for a contractual or other injustice should be fundamental to the decision to invest in a given country. If a nation has a reputation for having an unfair legal system, this must be factored into the risk assessment that is part of decision-making process. The investor must be prepared to research this issue, because statutes and legal practices differ from country to country, and often there is a lack of transparency.

In some countries, including China, foreigners who own real estate are required by law to have a local partner. Foreclosure and bankruptcy laws in the United States are courses of action that are clear to Americans; however, such laws simply may not exist in other countries. In a foreclosure or bankruptcy, an owner in the United States would typically lose the property pledged as security, but in some countries (e.g., Indonesia, Thailand), owners have been known to default on their obligations to foreign lenders, yet manage to retain ownership of the mortgaged property.

Currency Risk

Like other factors that affect economic risk in a real estate investment, American investors must consider the fluctuation of the local currency against the U.S. dollar. The volatility of a nation's currency against the U.S. dollar over periods of time is quantified by research groups. For example, the PRS Group (www.prsgroup.com) produces the *International Country Risk Guide,* a publication devoted to political, financial, and economic risk analysis for 140 countries. Thus, when the author's current (American) company was contemplating the acquisition of a hotel in Amsterdam in late 1999, research led the executive team to conclude that the investment represented a relatively low currency risk. This was because the Netherlands was already committed to joining the European Union, and its currency was rated as one of the strongest and most stable to be eventually converted into euros. Similarly reassuring was the evaluation derived from the *International Country Risk Guide,* which ranked the Netherlands as one of the least risky countries in the world and rated its currency among the three strongest in Europe.

From a lodging investment perspective, an interesting phenomenon is occurring in selected eastern European lodging markets such as Warsaw, Prague,

Budapest, and Moscow. Properties in these cities are able to collect their room revenues in U.S. dollars or in euros, but pay their employees in local currencies, creating an arbitrage that benefits the owner significantly. Parallel situations also occur in numerous markets in Asia, although the Asian currency crisis of 1997 greatly reduced the benefit of this dynamic, particularly in Thailand, Malaysia, Indonesia, and the Philippines—the countries, along with Japan, most affected by the region's financial crisis.

The Asian currency crisis has also affected real estate values throughout the region. In Hong Kong and other major Southeast Asian cities, seven years after the real estate bubble burst, values still have not returned to pre-1997 levels. The decline in average room rates and total revenues, which was exacerbated by the SARS (Severe Acute Respiratory Syndrome) scare, has left numerous hotels unable to make debt-service payments. Years after the onset of the crisis, several major hotel markets, including Beijing and Singapore, still do not have citywide average room rates above $100 (U.S.). As such examples demonstrate, currency risk is very real. Investors in foreign markets must do their research, evaluating currency risk as rigorously as they do any other component of the project's risk.

Local Business Practices and Conditions

The fundamentals that make a hotel or office building an attractive real estate investment in the United States also apply to foreign situations. However, Americans conducting business overseas will find great variation in customary business practices among these countries, as well as variation in the weighting of importance ascribed to the fundamentals. In most of the larger European metropolitan areas, where active trading of large real estate projects exists, institutional investors typically take a leading role in these markets. Institutional investors are also active in the larger metropolitan areas of Asia, although there is also a large contingent of entrepreneurial investors, particularly the ethnic Chinese, who are active in Asia's urban centers. In some countries, knowing the local real estate market is crucial to risk reduction and the ultimate success of a foreign hotel investment.

The assumption that a foreigner can "beat the locals" is usually a faulty one. The locals have access to information, and possibly analysis, that the typical American investor does not. Thus, the best way to keep pace with indigenous real estate professionals is to align with one at the partner level. In addition, the foreign investor is well advised to retain local hospitality experts and consultants, as well as building an overseas network through relationships with foreign hospitality brokers, consultants and appraisers, hotel company development and operations personnel, and financing sources. Nurturing these relationships through specific visits and attendance at foreign hospitality-industry conferences is expensive and time-consuming to do from the United States; however, it is necessary if a company wishes to be taken seriously as an investor by foreign sellers, brokers, and other hospitality professionals. Larger hospitality investment organizations with many assets in their portfolio will often open an affiliate office in the appropriate region overseas, but this can be prohibitively expensive unless the organization has a sufficient number of assets to justify an office.

The inherent difficulties of investing in foreign hospitality assets overseas can be compounded by corruption, red tape, and public or private monopolies at work in many of the developing countries, particularly in Asia and some eastern European countries. These complexities can greatly increase the time it takes to complete a transaction, and more time always means higher costs. A general rule when acquiring properties overseas is to assume that closing costs—legal fees, consultants, due diligence, financing, and other costs—will be at least twice what they would be if the transaction were completed in the United States.

Finally, the time-distance gap from the location of the asset to the foreign investor's home office is a consideration if the entity does not have an office in the same overseas region. Europe is a five- to seven-hour time difference from the east coast of the United States, and Asia a 12- to 14-hour time difference. When the author lived and worked in Hong Kong, telephone calls from the corporate office, located in the eastern time zone of the United States, were rare. Because of the 12-hour time difference, to reach an associate during business hours in Asia, a U.S.-based employee must telephone from home at night, just as the Asian-based employee must call during the night to reach an American-based counterpart during North American business hours. As a result of this inconvenience, electronic mail was the preferred method of communication.

Tax and Financial Considerations

Investing in foreign real estate gives rise to taxation issues that can greatly affect the potential to achieve the desired investment returns. In some countries, the tax laws are intentionally designed to discourage, or even prohibit, foreign ownership of real estate. In other countries, foreign ownership of real property is restricted to a defined percentage of the equity in a project.

Not unlike the United States tax code, foreign tax laws are also constantly changing. For example, Germany has never been considered a favorable tax environment, primarily because its tax rates are among the highest in the European Union. Moreover, Germany's tax laws have typically proven very difficult for foreigners to understand. Adding to this confusion, three different tax acts were passed in 2001—the Tax Amendment Act, the Act to Combat Tax Evasion, and the Corporate Tax Development Act. All three of these acts could affect foreigners contemplating investment in Germany. Thus, retaining an advisor experienced in local tax law and the particular character of hospitality investments is one of the first priorities of due diligence.

Regardless of the foreign investment locale, for the American investor, overseas investing creates more complex tax issues than investing domestically. This is particularly true for U.S. tax-exempt investors, such as pension funds. Thus, legal, accounting, and tax advisors familiar with current regulations are a requirement from the outset of any potential acquisition or development in a foreign land. The goal for the American investor is to create a corporate structure in the overseas nation that best facilitates the repatriation of returns and minimizes tax liabilities or—ideally—is tax neutral. Because the domestic parent company must pay U.S. income tax on the income brought into the U.S., the dual objectives are (1) to find legal vehicles for transferring income (2) from countries with favorable tax treaties, so that the ultimate structure permits the parent company to pay taxes only at the American level. For example, an American entity controlled by the author's company invested in the hotel in the Netherlands described previously by acquiring the shares of the single purpose entity that owned the hotel. The Netherlands has a favorable tax treaty with Denmark, which enjoys a favorable tax treaty with the Isle of Man, which in turn has a favorable tax treaty with the United States. Thus, to minimize the tax consequences of the investment, the structure provides for the flow of funds through corporations set up in two other countries before the funds enter the United States. These companies have bank accounts and are audited each year, along with the U.S. company and the Netherlands company.

As the preceding example illustrates, it can be cumbersome and expensive to devise a tax efficient investment structure for the ownership of a foreign asset. Moreover, as already suggested, tax rates and tax laws change constantly, making it prudent to maintain advisors to keep the overseas investor abreast of these changes.

Financing foreign acquisitions or developments can also be challenging. Unless the American investor has a pre-existing relationship with a domestic institution willing to lend on projects in the foreign country or there is a local joint venture partner with access to financing, the U.S. investor will likely be seeking financing from a local or regional financing source located in the foreign country. Since lenders are as concerned as the equity investor by project economics and risk reduction, they may impose requirements on their loans that reflect their own predispositions, but which are atypical for a loan in the United States. For example, many hospitality lenders in Europe will make loans only if the hotel operator leases the building or, alternatively, provides a minimum performance guarantee.

Lenders are also concerned by the legal and political risks associated with particular countries. Since the terrorist attacks of 9/11, coverage for acts of terrorism has been excluded from the standard hotel insurance policy. Yet many financing institutions require owners to carry terrorism insurance for hotels in selected locales.

Political Stability

American investors are primarily concerned that the foreign nation where they invest funds maintain a system of government that is stable. They also expect that the government will not implement unanticipated policy changes that disrupt the country's economic and social stability or prove detrimental to investment performance. While most of the western European countries generally meet these expectations, some eastern European countries and many Asian countries do not.

Terrorism has added a new dimension of concern for investors in international real estate, especially for hotel investors. The terrorist attacks of September 11, 2001, showed that, even in the world's strongest economy, economic stability can be disrupted. Although we now know that the U.S. economy was headed toward a recession before the events of 9/11, the attacks accelerated the decline precipitously. While all business activity suffered in the aftermath of 9/11, hotels especially were affected as uncertainty and the fear of additional attacks resulted in cancelled conventions, meetings, business trips, and vacation travel.

The recent run-up to the Iraq war caused corporations in the United States and Europe to view business growth with a very cautious eye, and business travel declined. Similarly, an examination of hotel occupancy statistics in the United States following the Persian Gulf War in 1991 (see Exhibit 6) shows just how sensitive the hotel industry can be when there is war or instability, even if it is halfway around the world.

An unstable economy can cause political instability, as witnessed by the case of Indonesia. During the mid-1990s, most Asian countries were experiencing record growth and, in some instances, citizens of these Asian nations were beginning to enjoy unparalleled prosperity. One such country was Indonesia, and in particular the citizens of its capital city, Jakarta. However, in the aftermath of the Asian currency crisis of 1997, Indonesia's currency experienced a disproportional decline (35 percent) in value against the U.S. dollar, causing members of its emerging middle class to lose much of what had been gained. Major social unrest followed, with rioting, looting, and the loss of 500 lives. Ultimately, the country's dictator, Suharto, was forced to resign after 32 years of governing the world's fourth most populous nation. Tremendous losses were sustained, much of it in real estate, and several hotel projects under construction were simply abandoned. Japan, by far the largest lender to Indonesia with $23.1 billion in bank debt, was left to write off a large portion of its loans.

Communication

The ability to communicate effectively (or not) can influence the outcome of an international real estate transaction. Although English is generally considered the language of global business, it can be very difficult for Americans to negotiate transactions in English in a faraway nation with foreign counterparts and with foreign laws governing the transaction. In Europe, a densely populated continent with numerous nations occupying a relatively small geographic region, multilingual skills are a high priority in the education systems of most countries. English is typically an optional language; however, in the Netherlands, English is a required language. Consequently, American companies are finding Holland an attractive place to locate their European offices.

In Europe, local English-speaking consultants, accountants, legal advisors, etc., who also speak the indigenous language can usually be retained. It is important for the American investor to engage such expertise because these local professionals understand the norms, customs, etiquette, and protocol of a particular country; they can help effect a smooth negotiation between an American buyer or seller and a foreign counterpart. In Asia, with the exception of Hong Kong, Singapore, the Philippines, and, to a lesser extent, Japan, the availability of English-speaking ethnic consultants and advisors is more limited. Typically, however, English-speaking ex-patriots of British, American, or other national descent are available to fulfill the roles required.

In some European and Asian countries, there is resistance to the use of English as the sole or "ruling" language for contracts. Often contracts, building plans, consultants' reports, loan documents, etc., are prepared in English and in the native language of the country where the hotel is located. For Americans, English is the

Exhibit 6 Historical Trend: United States, 1990–1992

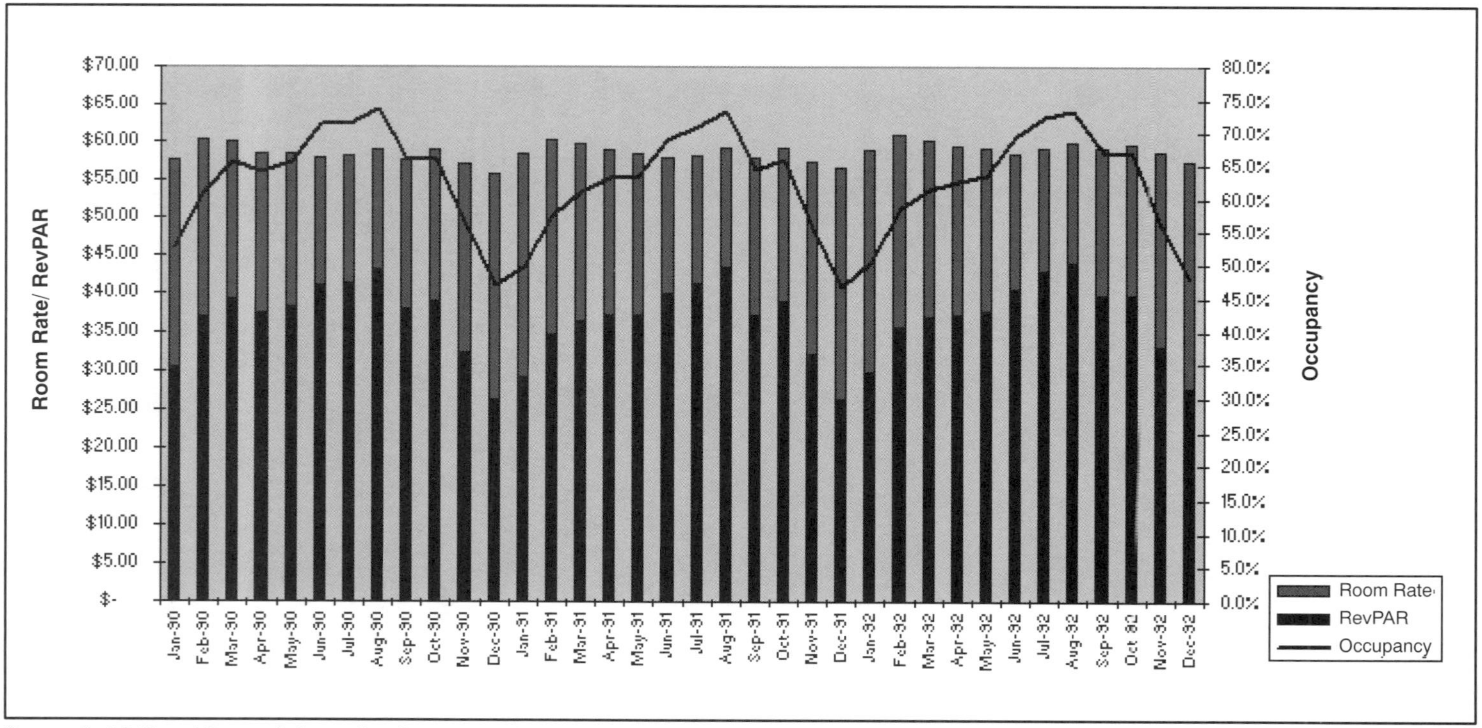

Source: Smith Travel Research (www.hotelreports.com).

preferred language to rule in a dispute resolution, particularly if the dispute is to be resolved through international arbitration. In some countries, such as China and Japan, securing agreement to the use of English as the ruling language for dispute resolution is much more difficult to negotiate.

When making international investments, Americans need to be sensitive to how they conduct themselves and how they are perceived by their foreign counterparts. Based on personal experiences living in Asia and conducting business in Europe over the last several years, this writer concludes that anti-American sentiment is prevalent across both continents. The likelihood of a successful transaction is improved if the foreign investor is aware of and sensitive to local customs and etiquette.

Europe Contrasted with the United States

American investors seeking to develop or acquire hotel assets in Europe will note certain characteristic differences when comparing lodging markets and opportunities to those available in North America. For example, in contrast to the United States, the percentage of branded hotels is significantly lower. As pointed out on p. 118, 55 percent of the properties and 67 percent of the U.S. rooms inventory carry a flag. Because most European cities are far more mature from a development standpoint, they typically have enjoyed a sufficient supply of well-located, high-quality independent hotels. Over the past twenty years, branding has become the preferred method of new hotel development in Europe. Nevertheless, a much smaller percentage of hotels in Europe are branded properties.

Other differences between Europe and the United States are the more widespread use of ground leases and frequent share transactions, where the shares of the company owning the asset are transferred instead of the property itself. Ground leases are more common in Europe because prime real estate locations in major European cities were originally the property of the aristocracy or the government. Over the centuries, this feudal right to the ownership of land has been staunchly preserved, and land has continued to be held by families, estates, royalty, or governments that confer the right to use of the land through ground leases. The prevalence of share transactions is explained by the tax policies of many European countries. Governments assess large transfer taxes—up to five or six percent of the total purchase price—when a fee simple interest is conveyed. Although a significant transfer tax is avoided by selling the shares of the owning company, the purchaser typically assumes the seller's depreciated basis in the assets acquired, reducing the tax-shelter benefits of ownership.

According to a report assembled by Jones Lang LaSalle Hotels (an international lodging investment advisory service) titled *Management Agreement Trends Worldwide*, "almost half (44.8 percent) of European management contracts contain performance guarantees by the operator in favor of the owner. An operator guarantee gives a degree of certainty of return to the owner (and the lender), but it comes at a price. It is interesting to note that in Europe, more owners are prepared to trade off greater upside for a guarantee than in the Americas."[5] None of the

American management agreements included in the Jones Lang LaSalle survey contained a guarantee by the operator.

European financial institutions, such as commercial banks and insurance companies, demonstrate a high degree of risk aversion, accepting yields that, by North American standards, are modest in exchange for guarantees. In addition to management contracts with operator guarantees, European financial institutions favor operating leases, whereby the hotel company shields the owner from the hotel's operating risk by agreeing to pay a specified amount of rent.

In general, European capitalization rates and investor return expectations are lower than in the United States. Jones Lang LaSalle Hotels surveys hotel investors semi-annually for its *Hotel Investor Sentiment Survey (HISS)*. According to the *HISS* survey, on average the capitalization, or cap, rate for a new acquisition is usually 200 basis points or more lower in Europe than in the United States. Similarly, according to the same survey, the average leveraged internal rate of return (IRR) for a new acquisition is 16 to 17 percent in Europe and 22 to 23 percent in the United States.[6] This is a significant difference in return expectation. Europe's generally lower and more stable interest rates, coupled with comparatively modest equity return expectations, explain why the cap rates observed in Europe are so much lower than in United States.

With wages the largest cost of hotel operations, American investors contemplating European investments must be very attentive to local labor laws. Some countries in Europe, such as France and the Netherlands, have very stringent labor laws that favor the worker over the employer. However, in certain countries in Eastern Europe, such as Poland, the Czech Republic, Romania, and Hungary, the opposite is true. Moreover, as previously discussed, in addition to paying relatively lower levels of wages and benefits in the local currencies of these countries, room revenues are collected in dollars or euros, significantly enhancing a hotel's operating profit.

Asia-Pacific Region Contrasted with the United States

Economically and demographically, the Asia-Pacific region has been, and will continue to be, the fastest growing region in the world. Despite the attractiveness of this growth, on a relative basis American institutional real estate investors have avoided investing large sums of money in hotels or other commercial real estate located in Asian-Pacific countries. A primary reason for this reticence is that many Asian countries still have unreliable legal systems. In Australia, New Zealand, Hong Kong, and Singapore, the legal systems are equitable and rooted largely in Anglo-Saxon law. In certain countries in the region, however, the risk of losing some or all of an investment becomes much larger because, if a dispute must be resolved, the American or other foreign investor is not likely to receive fair treatment.

In Japan and Thailand, until recently, foreigners were not legally permitted to own real estate. Other Asian countries still do not permit foreigners to own real estate. In communist countries (e.g., China, North Korea, North Vietnam) or totalitarian countries ruled by dictators (e.g., Indonesia, Malaysia), American investors seeking to resolve disputes are not likely to receive fair treatment, making hotel investments in these countries very risky. In addition, the Asian currency crisis of 1997 slowed the "Asian Miracle," yielding the "Asian Meltdown" that stanched the inflows of foreign investment. As growth stalled, the bubble burst, and the Asia-Pacific region has yet to recover fully.

Over the past two decades, Western hotel chains (e.g., Hyatt, Hilton, Sheraton) have enjoyed some success expanding their brand presence in the Asia-Pacific region. However, they must compete with numerous Asian and European brands that are well established in the region. For an Asian hotel owner, the attraction of a Western brand over an Asian brand is that American business and leisure customers are generally loyal to Western brands. American guests are preferred because historically they have been the least price sensitive and they pay for their rooms in U.S. dollars, whereas native customers typically pay less for their accommodations and settle their bills in local currency. Additionally, with some exceptions (e.g., Japan, Australia, South Korea, Singapore), most Asia-Pacific region countries have plentiful supplies of cheap labor, making hotel profit margins very attractive when revenues are collected in dollars and wages are paid in the local currency.

In some Asian-Pacific countries, such as Thailand, Malaysia, China, Indonesia, and the Philippines, the development of modern urban infrastructure (transportation, utilities, streets) has not kept pace with the demand for commercial real estate, with the result that traffic congestion and air pollution are major problems in many large cities. In some of the region's cities during peak periods, it can take an extraordinarily long time to travel just a few miles. From a hotel investment perspective, this phenomenon yields two challenges: a superior location is essential to the success of a hotel and the cost of land typically represents a larger percentage of overall project cost than in most other parts of the world.

Another interesting phenomenon of Asian hotel investments is the relatively high percentage of food-and-beverage revenues to total revenues. In the United States, hotel guests typically do not eat lunch or dinner where they are lodged, and with the exception of signature restaurants, most hotel food-and-beverage outlets do not attract local customers. In the Asia-Pacific region, hotels are often the focal point for leisure as well as business activity. Thus, hotels will have multiple food-and-beverage outlets that enjoy heavy usage by both hotel guests and local patrons. As a result of high volumes and multiple food-and-beverage outlets, the percentage base fee under management contracts tends to be lower in Asia because the operator's fees are significant in absolute dollars, even if the percentage applied to gross revenues is less than the typical three percent fee paid to branded operators in the United States.

When compared with management agreements in force in Europe and the United States, the typical management contract for a chain-affiliated hotel in Asia is more favorable to the owner. According to Jones Lang LaSalle's *Management Agreement Trends Worldwide*, Asian management agreements have shorter terms, feature lower fees, and provide for greater owner involvement.[7] This is consistent with the author's personal observations while living and working in Asia.

Return expectations in Asia also vary from those in the United States and Europe. Investment yields reported in Jones Lang LaSalle's *Hotel Investor*

Sentiment Survey indicate that Asian investor expectations for new acquisitions are higher than those reported in Europe but lower than in the United States.[8]

Debt financing as well as equity for hotels in Asia is typically provided by institutions in Singapore, Hong Kong, Japan, South Korea, or Australia. Native regional and local entrepreneurs also provide large sums of equity. In several emerging Southeast Asian countries, such as Thailand, Malaysia, Indonesia, and the Philippines, a large portion of the country's wealth is controlled by a small percentage of its citizens. These wealthier citizens tend to be hotel owners, and typically these individuals are in a variety of businesses, of which hotel real estate is just one. Foreign lenders have the same concerns as foreign equity investors when lending in certain countries (such as Indonesia) where the legal system favors the nation's citizen—especially a powerful local figure—over the foreigner, regardless of the facts in a dispute. Many Asian lenders, particularly Japanese creditors, learned this lesson during the currency crisis that commenced in 1997. Local borrowers defaulted on loans made by foreign lenders, but the foreign lenders found no redress in the courts, as the borrowers not only withheld debt-service payments but also succeeded in retaining ownership of the assets pledged as security for their debts.

Conclusion

After weighing all the factors, most American investors have concluded that the United States is still the best choice when investing in hospitality real estate. Higher investment returns, free market principles supported by regulations and conventions that facilitate the conveyance of real estate, and a legal system that ensures fair treatment in the event of a contractual or other dispute render the United States attractive for hotel investors.

Investing overseas can also be lucrative and provides a measure of diversification. However, hotel development overseas without a local partner is extremely difficult. When attempting offshore acquisitions, American investors need to be concerned with the many nuances of operating in a foreign environment, as well as with the additional costs and risks—all of which are best mitigated by having a local presence or partner.

Endnotes

1. Ernst & Young, *Opportunistic Investing: Real Estate Private Equity Funds* (New York: Ernst & Young LLP, 2002), p. 3.
2. Ernst & Young, p. 2.
3. National Association of Realtors, *Foreign Investment in US Real Estate* (Chicago: National Association of Realtors, 2002), p. 2.
4. See www.afire.org/foreign_data/2002fis_stable.shtm.
5. Jones Lang LaSalle Hotels, *Hotel Topics: Management Agreement Trends Worldwide* (Sydney: Jones Lang LaSalle Hotels, 2001), p. 7.

6. Jones Lang LaSalle Hotels, *Hotel Investment Sentiment Survey (HISS)*, Issue 5, July 2002, p. 1.
7. Jones Lang LaSalle Hotels, *Hotel Topics: Management Agreement Trends Worldwide*, pp. 2–5.
8. Jones Lang LaSalle Hotels, *Hotel Investment Sentiment Survey (HISS)*, Issue 5, July 2002, p. 1.

Part II

Management Contracts and Franchising

5

Management Contract Terms and Trends

By Greg Denton and Paul Beals

SINCE THE ADVENT OF DOMESTIC hotel management contracts in the 1970s, contract negotiations and the owner-operator relationship have been dictated by a volatile combination of economics and power. In some respects, the relationship can be likened to a mixture of nitroglycerin—benign, with many useful applications under normal conditions, but capable of exploding if disturbed by outside forces.

In the early years of hotel management contract negotiations, operators wielded considerable control over the process, owing to the combination of (1) higher levels of expertise in operations and contract negotiation and (2) control over the brand affiliation. Thus, branded operators more or less dictated contract terms to owners—who usually had little hospitality industry knowledge or experience—yielding management agreements heavily favorable to the operator. The occasional pension fund or large institutional investor was able to stand its ground in management contract negotiations due to the size of its portfolio, but in general the negotiating power rested with the operator. In such an environment, the owner's level of oversight and approval once the contract was in force is best described as blind faith.

During times of economic growth and prosperity, relations between hotel owners and operators were relatively peaceful. Owners reaped the economic benefits of hotel ownership, which outpaced returns from most other real estate investment vehicles, while operators were able to increase the number of rooms managed and their brand distribution networks without significant capital investment. Both parties benefited from the relationship, and little attention was paid to evaluating whether or not the rewards were proportional to the financial risk assumed. Since properties were performing satisfactorily, contract termination provisions were rarely invoked.

Over the past few years, the hotel owner's mentality has evolved. Owners now give serious consideration to the effect that management contract provisions have on the value of their investments, their ability to realize that value through a sale, and the balance of risks and rewards available to the owner and the operator. In addition, owners now realize that the operator's interests are not always aligned with theirs and that a degree of control over the hotel management function is necessary to protect their investment value and their flexibility.

In part, this evolution can be attributed to the economic downturns that have tested the relationship between owners and operators, revealing imbalances that owners did not previously comprehend. However, the most important factor driving the shift in owners' thinking is simply the higher level of sophistication and experience found in today's hotel owners. Contemporary hotel owners are significantly more knowledgeable about the hospitality industry than their counterparts in the 1970s and 1980s. Moreover, today's owners often employ, either internally or externally, dedicated hotel investment specialists, asset managers, and legal counsel to represent their interests. Today's hotel owners have seen the powerful effect that a long-term, "no-cut" management contract can have on the value of their properties in the event of sale. They have witnessed or experienced directly the negative effects on a property of brand impact and have read court decisions such as *Woolley v. Embassy Suites*[1] and *2660 Woodley Road v. ITT Sheraton*[2] that affirm owners' rights and the operator's fiduciary responsibilities to ownership.

Many industry observers would agree that the most tumultuous period for hotel management contracts is past and that the current environment represents a closer approximation of balance between the negotiating powers of the owner and the operator. We no longer have an environment in which operators receive fees dramatically out of proportion to their levels of risk or value added, basking in the glow of a 50-year, non-terminable contract while managing properties with little regard for the owner's return requirements. In cases where operators *do* engage in these tactics—typically in older contracts—owners at least have legal precedents and resources they can turn to as means of protecting their interests. Finally, although operators represent themselves as partners, owners have learned that the commercial maxim of *caveat emptor* applies to the selection of a property manager as much as it does to any business transaction.

If there is a more sustainable balance of power between owners and operators, it is because of the increased sophistication of owners and because of the heightened competition among hotel operating companies, including especially the larger branded hotel management companies. As discussed in Chapter 1, the increased sophistication of owners corresponds to the advent of the asset management function in the lodging industry. As hotel ownership has been consolidated in the hands of larger, more sophisticated owners, management companies have found ready customers for their services. Several have grown as publicly traded entities, reaching imposing mass, but with none controlling the market. It is not unusual, therefore, for lodging-ownership entities of even modest size to work with multiple brands and operators, each in its own way meeting the owner's needs, depending on the investment objectives, market positioning, and operating requirements of a particular asset.

The following pages in this chapter describe the current balance of power between hotel owners and operators. This is done by first analyzing the owner's and operator's outlooks on six critical provisions of management contracts:

- Contract duration
- Fees and fee structures
- Operator financial contributions

- Performance clauses
- Termination provisions
- Budgetary and spending limitations

After presenting the owner's and operator's vantage points on the individual contract provision, we report the broad outlines of current practices, as found in today's management contracts, for addressing the issues raised by the provision. The current practices were drawn from recent research with executives at larger branded hotel management companies operating in North America and discussions with the owners who employ them. Observations on management contracts in force between owners and unbranded operators as well as prevailing provisions other than the six identified above are beyond our scope here and will be offered only anecdotally.

Contract Duration

The issue of management contract duration or term can be simplistically summed up by observing that the operator wants a long-term contract, while the owner will always favor a shorter term. The respective rationales for these apparently irreconcilable stances deserve exploration, however, to appreciate the compromises reached in the contracts that do (or do not) result.

The Management Company's View: What's in a Brand?

Above all, branded operating companies recognize that short-term contracts are incompatible with their fundamental mission of building an enduring brand, one that enjoys a steady, predictable stream of fees that enables it to evolve and adapt to maintain its franchise with the consumer. Moreover, as most of the largest brands are publicly traded, fee-driven companies, their valuations depend on the duration of their management and franchise contracts. If there is a drift toward shorter terms, these annuities will inevitably decline in value, reducing a brand's share price. (It is interesting to note, however, that among the largest brands, not all companies take advantage of the financial strength represented by the duration of their contracts, while others trumpet them to analysts and shareholders.)

Contracts of longer duration give branded operators greater bargaining power with owners, both at the negotiation stage and when modifying or implementing new brand standards. Since owners are purchasing not only operating expertise but an identity, the existence of a stable system likely to endure in the consumer marketplace is a reassurance to the owner contemplating a 20-year contract with a branded management company. In short, the owner has difficulty arguing that requirements imposed on other owners and salutary to his interests should not also apply to new contracts. Similarly, the existence of long-term contracts reassures the owner that the management company is more likely to attract and retain competent managers, providing a depth of talent that might not otherwise be available to the individual owner. Finally, the existence of a long-term contract provides the operator with increased leverage when imposing new brand standards. Financially (and emotionally), it is easier for an owner to accept a controversial brand standard if the costs are amortized over multiple remaining years of an existing contract. Even if the owner contemplates selling in the short term, the new brand standard is more readily justified if there are multiple years left to run on the contract. At best, the owner can only defer the cost of meeting the brand standard, since a new owner stepping into the management contract would discount the purchase price to reflect the cost of bringing the hotel up to standard.

For many assets, the branded operator's strongest argument is that the longer the management contract, the greater the value added. Surely, for a significant portion of the undistinguished boxes—large and small—found in roadside and suburban locations across the United States, this is a valid argument. Many of these hotels rely on their brand identity for their value. It is impossible to imagine their having greater value under another flag. Often the choice of the brand is dictated by the *absence* of the brand in the local market, rather than a perfect fit between the property's physical plant and the segments served. When the power of the brand is such an important determinant of a property's success, a long-term contract with multiple years left to run can significantly enhance the value of the asset.

The Owner's View: Value Added or Encumbered?

The length of the management contract and corresponding termination provisions are two of the most critical issues for owners in the contract negotiation phase. Owners recognize that the brand affiliation can add significant value to their property and are not opposed to granting the operator a valuable management contract. They are, however, reluctant to encumber their asset with a franchise or management contract that might hamper their ability to make needed changes in management or to sell their hotel.

Owners view the selection of an operator for their property as entering a contract that may, for a variety of reasons, ultimately need to be terminated. Perhaps the management company will not prove to be the most appropriate for the property; or perhaps another management company more desirable to the owner will surface. Alternatively, the ownership entity itself may decide to enter the property management business, or it may want to reserve the option to combine the property with other hotels in a larger venture involving other operators. In some instances, management companies have simply proven to be ineffective operators, generating high revenue levels accompanied by bloated expenses, thus rendering the property unprofitable for ownership. Even if no reasons for termination are immediately apparent, astute owners will simply want to retain as much flexibility as possible, leaving them free to explore options that arise in the future.

Examples abound of hotels that have been marketed for sale under non-terminable management contracts or right-of-first-refusal provisions favoring the operator. The all-too-common result of these provisions is that a number of prospective buyers elect not to pursue the property, either because they do not favor the operator in place or because they are aligned with a competing branded manager. By limiting the pool of prospective buyers interested in the property, these provisions curtail the bidding process and result in the owner's receiving a reduced sales price. Since owners often make a sizable proportion of their total returns from trading the asset, being unable to execute a successful sale of the property can have a devastating impact on the productivity of the investment.

Committing to a management company for a 20-, 30-, or 50-year term can have catastrophic consequences if changes in the property, the market, or the management company during that time dictate another course of action. A property or location that is suitable for a specific brand today may evolve over the life of the investment, becoming more appropriate to a different brand or tier of the lodging market in the future. Moreover, particularly in an environment of consolidation and mergers, the company the owner contracts with today may not be the same company in the future; it may instead have vastly different capital, operating, and management structures. As an example, Sheraton and Westin Hotels have each gone through at least four different ownership structures over the past 20 years, operating as independent hotel companies, divisions of large conglomerates, and divisions of Starwood Hotels in its incarnation as a paired-share REIT and today's C-corporation. Owners who contracted with the Sheraton and Westin brands in the 1970s may still be bound by their original contracts, but they probably did not bargain for their operators becoming the quite different entities they are today. Under such circumstances, owners need the flexibility to change or terminate management contracts.

Moreover, owners take exception to the operator's stance that its fundamental mission is to build an enduring brand, arguing that they are paying the branded operator significant sums of money to manage their specific hotels. The owner would clearly prefer the operator to have brand value, if that value translates into higher performance for the owner's property. However, if the brand value comes at the owner's expense, or if the operator engages in activities that detract from the profitability or marketability of the owner's specific hotel for the good of the brand, the brand's value added is more than offset by the decline in the value of the owner's property. Effectively, the owner is subsidizing the brand's stock price.

As discussed throughout this text, the hospitality industry as a whole is becoming increasingly attentive to the inherent conflicts of interest between the operator's fiduciary responsibility to the individual owner and the operator's fiduciary responsibility to its shareholders. Decisions that an operator makes may be in the best interests of the firm's shareholders, but may be detrimental to specific owners or groups of owners, thus putting the operator in the difficult position of having to decide which of two masters to serve. A number of lawsuits have been waged against operators that do not act in the best interests of their owners, lending greater credence to owners' concerns for where operators' loyalties lie and the fairness of management contracts binding them to operators for long terms.

Current Trends: Contract Duration

The strength of branding is evident in the contract durations regularly negotiated by large branded operators—20-year terms with renewal at the operator's option. On renewal, contracts are extended for multiples of 10- or 20-year terms. The typical contract for full-service branded hotels will provide the operator the option of extending the contract for two 10-year periods, while contracts for the management of luxury hotels can be extended for longer periods of 30 to 60 years. Some branded operators report accepting 10-year initial terms to manage assets that offer particularly appealing strategic opportunities.

Owners report increasing levels of success negotiating renewals to the initial contract term that are not at the operator's option but are instead subject to mutual agreement between the owner and the operator, or available to the operator only if certain financial thresholds are achieved during the initial term. Astute owners generally agree to longer initial terms only if they are able to negotiate termination provisions that provide some flexibility to sell the property or terminate management in the intervening years. Owners may agree to accept less flexibility in termination-on-sale and performance clauses if they win shorter initial terms, reasoning that the shorter terms at least give them the ability, if warranted, to terminate the arrangement after 10 years instead of 50 years. The objective of such compromise provisions is to give the operator the potential to remain in a long-term contract while ensuring that the owner achieves at least minimum returns and levels of competitiveness in the property's local market.

Another acceptable compromise that assuages some owners' concerns yet keeps the asset in the brand's system is to negotiate a 10-year management contract that is replaced by a 20-year franchise agreement on expiration. This compromise provides the owner the possibility of installing a different management team, yet protects the brand from the loss of market penetration, since it preserves the rooms in the system. In the role of franchisee, the owner may actually gain some flexibility in the implementation of brand standards, since the requirements can be negotiated at arm's length rather than being imposed as a matter of course by property managers in the employ of the branded management company. Moreover, in strictly pecuniary terms, conversion to a franchise may benefit the brand, since franchise fees can exceed the fees collected under management contracts.

Although branded companies are compelled by their strategic objectives and the pressures of the public markets to hold adamantly to the principle of contracts of long duration, they attempt to compensate for this competitive disadvantage in several ways. Some branded companies have aligned themselves with capital sources or types of ownership entities (e.g., institutions) that have longer holding periods or that prefer to invest in the type of hotel assets whose values are enhanced by the presence of long-term management contracts. An even more proactive approach is for the branded management company to seek out opportunities, securing land or development rights and advancing in the entitlement process before "shopping" the project to prospective owners. By this tactic, the branded company effectively chooses the investor rather than the investor's selecting a management company. The tactic is especially attractive to publicly traded brands, since the investments represent relatively limited dollar amounts and are not held for extended periods on the balance sheet. This allows these brands to retain the character of fee-driven service companies rather than real estate entities warehousing product. Finally, in some instances, branded companies decide that their long-term orientation simply renders them incompatible with selected owners whose investment objectives and preferred property types require short-term contracts. Although the decision to omit a class of hotel investors from its universe of potential customers is difficult for the branded management company, there is one consolation: aggressive short-term investors are most active at the height of real estate cycles, when other, more compatible opportunities are also likely to be abundant.

The strength of branding is also evident in the growth of third-party independent management companies that align themselves with a brand or a select number of brands. Often these companies both own and manage hotels and are therefore known to the brands and have experience operating to the brands' standards. Effectively, these independent management companies are extensions of the brand, bringing both operating expertise and, through a franchise agreement, a brand affiliation not readily available to the small or inexperienced owner.

Ostensibly, the economics of employing an independent management company and entering into a separate franchise contract with a brand operator are unfavorable to owners because they must pay both a management fee and franchise fee. However, there are often compelling reasons for owners to contemplate this type of arrangement. First, independent operators tend to be more flexible, demonstrating a willingness to accept shorter-term contracts with more reasonable termination provisions, thus giving owners greater control over their properties. Further, independent operators are likely to have fewer conflicts between defending ownership's interests and defending the brand's best interests, even going so far as to assist owners in evaluating if a brand's proposed standards are cost-effective and in the best interests of ownership. Thus, a number of owners are willing to accept a higher annual fee structure in exchange for the ability to terminate a management contract after three to five years as an alternative to being locked into a 20-year contract.

Fees and Fee Structures

As mentioned earlier, the balance of power between owners and operators has shifted, providing a more equitable sharing of risks and rewards between owners and operators. Perhaps the most surprising aspect of the shift in the balance of power is that it has occurred not because one party has gained ascendancy over the other, as was the case in the 1970s and into the 1980s when management companies dictated terms to owners. Rather, the new balance of power results from the increasing strength of both parties. This is nowhere more evident than in the fees and fee structures currently practiced in management contracts between owners and branded operators.

The Management Company's View: Fair Compensation for Value Added

Executives at branded management companies concede readily that earlier fee structures and operator compensation were inequitable and excessive. However, the same executives argue forcefully that if the operator reduces the owner's business risk and builds asset value, then fair compensation is due the operator. Similarly, they argue that owners must appreciate the need for the brand to evolve to meet guest preferences, expand systemwide services, and provide new technologies. These incremental expenditures benefit participants in the system. The costs must therefore be passed along to owners and cannot be absorbed by the operator, especially if the operator is a publicly traded entity that must meet growth and earnings objectives to protect shareholder value.

Notwithstanding this stance, operators are willing to exercise patience, accepting lesser fees in the early years of the management contract's term. In some instances, the operator's patience is motivated by a desire to do "strategic" deals—i.e., accept contracts whose fees are inferior to the norm in exchange for gaining market penetration, or "distribution," for the brand. In virtually all cases, the competitive landscape demands that the operator subordinate incentive fees to an owner's return, although the level of appropriate preferential return to the owner varies significantly according to the specifics of the deal and concessions the owner and operator might win in the negotiation of the management contract.

The Owner's View: Sharing Risks and Transparency

Most owners agree with the basic concept of compensating operators for the value that they bring to a project. But from the owner's perspective, the balance between just compensation and the sharing of risks is best achieved by structuring appropriate levels of base and incentive management fees in the management contract. Historically, owners considered the base management fee the operator's vehicle for recovering corporate overhead expenses and ensuring a minimal level of profitability. In contrast, the incentive management fee has been the means for the operator to share in the hotel's profitability, thus receiving compensation for the value the operator provides through its management and brand. This balance mitigates the operator's risk by ensuring receipt of a fee stream that is not contingent on the hotel's profitability, but also rewards the operator for superior performance by giving up a portion of the property's profits via the incentive fee. Additionally, motivating the operator to earn incentive fees gives owners comfort that the operator is driving profits at the property instead of focusing solely on revenues. From the owner's vantage point, the operator should realize a modest profit from the base management fee in exchange for reducing the owner's financial risk, but the operator should enjoy the opportunity to realize substantial profits only if the property achieves a reasonable level of profitability.

However, the roles of these fees, particularly the base management fee, have blurred over recent years, thus shifting the debate from "What is fair compensation to the operator?" to "What are we getting in exchange for the base management fees?" Currently, the most contentious issues between owners and operators involve the recovery of shared costs and overhead expense pass-throughs that owners formerly considered included in the base management fee but which are now invoiced *in addition to* the base management fee. Examples of such operator services and costs that are now billed to hotels separately in addition to the base management fees include the following:

- Centralized marketing services
- Group sales offices
- Frequent guest programs
- Purchasing programs

- Accounting fees
- Software licensing and support fees
- Network/management information services licensing and support fees
- Employee training/satisfaction programs
- Guest satisfaction programs
- Brand compliance inspections
- Internal audits

In the aggregate, these corporate expenses and fees can represent as much as three to five percent of total revenues in addition to the base management fee paid to the operator, thus converting the base management fee from a modestly profitable item to one of substantial profitability for the operator, since a large proportion of the operator's expenses are reimbursed from the properties. In addition to the sheer magnitude of these expenses, owners are often dissatisfied with the specific items that are included within the reimbursements, such as the recuperation of corporate research and development expenses and personnel costs that were formerly covered by the base management fee. Owners' concerns have been heightened by inadequate disclosure and the lack of transparency in operators' financial reporting, which has failed in a number of cases to account properly for expenses charged to properties in the system.

As stated, the net result of these increased cost allocations to the properties is that the base management fee is now perceived by owners as constituting a significant profit component instead of being largely a vehicle for recovering corporate overhead expenses and a modest profit component. Indeed, operators estimate that one percent of the average three percent base management fee represents profit to the management company. (One of the largest companies, however, places the estimate at two percent, which owners view as shifting more expense—and risk—onto their shoulders.) Owners often cite this as justification when asking for reduced term lengths and more meaningful termination provisions, because the operator is no longer perceived as a partner sharing in the risks of the venture but as an agent of ownership who profits regardless of whether or not the hotel is successful.

Trends: Fees and Fee Structures

Base fees in management contracts with branded operators range from 2.5 to 4 percent of total revenues, with the average fee remaining relatively stable over time at 3 percent. The "ramp-up" of fees—a progressive increase, in increments of 25 or 50 basis points, in the percentage of gross revenue collected as a base fee over two to five years until a stabilized percentage is reached—occurs in contracts for both conversions and new properties. Owners are more likely to prevail in negotiating a ramp-up of fees for larger properties or when the initial term of the management contract is longer, since the absolute dollar amount of the fees is more significant.

Incentive fees are negotiated based on pro forma estimates of cash flows. As a general rule, the farther down in the cash flow "cascade" the operator stands, the larger is the percentage of cash flow accorded to the management company. One common formula provides for a return to the owner ranging from 8 to 12 percent of total project cost (plus major capital additions) before the operator is eligible for an incentive fee. Once the owner's priority return requirement is met, the operator's incentive fee ranges from 15 to 35 percent of the remaining cash flow. Another formula provides for a return on the owner's invested equity, typically in the range of 10 to 15 percent, before the operator receives an incentive fee that ranges from 15 to 25 percent of the residual cash flow. One company reported that, while most contracts required subordination of the incentive fee to an owner's return, it has negotiated occasional contracts where incentive fees are based on a share—10 to 15 percent—of house profit.

All branded management companies surveyed reported that, to be accepted, a new management contract must yield a minimum economic value. The executives interviewed, however, were reluctant to identify the threshold dollar amounts required or the discount rates applied to derive the requisite minimum value added from incremental contracts. Above all, branded operators report that, as currently structured, incentive fees provide them a meaningful return only when the hotel investment cycle peaks. This observation suggests that operating companies at least believe that current management contract fee structures provide for an equitable sharing of risk and returns between the owner and operator.

Operators that offer both franchise agreements and management contracts observe that the brand's fee stream is typically greater from a franchise affiliation than from a management contract. If the franchisor is able to command franchise terms that require the owner to pay five or six percent of room revenue and two or three percent of food and beverage revenue, the arbitrage between the top-line franchise fees collected and a management contract's three percent of revenue pushes the brand toward franchising. Moreover, as executives at branded companies are quick to point out, the financial and contingent risks of management contracts far exceed those of franchises, and the administrative burden of a franchise is far less than that of a management contract.

Branded operators agree that more transparency and greater precision are necessary to determine and allocate systemwide costs. For certain companies, insufficient cost accounting and administrative systems hampered their ability to provide the requisite information. However, as these companies settle fully into their role as publicly traded firms, the rationalization of their procedures continues, providing the tools to analyze and allocate costs in a more transparent and logical fashion. Finally, increased emphasis on transparency in financial reporting and recent lawsuits brought by owners against hotel management companies have further sensitized operators to the necessity of open and frequent communication with their owners.

Operator Financial Contributions

Although publicly traded hybrid lodging companies that are owners, operators, and franchisors continue to exist, none currently plans to grow systematically by increasing its ownership of assets. Hybrid companies may occasionally grow opportunistically by acquiring key strategic assets or joint venturing with private ownership entities, but the emphasis will continue to be on growing earnings streams by adding managed and franchised rooms. Not surprisingly, in the current environment, the outlook on operator equity investments in lodging projects has changed considerably from the earlier days of management contracts, when owners demanded that operators put significant dollars at risk—a mentality summed up by the observation of one owner: "If I have the hurts, I want him [the operator] to have the hurts, too."

The Management Company's View: Lean Earnings Machines

Most branded management companies identify themselves resolutely as publicly traded service firms that eschew, where possible, the ownership of real estate. For companies practicing this strategy, an investment in a hotel project is a threat to the earnings stream that underpins their value on Wall Street. Under increasingly stringent post-Enron accounting rules, even modest minority interests may be required to be reported under the equity method, resulting in the consolidation of accounting losses with the operator's earnings and a decline in the company's balance-sheet value as a result of the minority interest.

Debt investments and credit enhancement also represent disadvantages to publicly traded operators. Loan guarantees that operators might offer to secure management contracts must be disclosed as contingent liabilities, and analysts routinely include these contingent liabilities as part of operators' debt, adjusting their risk assessment accordingly. Similarly, loans made to secure management contracts must earn at least market returns or analysts adjust downward the value of the fee stream purchased by extending subsidized credit.

Finally, branded management companies incur an opportunity cost when a given management contract is accepted, especially if the contract is for the operation of a property in a particularly desirable market. Development officers at branded management companies acknowledge that one of their functions is to act as gatekeepers, ensuring that only the most promising opportunities and partners gain access to the brand's expertise. The same concern for reducing operators' opportunity cost has led to the development of the previously described network of third-party independent property management companies aligned with brands. In this environment, executives at branded management companies are chary of making financial contributions in any form to some deals, reasoning that by passing on other projects to accept the opportunity and subordinating their incentive fees, they have shouldered adequate risk.

Independent, unbranded management companies have a similar outlook on investing in hotel projects but are typically less constrained by balance sheet issues (unless they, too, are publicly traded). The intensely competitive environment for all management companies, whether branded or unbranded, and the strong financial returns available from investments in lodging assets are an incentive for independent management companies to provide capital to projects. When coupled with their management fee stream, independent management companies' cash-on-cash returns can reach 20 to 25 percent; it is not surprising, therefore, that an increasing number have allocated investment capital for the purpose of making "sliver" equity investments or other forms of financial contributions to win management contracts and grow their inventories of managed rooms.

The Owner's View: Expensive Capital or Grease that Gets the Deal Done?

The owner's view of management company investments varies dramatically, depending on (1) the project economics, (2) the capital resources and investment philosophy of the individual owner, and (3) the salient terms of the management contract—e.g., length of term, termination provisions, etc.—that affect the owner's risk exposure and the potential value of the property.

Owners seeking aggressive investment returns or those willing to accept higher risk often view operator contributions as a critical source of capital and a means of reducing their financial commitment to a project. They evaluate operator capital contributions, both financially and in terms of other contract concessions, comparing them to the cost of mezzanine debt or other high-cost components of the project's financial structure. This type of owner will pursue operator contributions so long as the capital is "accretive"—i.e., the cost of the operator's money is lower than the projected yields on the investment.

More conservative owners often have a different outlook on operator contributions, viewing them as an unnecessary complication in the deal structure and capital that is expensive in more than a strictly financial sense. By taking a minority equity position in hotel properties, operators have claimed the legal status of an "agency coupled with an interest," using the status to avoid termination of the management contract on the basis that their equity position makes them a partner and protects them from termination under any circumstances. These arguments have met with varying success in the courts. However, even if the arguments are not ultimately sustained in court, accepting equity contributions from the operator (thus opening the door to this potential issue) is undesirable to many owners. These owners prefer to maintain more of an arm's length relationship with their operators and recognize that they may be able to negotiate other concessions from the operator that are of more importance to them if they do not require an equity investment in the property.

The one arrangement whereby both aggressive and conservative owners appear to accept contributions from operators is in the form of "key money"—outright contributions to the project that are typically only repaid if the management contract is terminated prematurely. Operators' willingness to provide key money contributions can be considered a tacit admission of the profitability of today's management contracts. It is often viewed by owners as the owner's version of an incentive management fee—i.e., a means for the owner to share in the profits of the operator.

Current Trends: Operator Financial Contributions

Early in the evolution of management contracts, both the argument for operator equity contributions and the argument against them seemed compelling. Owners in favor of equity contributions held that the dollars advanced put operators at risk and gave them a meaningful incentive to perform. Owners opposed to operator equity contributions argued that if operators held a security interest in properties they managed, it created a conflict of interest with their role as agents, making it problematic to discipline or terminate operators. Today, the consensus view among owners and executives at branded management companies is that operator equity contributions are to be avoided. When there is equity participation by the branded operator, it is usually either because the operator is the sole recourse, providing the last dollars needed to make a deal work, or because the operator brought a partial ownership interest to the project. In such circumstances, however, the operator is a passive investor and does not participate in decisions affecting the management company.

As discussed, branded and independent operators alike do "buy" management contracts by providing key money. Key money amounts generally range from $1 to $2 million, or one to three years' base management fees for a five- to ten-year contract, and are usually the last funds paid into a project. Some operators earmark key money to cover pre-opening costs, reasoning that the contributions are going primarily to compensate their own employees.

Publicly traded management companies view operator loan guarantees as the virtual equivalent of holding an equity position in a project. Most executives surveyed were resolutely opposed to owners' requests for loan guarantees, although owners with highly desirable properties or strong relationships with the operator maintain that credit enhancements and loan guarantees are still available under the right circumstances.

Some branded operators report a willingness to provide mezzanine financing in amounts representing 10 to 15 percent of project cost up to a debt-to-asset ratio of 70 percent. Mezzanine loans are offered at market rates and market terms (e.g., relatively short amortizations and immediate repayment if the project is refinanced). At least one branded operator has attempted, with mixed success, to move mezzanine debt off its balance sheet, reselling it to financial intermediaries.

As with the length of management contract terms, the operator's equity investment is another area where independent, non-publicly-traded management companies are able to differentiate themselves from the large, branded hotel companies. By having the flexibility to provide capital contributions without concern for the effect on their stock price, non-public companies can often outmaneuver the publicly traded companies in the terms they are able to offer to owners.

Performance Clauses

Over recent years, performance clauses appear to have become a regular feature of hotel management contracts. Executives at branded management companies could not recall a recent management contract that did not contain a performance clause, and all agreed that they will be a fixture of future management contracts. Despite the apparent agreement between owners and operators that the inclusion of performance clauses in management contracts is prudent and necessary, structuring an effective performance clause is not an easy exercise. On one hand, performance clauses must provide reasonable flexibility to the operator in the face of unforeseen market conditions and other exigencies, while on the other hand, they must represent meaningful performance standards that owners can invoke to protect their interests.

The Management Company's View: Flexibility and Reasonable Tests

Executives at branded operators express the view that, if the management company is not performing adequately, the owner should have the right to terminate the contract. Further, they appreciate that if the operator has relatively little cash at risk in a project, it is reasonable for the owner to seek an effective means of ensuring that the property is managed to achieve optimal results for the owner.

However, while operators accept that they should be held to performance standards, they maintain they should be protected from market vicissitudes outside of their control and that standards must be set to allow some shortfall. In a similar vein, they hold that there must be a reasonable period after the management company takes control of an asset before the performance standard can be invoked and the contract potentially terminated. Finally, while they want the option to contribute cash to cure shortfalls from performance standards, they acknowledge that, if the property consistently under-performs, going out of pocket repeatedly does not adequately address the owner's concerns.

The Owner's View: Last Line of Defense to Remedy a Bad Situation

It is rare to find a hotel owner who disagrees with the logic that performance standards should be reasonable and operators should have the opportunity, within defined limits, to cure shortfalls to avoid termination. The primary difference between owners and operators lies with the definitions of what is a reasonable standard and what counts as a market factor or *force majeure* event that would preclude termination.

It is important to point out that the increased use of performance standards is viewed as largely a result of operators' insistence on long-term contracts. Further, the perception that operators no longer share in the risk of the property because they recoup a substantial portion of their overhead costs through add-on fees—while pocketing much of a base management fee as profit—contributes to ownership's need for an "out" if the property is not achieving acceptable returns. The combination of these two factors means that, in the absence of performance standards, an operator may have a highly profitable, long-term income stream from the base management fees, service fees, and expense pass-throughs, while the hotel itself is losing money. Absent a mechanism for remedying this situation, owners could be driven slowly (or rapidly) into bankruptcy, while the operator lives well because of its top-line-oriented fee structure.

Performance clauses most often proposed by operators are revenue-per-available-room (RevPAR) tests whereby the owner may terminate the manager if the property fails to achieve a predetermined percentage of its competitive set's RevPAR levels. These strictly top-line tests are not particularly meaningful to owners because they do not measure the property's profitability. An operator can achieve strong RevPAR levels by providing extremely high levels of service and amenities, but if doing so impedes the property's profitability, then meeting the RevPAR test should not protect the operator from termination.

The reassurance that owners seek from performance standards is that minimum profitability levels will be achieved, enabling the property to meet its debt service and other obligations and remain a viable hotel investment. To ensure that ownership's objectives are met, a bottom-line performance test is a *sine qua non*. Focusing on profit measures leaves the day-to-day management decisions in the hands of the operator (where they belong). However, it commits the operator to generating a minimum level of profits based upon either (1) the projections originally agreed upon at the commencement of the investment or (2) a predetermined percentage return on the total investment that enables ownership to make debt-service payments and provides the minimum return needed to induce equity investment in the project.

Owners see termination provisions as a fail-safe mechanism that allows them to salvage a property when the operator is failing to manage effectively, not a weapon enabling them to terminate operators indiscriminately. Owners also point out that terminating and replacing a management company is an expensive proposition that is often disruptive to the property; therefore, it is not an action undertaken lightly. Thus, even when termination provisions may allow them to replace the operator, owners are unlikely to do so unless there is good cause or there is another operator that is realistically expected to perform significantly better.

Current Trends: Performance Clauses

Management contracts for both new development and conversions regularly specify a honeymoon, or transition, period before the owner can invoke performance clauses. The honeymoon period ranges from three to five years. Typically, the operator must fail the performance tests either two years out of two consecutive years or two consecutive years out of three years before the owner either must accept a cure or seek termination.

Standard performance tests are conjunctive—the operator must fail both a top-line *and* an operating results test for the owner to exercise termination or cure options. As mentioned, a common top-line test measures the subject's RevPAR penetration against the RevPAR achieved by a pre-determined competitive set. The most frequently encountered operating results test is the achievement of a budgeted house profit.

Neither test is entirely objective, which reduces the comfort level of both owners and operators. The subject hotel's RevPAR penetration will depend on the appropriateness of its competitive set, which can prove fluid across the life of a 20-year contract. The best owners and operators can do to mitigate the risk of choosing an unfair competitive set as a benchmark is to stipulate that the competitive set be carefully negotiated—or, as one executive observed, the parties "agree to agree" to an appropriate competitive set. Similarly, the standard operating results test lacks some precision if it is based on a budgeted figure that is negotiated annually.

The operator usually succeeds in setting the RevPAR penetration threshold at less than 100 percent, with the result that the subject hotel will pass the top-line test if it achieves a RevPAR penetration in the range of 80 to 90 percent. The threshold for the operating results test is typically set at 80 to 85 percent of the budgeted house profit.

The number of times an operator may cure a shortfall from budgeted house profit ranges from once to three times in a 20-year contract term. Other contracts are silent on the number of times the operator may cure, leaving the issue to negotiation as necessary over the life of the contract. When the operator cures a shortfall, it effectively resets the clock, gaining another two- or three-year period to improve operating results or face the option of curing or exiting the contract. Cures are not cumulative; the cash advanced by the operator makes up the shortfall of the second or third consecutive year only. Moreover, the cure makes the owner whole only up to the threshold specified in the contract, not the sum necessary to bring operating cash flow up to the full budgeted level.

Termination Provisions

Although we (and our spouses) find analogies comparing management contracts to marriages unsettling on several levels, the negotiation of termination provisions in a management contract can be loosely compared to the negotiation of a prenuptial agreement. Under normal circumstances, the termination provisions are not enforced, but rather they exist as a safety net for both the owner and the operator to fall back on if, for whatever reason, the union is not working.

The increasing strength of branding militates against owners' natural inclination to seek termination clauses to ensure flexibility in managing and disposing of their assets. Assuming they have negotiated a contract term of acceptable duration, owners who are convinced a given brand is the optimal choice for maximizing the value of their assets are less inclined to put a high priority on termination clauses in the negotiating process. Similarly, operators who perceive that their brand represents a superior—or the only—fit with owners' investment objectives, market positioning, and operating requirements are likely to be even firmer in their resistance to termination provisions.

The pressure to increase the number of rooms in their systems appears to be leading branded operators to focus less on management contracts and more on the durability of the franchise agreement, preferring more readily achieved increases in their system distribution and the brand's royalty fee stream to the incremental fees potentially derived from managing. Independent operators, however, have no such assurances of residual income streams in the event of management termination and therefore tend to cling more forcefully to tempering the impact of termination provisions.

The Management Company's View: Protecting Share Price

For branded operators that are public companies heavily dependent on a long-term earnings stream to support their market valuations, preserving consistent fee revenue is of paramount importance. To the extent that termination provisions threaten future earnings and diminish current market valuations, they are anathema. When buyout provisions are admitted in contracts, branded publicly traded operators strive to achieve terms that make the company whole, attempting to negotiate a lump-sum buyout payment equivalent to the present value of the fee revenue forgone. Termination-on-sale provisions, regardless of how they are priced, are viewed as especially detrimental to the operator's interest because they invite renegotiation of the contract.

The Owner's View: Protecting Asset Value

Owners that allow management companies to impose long-term contracts with no termination provisions run the risk of seriously impairing the value of their investments. Investing in hotels is not an activity for the fainthearted, as investors are buying into one of the most difficult real estate property types to develop and manage. Moreover, hotels are highly subject to the risk suggested by the real estate aphorism "locations don't change, but neighborhoods do." If owners are to protect the value of their assets, they need some basic level of flexibility over the long term to make needed changes to the property.

For an owner cognizant of the potential effect that an encumbered asset has on market value, a long-term contract with no performance clauses or other termination provisions is the worst possible management structure. An alternative that is somewhat less painful for the owner is the inclusion in the management contract of a termination-with-fee provision or buyout clause that enables the owner to compel the manager to leave the property at the owner's discretion, but at a steep price. The negotiation of a buyout clause at least caps the diminution in value the owner will be forced to bear. When the time comes to sell, if the property is performing well and the buyer wishes to retain the manager, the owner is not harmed financially. However, if the buyer does not wish to retain the current management, the owner can quantify the downside impact.

Another area of concern for owners in the negotiation of termination provisions is the attempt by operators to incorporate language enabling them to terminate the brand affiliation for vaguely worded actions (or inactions) of the owner. Such provisions are perceived by owners as depriving them of their rights to question or approve the actions of the operator, effectively forcing them to relinquish control over their properties. For example, categorizing the failure to approve the annual operating budget as an ownership default—thus grounds for termination—removes owners' ability to question the budget unless they are willing to forfeit the management and brand affiliation. Similarly, if owners deem capital expenditures inappropriate or lacking in cost-effectiveness, they need to maintain the ability to withhold the funding reasonably, without triggering the operator's right to terminate the contract.

Owners are also increasingly aware of the risks imposed by a change in control of the management company; accordingly, they are seeking additional rights to terminate the management agreement when such events occur. A change-in-control clause is largely a defensive mechanism on the part of owners who are concerned that the company they have contracted with may not be the same company in the future or may undergo changes at the upper levels of the executive team that dramatically alter the philosophies or management capabilities of the operator. Similarly, the risk of a diminution in brand distribution, particularly for small boutique hotel brands, has led some owners to seek the ability to terminate the contract if the operator does not achieve or maintain a defined portfolio size over the course of the contract.

Current Trends: Termination Provisions

Termination for cause, including material default, incompetence, gross negligence, and fraud, offers standard contractual protection to owners. It is interesting to note that operators in material default on substantive contractual terms (e.g., audit and reporting requirements, employee bonding, and insurance coverage requirements) but otherwise managing an asset successfully are vulnerable to contract renegotiation. In the face of termination without a compensatory payment, operators find it more palatable to accept reduced fees or other constraints than to be removed altogether and suffer the loss of all fee revenues and the loss of rooms from the system.

When required to negotiate buyout clauses in management contracts, branded operators attempt to price them at the value of the fees forgone, using one of two basic formulations. The look-back approach, used most often in ten-year contracts, prices the buyout at three to seven times trailing fees. Multiples, of course, tend toward the higher end of the range for contracts with more years remaining. The second formulation prices the buyout as the present value of the remaining stream of fees. A separate multiple, equating to a discount rate in the range of seven to nine percent, is applied to the basic fee. The multiple applied to the incentive fee is the equivalent of a discount rate in the range of 11 to 13 percent.

As noted, if the owner must be provided an exit from a management contract, the preferable resolution for the branded operator is a ten-year contract that converts to a franchise agreement.

Budgetary and Spending Limitations

As hotel asset managers recognize daily, owner-operator relationships are necessarily collaborative and consultative. This principle is nowhere more evident than in the negotiation of a property's budgets. The relationship represents a careful balance, preserving the operator's right to maintain brand standards and operating norms while providing ownership with input into decisions requiring the disbursement of significant sums of the investor's funds.

The Management Company's View: Strength in Numbers

The branded operator's insistence on preserving the right to mandate expenditures turns on two fundamental arguments. First and foremost, the branded operator maintains that what is good for the system is good for the individual owner. Expenditures are required to protect and enhance brand integrity and pricing power. As the brand is strengthened and its consumer franchise extended, all owners' asset values increase. Second, the branded operator maintains that system-wide efforts are cost-efficient, providing owners with services and enhancements to the guest experience that owners could not afford individually.

The Owner's View: Good for All?

Owners maintain—and recent history has confirmed—that the conflicts and misalignment of interests between owners and operators precludes owners from accepting the "trust me, I know what's right for you" stance often taken by the operator. The notion that the operator will spend the owner's money in the wisest, most prudent manner has been debunked all too often, in the field and in the courts, to be relied upon by any but the most naïve of owners. Indeed, as noted in Chapter 1, one of the reasons that the Hospitality Asset Managers Association (HAMA) exists today is that practicing asset managers sought a professional forum to address their frustrations and resolve the issues brought on by the operators' "I know what's best" philosophy.

Evidence assembled among the HAMA membership shows a strong correlation between the intensity and sophistication of the asset management techniques employed in overseeing a property and the financial returns the property generates for ownership. Active oversight produces higher returns than passive ownership, and one of the basic and most critical of asset management techniques employed is to review and critique operating budgets and to hold management accountable for expenditures that are either imprudent or poorly managed.

To their credit, the majority of management companies have acceded to owners' desires to be actively involved in the budgeting process, although owners must still insist on full approval rights and not settle for watered-down provisions allowing them only to comment on areas of concern. This change in thinking represents a watershed that was unimaginable 20 years ago and is largely attributed to the coordinated efforts of a number of owners who insisted upon having these rights.

Current Trends: Budgetary and Spending Limitations

Operators report that management contracts regularly contain language specifying that budgets are subject to the owner's review. As a minimum, operating, marketing, FF&E (furniture, fixtures, and equipment) replacement, and capital expenditure budgets are subject to the owner's review. The typical language of management contracts stipulates, however, that the owner cannot refuse to budget the necessary expenditures to meet brand standards or pay fees for services received as a member of the brand's system.

In addition, the owner cannot unreasonably withhold approval of the budgets presented. Tests of the appropriateness of budgets presented to ownership include a historical test to verify consistency with the subject property's past expenditure patterns and a comparison of the subject property's level of expenditures to the norms for similar properties within the brand. If budget approval is withheld despite the successful application of the tests provided for in the contract, the conflict is ultimately subject to arbitration.

Executives surveyed reported that the reserves for FF&E replacement stipulated in management contracts were typically in the range of four to five percent of gross revenues, with resorts requiring an additional set-aside of 50 to 150 basis points of gross revenue to maintain their extensive amenities adequately. Some ramping-up of the percentage applied to gross revenues is permitted for new hotels or for hotels having recently undergone product improvement plans (PIPs). Reflecting the increasing distrust of percentage-of-revenue formulas for determining the appropriate levels of FF&E reserves, some executives noted that a cost-per-key analysis is a more reliable approach to determining adequate dollar reserves for FF&E replacement. Although the adequacy of the FF&E reserve, as discussed in Chapter 11, is a critical issue in determining the overall success and long-term viability of the property, as yet there has been surprisingly little conflict in the management contract negotiation stage regarding the appropriate levels of FF&E reserves.

Conclusion

As with any negotiated working arrangement, the specific provisions agreed upon between an owner and the operator are subject to wide variation, depending on the balance of power between the two parties and the level of motivation of each. Large, sophisticated owners with multiple high-profile properties negotiating against smaller independent or highly motivated branded management companies will win more concessions from the operator than will a small owner with one hotel in a secondary location.

However, two important trends appear to have surfaced in the negotiation of hotel management contracts over recent years. First, the onerous contract length and non-termination provisions formerly imposed by managers appear largely to have come into a more equitable balance, with operators still receiving relatively long-term contracts but with owners enjoying a basic level of rights over performance and termination. Second, evidence suggests that owners have become markedly more astute, knowing better what to ask for in their negotiations. We attribute this to a combination of increasingly sophisticated owners and greater dissemination of information and counsel from industry commentators, consultants, asset managers, and attorneys.

The reader who has followed the give-and-take of the preceding pages might wonder if the authors—each of whom has purposely adopted (evenhandedly, it is hoped) the mantle of the owner and the operator—are able to agree on any aspect of the preceding debate. If there is an area of agreement, it is in what the future is likely to hold for branded management companies.

Recent issues highlight the inherent conflicts of interest when a branded hotel company is (1) an owner of hotels, (2) a manager of others' hotels, (3) a franchisor, and (4) a publicly traded company. The dynamics suggest that the trend toward multiple business models in the same lodging industry enetrprise—which, for some entities, is an artifact of the mergers and acquisitions that occurred in the industry in the 1990s—will reverse. Branded management companies will tend toward either the management business (e.g., Hyatt, Four Seasons, and Ritz-Carlton Hotels) *or* the franchising business, but staying in both in a meaningful way will increasingly conflict with their status as public companies. To the extent that branded management companies do move toward a franchising "pure play," the balance of power may swing in favor of the owner, as control over the brand affiliation is one of the management company's most effective bargaining chips. The landscape will also favor non-public, entrepreneurial operators that are able to align their interests (and their dollars) more effectively with owners' interests.

Endnotes

1. *Robert E. Woolley, et al, v. Embassy Suites, Inc., et al.* 227 Cal App 3d 1520 (1991).
2. *2660 Woodley Road Joint Venture, et al, v. ITT Sheraton Corporation, et al.* D Del WL 1469541 (1998).

6

Negotiating the Hotel Management Contract

By Chad Crandell, Kristie Dickinson, and Fern I. Kanter

Chad Crandell *is a co-founder of Capital Hotel Management (CHM), where he serves as President and operations leader of hotel investment advisory and asset management services. Since its inception, CHM has provided asset management services to investors and developers holding hotels and resorts valued at more than $1 billion and located throughout the United States.*

Before forming CHM, Mr. Crandell held a senior-level position at a major consulting firm. His 20 years of hospitality industry experience includes management company and franchise selection and contract negotiation, operational reviews focusing on market positioning and financial performance, and the development of hotel acquisition and disposition strategies. Mr. Crandell has held numerous positions in operations and development with InterContinental Hotels, Chalet Suisse International, and Koala Inns of America. He currently serves as a member of the board of directors of the Hospitality Asset Managers Association (HAMA).

Kristie Dickinson, *Vice President of Portfolio Management for Capital Hotel Management, has nearly a decade of experience in hotel operations, development, and advisory services. At CHM, Ms. Dickinson is responsible for overseeing portfolio projects, including implementing revenue-enhancement programs, conducting pricing analyses, monitoring labor productivity and market trends, and identifying profit improvements.*

Before joining CHM, Ms. Dickinson was a member of Doubletree Hotels Corporation's development and franchise team. She has consulted on hotel development, positioning, management, and disposition projects, completing over 60 research assignments for a variety of hospitality-related land uses. In addition, Ms. Dickinson has been involved in numerous strategic planning studies, developing strategic plans for food, beverage, entertainment, and lodging facilities for the United States Air Force in Korea, Japan, and Germany, as well as undertaking a national growth plan for an international hotel company.

Fern I. Kanter, *Executive Vice President of Strategic Planning for Capital Hotel Management, has over 20 years' experience in the hospitality and tourism industries, specializing in South Florida and international hotel markets, including the Caribbean, Mexico, and Central and South America. Before joining CHM, Ms. Kanter held senior-level positions with various international hospitality consulting firms.*

Ms. Kanter's experience includes a variety of visitor-based land uses, mixed-use resort developments, and tourism destination projects. She has consulted on master planned mixed-use resort communities, assisting in programming a variety of different land uses, including hotels and resorts, vacation ownership, golf and club programs, marinas, resort residential, and commercial uses. Ms. Kanter has also served both domestic and international hotel companies, performing due diligence for acquisition opportunities and developing market-entry strategies for international locations.

THE MANAGEMENT AGREEMENT IS the single most important contract entered into by the hotel owner. Careful negotiation of this legally binding document is critical, as it sets the rules that define the long-term relationship between the owner and operator and is referenced routinely throughout the life of the contract. This chapter outlines the key steps in the process of negotiating the management agreement, beginning with the selection of an operator and setting the stage for negotiations through the introduction of the owner-operator bill of rights, which establishes the desired posture of the owner with respect to the salient terms of the agreement.

The present chapter was prepared based on the authors' experience negotiating hotel management contracts. We also draw on reference material from two leading authorities on the subject, James J. Eyster and Stephen Rushmore. Our intent is to provide an overview of the recommended process for negotiating hotel management contracts. The process described in the following pages is summarized graphically by the diagram appearing in Exhibit 1. For a comprehensive review of all the intricacies that surround hotel management contracts, readers are referred to the works of Eyster and Rushmore that are either referenced in the course of the chapter or presented in the bibliography at the end of the chapter.

The discussion that follows is limited to a treatment of management contract negotiations for full-service hotels; the contract variations that may occur in select-service properties are not addressed. Further, the chapter focuses on agreements between an owner and a branded management company, omitting discussion of the model where contracts are negotiated separately with a franchisor and an independent third-party operator.

Getting Ready: The Pre-Selection Process

Whether the owner's objective is to engage a property manager for a new development or for an existing property, there are several factors that warrant careful consideration before the search for an appropriate operator begins. The following discussion provides selected points to consider at the outset of the process, as they will affect the brand and operator chosen.

Owner Investment Strategy

Before the search for an appropriate operator begins, ownership's investment objectives must be clearly defined. Is the intent to maintain ownership of the asset

Exhibit 1 Management Contract Negotiation Process

as a long-term investment, a medium hold (five to ten years), or a quick turnaround (one to five years)? What are ownership's investment criteria and return expectations, including the minimum and target hurdle rates? Depending upon the strategy chosen for the asset, owners may need to limit or broaden their search for a suitable operator accordingly. For instance, most of the national branded operators are primarily interested in entering into long-term contracts and thus may not accept a contract provision that permits termination of the relationship upon sale of the asset. If a long-term management contract with no provision for termination on sale is in place, this could potentially limit the marketability of the asset. Therefore, a branded operator may not be a suitable match for an owner whose strategy is a quick disposition. However, there are some operators, typically not affiliated with a brand, that specialize in positioning assets for sale, should a quick turnaround be the owner's strategy. Whatever the owner's objectives, to ensure a proper fit between owner and operator, a clear investment strategy must be developed and considered during all stages of the selection process.

Creating a Competitive Environment

As with the brokerage process, creating a competitive bidding environment from the beginning of the operator-selection process will yield a more favorable negotiation for the owner. The more competitive the bidding, the more flexible management companies will be with respect to the contract's key provisions. Assessing ownership's relative bargaining power before entering into negotiations will expedite the process by setting realistic expectations from the outset. The following factors affect the owner's leverage in the negotiation process:

- *Property Location.* Whether it is a resort on a Hawaiian island or a commercial hotel in downtown Boston, certain locations are deemed more desirable than others, particularly by branded operators, due to the high barriers to entry that exist. This is not to say that branded operators are not interested in managing a property located in a second-tier city or an outlying suburb, but they may be more flexible in the deal terms to obtain a brand presence in a highly desired location. Conversely, there may be a situation in which national brands are well represented in the market, precluding owners from obtaining a brand within the same market due to radius-restriction limitations contained in management contracts for existing hotels. In this instance, location may serve to hinder an owner's negotiating strength because it limits the pool of viable operators.
- *Property Profile.* Like its location, the profile of a property may influence the operator's willingness to compete to manage the hotel. The higher the profile of a property, the more interest owners will generate from prospective operators. Examples of high profile assets include larger-than-average hotels (1,000+ rooms), strategically located properties (e.g., a hotel connected to a convention center), and properties with historical significance.
- *Branded vs. Third-Party Management.* Owners have options when it comes to selecting an operator and branding a hotel. One option is to enter into a separate franchise agreement to secure a brand and engage an independent third-party operator to manage the hotel. Another option is to select a single company, often referred to as a "brand manager," to provide both the brand and the operational expertise to manage the property. Most major brands, with the exception of a select few (e.g., Hyatt, Ritz-Carlton, Four Seasons), offer both options; however, owners may have more leverage if they elect to go with a brand manager, primarily because brand managers' fees are higher in absolute dollars. For example, franchise fees generally range from four to seven percent of gross rooms revenue. On the other hand, management agreements are most often based on total revenue. Furthermore, there are several add-on fees associated with a management agreement that do not appear in the base fee, such as incentive fees, mandatory contributions to sales and marketing funds, and accounting fees, to name only a few. A management

contract with a brand manager is not always the investor's best choice, but owners negotiating with major branded operators are better able to appreciate their relative bargaining strength if they are aware that management contracts typically equate to more fees for branded companies than stand-alone franchise agreements.

- *Deal Structure.* Sometimes owners look to operators to provide a financial contribution to a deal, either in the form of an equity investment or through loans or loan guarantees. The benefits of operator financial contributions are that (1) needed financing is obtained and (2) the management company's financial commitment aids in aligning owner and operator interests. Despite these benefits, the authors believe that an owner is better off if the deal can be financed by sources independent of the operator, and the owner is thus well advised to observe the maxim "if you don't need the money, don't take it." Equity participation changes the relationship between the owner and operator significantly, and by accepting an operator as a partner, owners should be prepared to relinquish a considerable amount of control in the negotiating process and perhaps in the subsequent administration of the contract. In short, the cost of concessions that owners are forced to accept typically outweighs the value of the funds received up front. This is not to say that operator equity participation is not an option worth considering, but owners need to understand the ramifications of the operator's becoming a partner in the project.

Identify Key Players

During the pre-selection stage of the process, owners should begin to identify the senior-level executives within the business development departments of the operating companies they expect to pursue. As discussed in greater detail in a subsequent section, the choice of operators that an owner will pursue is largely dictated by the market positioning of the hotel and the availability of one or more brands within the subject hotel's local marketplace.

Now is also the appropriate time to identify and retain legal counsel, as well as a hotel contract negotiation consultant, should one be required. All individuals retained to represent ownership's interest in the complex process of negotiating a hotel management contract should be specialists because hotels are truly different from all other classes of real estate. The more experience the team possesses in hotel contract negotiations, the more favorable the outcome is likely to be for the owner. The brand operators with whom the owner's team negotiates do this for a living, and they typically have deep experience and in-house counsel to guide them. Owners need to balance the scales with competitive representation, ensuring an equitable negotiation process and ultimately a fair agreement.

Timing

Because the process is complex, selecting an operator and entering into the negotiation process takes a lot of time. Even in instances where an owner and operator may have a history together, including perhaps existing contracts for other hotels managed for the owner by the operator, the process may take three months or longer because each contract entails new and unique issues. For an owner with no experience in selecting an operator, arriving at the completion of the contract negotiation process will require closer to six months. However, considering the term of the contract binding the owner and operator—ten to twenty-plus years—the process is not one that should be rushed.

The Operator Selection Process

Having decided to develop or purchase a hotel asset, ownership's selection of a brand affiliation and operator becomes the most important decision influencing the outcome of the real estate underwriting. A hotel's brand and operator have a direct impact on asset value, and the owner's selection therefore requires careful consideration.

Research Viable Candidates

The first step in the selection process is to develop a pre-qualified list of potential branded management companies that will receive a request for proposal (RFP). In developing this short list, owners need only consider brands that represent an appropriate match for both the subject hotel and the market. While there are a number of qualified operators and numerous brands to choose from, the short list should be limited to six companies, a manageable yet sufficient number of candidates from which to choose.

Brand. A hotel should be positioned within the market to maximize its operating potential, and branding is a critical component of establishing the hotel's positioning. Because different brands set different expectations in the consumer's mind, the selection of a brand determines how the hotel will be perceived. The brand chosen will also directly affect the level of services and amenities offered, as well as the hotel's price point, competitive set, cost of development or conversion, and cost of operation. The brand selected must convey an image commensurate with the physical product. Several brands should be researched and considered. Not infrequently, an owner's first choice among brands may not be available, either because the brand is already represented in the subject hotel's market or because of radius restrictions present in the chosen brand's contracts with other owners. Similarly, owners should not exclude desired brands from the selection process simply because they may already exist in the subject market, as agreements may be expiring or hotels bearing the desired brands may be positioned for sale. Another compelling reason for owners to pursue multiple branding options is that, although base fees may appear comparable, the all-in costs of brand affiliations, after taking into account mandatory participation in centralized services and brand standards, can vary significantly across brands. Owners should be sure to pursue several branding options so as not to limit the pool of suitable operators.

Operator. Although the selection of the operator is sometimes dictated by the brand desired (e.g., Hyatt, Ritz-Carlton, Four Seasons), most brands offer franchising as an option. As noted earlier, the emphasis in the present chapter is on the process of choosing a branded operator. However, owners should also consider the strategy of entering into a franchise agreement to secure a flag and employing an independent third-party management company to operate the asset. There are pros and cons to each approach, but some owners may find the reduced constraints of the franchise-with-independent-operator formula attractive. For example, as a franchisee, the owner may be able to opt out of costly programs offering little perceived value while the same programs are often mandatory for properties managed by the branded operator.

Request for Proposal

The request for proposal serves three primary purposes: (1) it is a formal invitation from an owner to an operator to bid on the management of the subject hotel; (2) it is the means by which pertinent information about the subject hotel is communicated to prospective operators; and (3) it facilitates the gathering of the same information on all operators for the purposes of comparing and ranking responses.

Through the RFP process, owners ascertain the level of interest from the operators selected and obtain the information necessary to compile a decision matrix that serves as the basis for ranking each operator's qualifications and ultimately developing a list of finalists. From an owner's perspective, the most critical components of the RFP responses are projected operating results, as reflected in the operator's pro forma, and the cost, as reflected in the operator's proposed contract provisions and conditions. The pro forma is critical because it represents the operator's projection of the subject hotel's operating potential under its brand and management. The operator's proposed provisions and conditions are of equal importance in assessing the RFP responses because they convey the cost and the key expectations of the operator, such as the duration of the contract and termination rights. As a minimum, operators should be asked to provide proposed base and incentive fees, length of term, chain fees and charges, termination-clause language, and estimated conversion costs in the case of an existing hotel.

The quality of operator responses depends on the specificity of information on the subject hotel and its market contained in the original RFP, as well on as the extent of the detail requested from respondents to the RFP. The more experienced the owner's team is in preparing RFPs, and the greater the time commitment to the preparation of a thorough RFP, the better will be the information provided by potential operators, ultimately simplifying the selection process. Exhibit 2 provides a sample table of contents for an RFP soliciting bids and related information from hotel management companies.

The questions included in the RFP will vary according to the project because the objectives and circumstances surrounding each deal are unique. However, the following list represents some of the typical questions posed to prospective operators in the RFP:

- What are the fundamental strengths that differentiate your organization from others in the field?
- What would be your operational approach to achieving the level of service outlined?

Exhibit 2 Sample Table of Contents: Request for Proposal from Hotel Management Company

1. Introduction and Objective
   a. Deal Highlights
   b. Hotel Facility History and Description
   c. Owner's Objectives
2. Property Overview
   a. Summary of Salient Data
   b. Photos
3. Overview of Subject Market
   a. Area/Location Overview
   b. Economic and Demographic Overview
4. Lodging-Market Overview
   a. Competitive Supply
   b. Demand
5. Analysis of Subject Operations (for existing property)
6. Requested Specifics of Submission and Time Line
   a. Request for Proposal (specific questions)
   b. Management RFP Time Line

Source: Capital Hotel Management.

- Provide the background and qualifications of your organization, providing particular discussion of those individuals who would be assigned to this asset.
- Provide a memorandum describing relevant proposed contract provisions and conditions, including the base and incentive management fee, term, centralized service fees, termination clause, etc. Include an estimate of expenses related to the transition.
- Provide a list of properties managed by your organization, giving particular attention to those similar in size and scope to the subject property. Address any similarities with your properties to the subject, if applicable. Please include examples of financial results achieved at similar properties under management, as deemed appropriate.

Review RFP Responses

The next step in the selection process is to review the responses to the RFP submitted by the operators. During this step, the owner must consider many factors reflecting the strengths and weaknesses of the respondent operators to determine those that will advance to the next round of the competitive process. The goal at this stage is to evaluate quickly the responses of each operator, assembling a short list of finalists that will proceed to the interview stage. The most efficient and effective method of conducting a review and comparison of the respondent operators is to create a decision matrix that permits the owner's team to organize responses to all pertinent questions and rate them accordingly. Stephen Rushmore, founder of HVS International, has developed the "Hotel Management Company Initial Selection Rating System" that appears in Exhibit 3. Using Rushmore's rating system, a specific weight is applied to each company's response to questions contained in the RFP, thus resulting in a numeric score that quantifies the responses and ranks the suitability of each management company under consideration.

Although decision matrices must be customized to reflect the unique aspects of individual deals, operator responses to the RFP can be generally categorized as either corporate or project-related. Corporate responses reflect decision factors such as the relative experience and suitability of the branded operator to the hotel asset in question. Project-related responses address specific questions concerning the project at hand, such as the proposed contract provisions and conditions, projected financial results and, if applicable, the operator's willingness to contribute financially to the project. The following list presents examples of both corporate and project-related factors typically weighed in the decision matrix.

Corporate Factors

- Size of managed hotels
- Size/experience of management company
- Brand recognition
- Distribution
- Management experience (turnover)
- Specialization/niche (e.g., resort, distressed property, secondary cities)
- Historical performance
- Corporate operating strategy (to test consistency with owner's vision of hotel's operation)
- Level of completeness/professionalism in response to the RFP
- Owner's instinct or "gut feel"

Project-Related Factors

- Proposed management contract provisions and conditions
- Projected operating pro forma
- Chain services and charges (*all* costs from conversion to operating should be enumerated)
- Brand value (for comparison to cost of chain services)
- Financial resources/willingness to invest (if desired by ownership)

Management Agreement Provisions: Key Points Checklist

There are numerous provisions and conditions essential to a well-crafted management agreement, and the list has grown with the complexity of hotel management

Exhibit 3 Hotel Management Company Initial Selection Rating System

Comparing the size of the hotels managed by the operator to the subject, most are:

Larger	-1
The same size	0
Smaller	-1

Comparing the chain affiliations of the hotels managed by the operator, most are:

Same affiliation	1
Similar affiliation	0
Dissimilar or no affiliation	-1

If the operator manages other hotels in the same market area, are these considered to be:

Directly competitive	-4
Somewhat competitive	-2
Non-competitive	1

Experience of the management company:

New company	-1
Moderate experience	0
Established	2

Management company's financial resources: ability to invest funds in the property:

Limited	-1
Moderate	0
Strong	2

Operator shows willingness to invest funds in the property as a loan (double amounts if funds are contributed as equity)

Initial inventories	+1
Working capital	+1
Pre-opening expenses	+2
FF&E	+3
Debt service guarantees	+3

If the management company appears to be flexible in accommodating the following specialized needs:

Short-term contract	+2
Termination buyout provision	+2

Management company's ability to generate profits (based on actual performance):

Normal—competent management	0
Better than average	+5
Exceptional operating ability	+10

Management company offers:

Ability to obtain specialized identification	+2
Ability to obtain financing	+4
Feeder city representation	+2
Track record of success	+2

Management company has exceptional expertise or offers specialized services in the following areas:

Centralized reservation system	+2
Centralized sales and marketing	+1
Regional sales offices	+1
Convention and group sales	+1
Frequent traveler program	+1
National advertising program	+1
Top-level personnel	+1
Financial systems and controls	+1
Other specialized services	+1
Personnel relations	+1
Development capability	+1

If management company has the following deficiencies:

Poor references	-3
Loss contracts (deduct for each loss)	-1
Limited home office structure	-1
High management turnover	-2
No growth plans	-1
Excessive growth plans	-1
Will not subordinate incentive fee	-3
Unwilling to provide restrictive covenant	-3
Fee based entirely on percentage of total revenue	-3

Response to RFP showed professional effort in:

Preparing operating budget	+1
Preparing sample marketing plan	+1

Exhibit 3 *(continued)*

If the management company has extensive experience in one of the following specialized areas that would directly benefit the operation of the subject		Opening new hotel	+2
		Distressed property	+2
		Bankruptcy	+2
		Unions	+1
		Operating in secondary cities	+1
Destination resort	+2	Property ownership	+2
Major convention operation	+2	**Your gut feel**	
Unique market	+1		
Major food and beverage operation	+2	Can you get along with this company?	+3
Development assistance	+2		

Source: © Copyright 2004—Stephen Rushmore. Used with permission.

contracts. Presented below are only some of the key provisions that warrant consideration and inclusion in the management agreement. Although not all of these provisions will be addressed in the RFP, it is a good idea for owners to review this checklist as operator responses are evaluated. Owners can then anticipate the respondents' respective stances on key contract points and prepare their desired position on each point before entering the initial negotiation phase. This checklist can also be used at the conclusion of the negotiations to ensure that the agreement contains all of the key provisions. Of course, the provisions considered key to a given contract will vary with the owner's objectives, the requirements of the deal (e.g., operator financial participation or not), the dynamics of the negotiation, and other circumstances of the project. For a more detailed discussion of the points contained in the following list, Eyster's *The Negotiation and Administration of Hotel and Restaurant Management Contracts* is recommended.[1]

Key Points Checklist

- Initial term and renewals
- Management fee structure
- Operator reimbursable expenses
- Operator loan or equity contributions (terms and conditions, priority, and payback)
- Operator performance standards
- Owner input in operational decision-making
- Operational and financial reporting
- Termination with cause, at owner's option without cause, on sale, and on foreclosure
- Non-compete covenants
- Dispute settlement mechanisms

Interview Finalists

Based on the outcome of the owner's review of the information contained in the decision matrix, two to three finalists will typically emerge as potential operators. Representatives of the finalist companies should be invited to meet with the owner's selection team so that each company's representatives are interviewed in person. The purpose of the interview is for owners and operators to ask any outstanding questions, gain further clarification of each party's intent, and ultimately to determine if a viable partnership is possible. This meeting also provides the owner with an opportunity to gain more insight into the intangible aspects of the union, such as the chemistry between the two parties—an essential component for successful negotiation and a durable relationship under the contract.

Final and Best Offers

Following the interviews, owners should take the opportunity to provide feedback and solicit final and best offers from each operator. Owners must continue to maintain the discipline of the selection process, ensuring that any information requested of one operator is requested of all operators. For instance, if an owner requests a final and best offer on the management fee from Operator A, the same opportunity must be extended to all other finalists to maintain a fair and competitive bidding process.

Selection

After all factors are weighed and interviews are concluded, the time has come to select an operator. Ideally, it would be most beneficial for an owner to enter into "hard" negotiations with more than one operator. However, due to the time and cost involved in moving to the next level of the process, it is not practical to enter into negotiations with two prospective partners—nor is it a practice generally accepted by operators, who often seek an exclusive commitment before entering into negotiations. Nonetheless, it is a good fallback plan to keep the second-choice contender interested and informed in case negotiations with the first choice falter.

Round One: Negotiating the Bill of Rights

At the outset of the management contract negotiation, the owner and operator are essentially on a level playing field—the owner seeks an operator to manage the asset and maximize investment returns, while the operator seeks an opportunity to manage and brand a property to enhance corporate fee revenue and increase distribution. Although this proposition is simple in theory, the process by which these two entities unite to create an equitable agreement is often arduous. To launch the painstaking process, the authors recommend introducing the owner-operator bill of rights.

The intent of the bill of rights is to recognize the core rights of both the owner and the operator. The first round of negotiations should revolve around the bill of rights, which is aimed at providing an equitable platform for negotiating the key provisions of the agreement *before* developing the legal document. The bill of rights suggests that owners and operators start negotiations not based on a legal document containing *a priori* positions, but rather parity of expectations for both sides, which becomes the premise on which the contract will eventually be drafted.

There are several benefits to conducting the negotiations in this manner. First, a discussion centered on the bill of rights allows the parties to debate and resolve key provisions before the legal document is drafted, fostering a positive relationship among the participants in the deal. It aids in creating an equitable agreement—one that provides operators with the flexibility to operate in accordance with their standards while providing owners the ability to protect long-term asset value and achieve desired returns consistent with their ownership strategy.

Another benefit of starting with the bill of rights as a precursor to drafting the legal document is that "show stoppers" can be uncovered before advancing too far in the contract negotiation process. At this stage of the process, owners typically expect that there is a fundamental level of understanding between the two parties that eliminates the need to revisit the operator-selection decision; however, there are instances where unresolvable conflicts are uncovered, even at this advanced stage of the process. It is far better to identify potential show stoppers during this phase rather than later in the process, after even more time and money have been expended. Typical show stoppers are often in the areas of the performance clauses, approval rights, and cash control. In the event the two parties cannot come to an agreement on the bill of rights, ownership can revert to its back-up selection among the operators interviewed.

To expedite the process, Eyster advises that both owners and operators should enter into the negotiations with a going-in position, a fallback, and even a second fallback position.[2] As Eyster's approach suggests, there will likely be a significant give-and-take in an effort to find the grounds for agreement on some of the key provisions. While there is a certain base level of rights that owners should expect to achieve, they should be prepared to extend parallel rights to operators to create an equitable relationship.

Owner's Bill of Rights

A summary statement of the owner-operator bill of rights is presented in Exhibit 4. The following discussion illuminates the key reasons for inclusion of the individual owner rights and explores the ramifications of selected rights.

- *Right that operator put owner's interests first.* Although it is seemingly logical that the operator, as the owner's agent, should work to advance only ownership's interests, an inherent conflict exists between building brand equity and owner's equity. Oftentimes the operator's decisions benefit the brand but do not necessarily add asset value—and, in some instances, may detract from the value of the hotel asset. Discussion of this right reveals the owner's expectations regarding the operator's fiduciary responsibility to place the owner's interest first and foremost, above obligations to the brand.
- *Right to absentee ownership.* Hotel owners' desired level of involvement in the operation of their assets varies. Some owners want to be apprised daily of operational results and decisions at the property level, and may even engage

Exhibit 4 Owner-Operator Bill of Rights

Owner's Rights

- Right that operator put owner's interests first
- Right to absentee ownership
- Right to active ownership
- Right to a fair and equitable management agreement (not operator biased)
- Right to approve a detailed annual operating plan
- Right to approve a detailed annual capital plan
- Right to provide input in the selection/removal of the general manager and other key management personnel
- Right to a reasonable restrictive (non-compete) covenant
- Right to operator performance standards
- Right for owner to terminate contract with cause or upon sale
- Right to control cash in excess of operating capital requirements and in the replacement reserve account
- Right to understand the costs and benefits associated with operator system reimbursable expenses
- Right to meet monthly with operator to review financial performance
- Right to have access to and audit the books and records of the hotel
- Right for the hotel to be managed consistent with maximizing long-term asset value

Operator's Rights

- Right to manage the hotel without undo interference from owner (reasonable non-disturbance)
- Right to manage the hotel consistent with an approved annual plan (operating and capital budgets)
- Right to limited financial risk
- Right to indemnification except for gross negligence or willful misconduct
- Right to cash for operating capital and approved capital-expenditure requirements
- Right to a stable, reasonable contract term, subject to performance standards
- Right to earn a fair base management fee and an incentive fee based on performance
- Right to demand that owner be well capitalized and the hotel not over leveraged
- Right to operate and maintain the hotel consistent with operator's standards
- Right to select, terminate, train, supervise, and assign all employees of the hotel
- Right to require the owner to maintain appropriate insurance coverage and hold operator harmless for any loss sustained.

Source: Capital Hotel Management (© 2003).

an asset manager to assume a very proactive approach to ownership. Other owners may take a more passive stance. Regardless of the extent of involvement ownership seeks, management should respect this position.

- *Right to active ownership*. Active ownership should be defined in terms of the owner's expectations, anticipated level of involvement, reporting requirements, intent to engage an asset manager, etc., so that both parties are clear and in agreement on how the relationship will function.

- *Right to a fair and equitable management agreement (not operator biased).* This is a right of both parties to the contract, and is simply a reminder that the goal of the negotiations is to arrive at an agreement mutually beneficial to the owner and operator. The negotiation process will be extended needlessly if either party proposes prejudicial contract terms.
- *Right to approve a detailed annual operating plan.* Although the operator assumes responsibility for the financial performance of the hotel, the owner should maintain approval rights over performance goals and objectives. Therefore, this right entitles owners to review the annual operating budget and marketing plan according to a pre-defined schedule, allowing ample time for necessary changes before approval. In anticipation of those instances where the owner and the operator might fail to agree on the budget or other issues related to the annual plan, the means for dispute settlement should also be addressed in the management agreement. The procedure for resolving such conflicts at various levels of disagreement should be mutually agreed upon and clearly stated in the contract.
- *Right to approve a detailed annual capital plan.* Similarly, owners should insist on the right to review and approve the annual capital plan. It is critical that owners maintain control of how the reserve for replacement fund is spent to ensure that capital projects enhance asset value rather than satisfying brand standards without commensurate economic return for ownership.
- *Right to provide input in the selection and removal of the general manager and other key management personnel.* Owners should seek approval rights over the key executives hired to operate the hotel and should retain the right to remove any member of the executive committee should there be sufficient cause.
- *Right to a reasonable restrictive (non-compete) covenant.* Although it is increasingly difficult for owners to ensure that their hotel is the sole beneficiary of a brand's strength in a particular market, careful consideration should be given to negotiating an exclusive trade area and the term or duration of the non-compete clause. Specific attention should be given to defining similar or "sister" brands under the same corporate management (e.g., Marriott full-service hotels and Renaissance, Sheraton and Westin), as well as to crafting carefully the legal language surrounding this provision (e.g., specifying the use of impact studies to determine infringement on a trade area). Further, as previously suggested, a means of resolving any disputes that may arise in the application of the non-compete provision should be incorporated into the management agreement.
- *Right to operator performance standards.* Owners should pursue minimum performance guarantees based on a "flow-through" measure (e.g., house profit, net operating income) and a performance-versus-market metric (e.g., RevPAR index or penetration). Although performance guarantees will likely represent a minimum threshold calculated as a percentage of budgeted expectations, it is important that the contract be very precise in specifying the metrics to be employed, as well as the conditions triggering the imposition of each

standard. Only by carefully specifying the measures and conditions of the performance clause can an owner pursue the right to terminate based on an operator's failure to perform financially. The current standards for performance clauses seem to provide for a four- to five-year ramp-up period before owners can invoke performance clauses. Once the specified period has passed, the operator's failure to meet performance standards for two years in succession triggers the owner's right to terminate, although operators usually have the right to "cure" shortfalls from the budgeted performance level for at least one year, effectively buying another two-year surcease to improve the hotel's performance.

- *Right for owner to terminate contract with cause or upon sale.* The right to terminate under all possible scenarios must be addressed in the management agreement. Owners should pursue the right to terminate in the event the operator fails to perform to an acceptable level, defaults on a substantive provision, or breaches its fiduciary duty to the owner. In addition, winning the right to terminate upon sale is an important option that can be critical to owners seeking a short-term exit strategy. When dealing with branded operators, however, owners can expect significant resistance to early termination on sale and should be prepared to pay liquidated damages to exercise this right. If the hotel is a new development, language should also be included specifying the owner's right to terminate should the project be sold before opening or, alternatively, fail to open.
- *Right to control cash in excess of operating capital requirements and in the reserve for replacement account.* Even with the right to approve capital budgets, only owners who maintain control of the replacement reserves can ensure that funds are being spent appropriately. Most branded national chains will want to control available cash at all levels; however, having control over the cash provides owners with a system of checks and balances.
- *Right to understand the costs and benefits associated with operator system reimbursable expenses.* Putting this point on the negotiating table should lead to a discussion of the full disclosure of existing chain service fees, the methods for calculating and allocating these fees, and fee caps. A discussion of the owner's expectations regarding the cost-benefit analyses to be presented for reimbursable fees resulting from future programs should also ensue. The owner has the right to know all related expenses and have an opportunity to verify that all future programs implemented are fair and reasonable and allocated accordingly. The key is for owners to identify and eliminate potential expenses that serve to enhance top-line revenues at the expense of net operating income.
- *Right to meet monthly with the operator to review financial performance.* Owners' reasonable expectations regarding the sharing of financial performance information should be honored. It is appropriate to discuss expectations of the level of detail to be presented, the format, and timing of delivery. Owners should seek to obtain information on a basis as close to real time as possible (e.g., receipt of financial statements within ten days of a period's close).

- *Right to have access to and audit the books and records of the hotel.* This right allows owners and their representatives full access to all records and explicit permission to conduct an audit of the hotel's financial and accounting practices at the owner's discretion.
- *Right for the hotel to be managed consistent with maximizing long-term asset value.* This right encompasses several of the items addressed above. It is similar to the owner's right to require the operator to put ownership's interests first, but reiterates the expectation that all decisions made with respect to the hotel should maximize the long-term value of the asset.

Operator's Bill of Rights

As practicing asset managers, the authors have presented the position of ownership first, but intelligent and efficient negotiations also require that both parties to the contract comprehend the rights of the operator. Accordingly, the following discussion illuminates some of the key reasons behind the individual operator rights contained in the bill of rights.

- *Right to manage the hotel without undue interference from the owner (reasonable non-disturbance).* This assures the management company that it will not be encumbered or prevented by ownership from doing the job for which the operator was engaged.
- *Right to manage the hotel consistent with an approved annual plan (operating and capital budgets).* Operators are entitled to the reassurance that owner-approved annual operating plans and capital budgets are working documents that will serve as a valid road map to achievement of the owner's objectives, and that the owners will not materially alter them after approval. The approved budget also serves to align the operating philosophy and the financial objectives of the owner and operator.
- *Right to limited financial risk.* This is the operator's expectation that the owner bears the risk of owning real estate and accepts the business risk of operations. Owners should not expect or require that operators respond to cash calls from ownership.
- *Right to indemnification except for gross negligence or willful misconduct.* Like the preceding right, acceptance of this provision protects the operator from liabilities associated with the asset, with the exception of liabilities arising out of gross negligence or the intentional misconduct of employees.
- *Right to cash for operating capital and approved capital-expenditure requirements.* Operators have the right to expect that owners will fund operating-capital requirements and capital projects on a timely basis, in accordance with the provisions of the management agreement and approved annual budgets.
- *Right to a stable, reasonable contract term, subject to performance standards.* Discussion of this operator's right should result in an agreed upon duration of the contract. Performance standards should be equitable and should consider the impact of economic cycles beyond the control of the operator. Although

owners typically attempt to limit the term of the contract, operators need long-term agreements. Branded managers will require ten- or twenty-year terms, with publicly traded companies especially reluctant to manage for fewer than twenty years. Unbranded independent management companies may accept terms ranging from three to ten years.

- *Right to earn a fair base management fee and an incentive fee based on performance.* Management agreements have evolved significantly from the operator-biased contracts of the early 1970s that were based solely on top-line results, yielding substantial fees to management companies regardless of whether owners were realizing bottom-line profits. Management fees are structured much more equitably today, typically including a base fee (ranging between two and four percent of gross revenues) and an incentive fee component (typically 10 to 12 percent of net operating profits after debt service). In some instances, the incentive fee is structured so that an owner receives a minimum return on equity before the distribution of the incentive fee. However structured, an incentive fee must be earned and should not be paid unless ownership has met its minimum return requirements.
- *Right to demand that owner be well capitalized and the hotel not over-leveraged.* The operator has the right to require that the owner be able to perform reasonably, supporting the provisions and intent of the management agreement by maintaining a minimum net worth. In addition, the owner should be required to maintain a prudent loan-to-value ratio when debt is used to finance the asset.
- *Right to operate and maintain the hotel consistent with operator's standards.* Operators should be able to operate the asset in accordance with their brand standards; however, an operator needs to provide clear and uniform standards across its brand. Further, brand standards need to be consistent with the owner's objective of maximizing long-term value.
- *Right to select, terminate, train, supervise, and assign all employees of the hotel.* By and large, under today's management contracts employees work for the operator, not the owner. The only limitation on the operator's right to manage its employees according to its standards and practices is the owner's right to selection and removal of executive committee members.
- *Right to require the owner to maintain appropriate insurance coverage and hold the operator harmless for any loss sustained.* Similar to the operator's right to limited financial risk, the owner must assume responsibility for all risk associated with the real estate, including the risk of business interruption.

Round Two: Negotiating the Legal Document

At this final stage of the negotiation process, the assumption is that the owner and operator have reached a consensus on the key provisions of the owner-operator bill of rights. Legal counsel should now become more active in the process, integrating the key provisions agreed upon and couching them in the legal language that constitutes the management agreement. The authors recommend that owners insist on drafting the management agreement because experience has demonstrated that the party that controls the development of the contract document controls the process.

With the legal document—preferably drafted by the owner's counsel—in hand, negotiation of the definitive contract can commence. Since numerous of the key provisions have been addressed in the first round of negotiations, this final phase requires only the fleshing out of the management contract's clauses according to terms already agreed to by the owner and operator.

Conclusion

The industry as a whole has made great strides in leveling the playing field in the negotiation of hotel management agreements, which for many years were drafted by—and in favor of—the operator. Owners who clearly define their investment strategy, create a competitive bidding environment, and assemble a team of qualified, experienced consultants and legal counsel will enhance their leverage going into the negotiation process. Owners and operators who use the bill of rights presented in this chapter as the basis for their initial negotiations will have the opportunity to create an equitable platform at the start the negotiation, thereby closing the gap between the parties' expectations, reducing the time and money invested in the process, and ultimately yielding a more equitable agreement for both parties.

Endnotes

1. James J. Eyster, *The Negotiation and Administration of Hotel and Restaurant Management Contracts*, 3rd ed. (Ithaca, N.Y.: Cornell University School of Hotel Administration, 1988). See especially pages 35–87.
2. Eyster, pp. 139–142.

References

Eyster, James J. 1997. *Hotel Management Contracts in the U.S.: The Revolution Continues and Twelve Areas of Concern.* Ithaca, N.Y.: Cornell University School of Hotel Administration.

———. 1993. "Hotel Management Contracts Under Fire and Change: A Perspective," *The Real Estate Finance Journal*, Vol. 8, No. 3, pp. 37–46.

———. 1993. "The Revolution in Domestic Hotel Management Contracts," *The Cornell Hotel and Restaurant Administration Quarterly*, Vol. 33, No. 4, pp. 16–26.

———. 1990. "Trends in Hotel Management Contract Provisions for the 1990s," *Real Estate Review*, Vol. 20, No. 3, pp. 28–34.

Rushmore, Stephen. 2002. "Performance Clauses Essential in Contract." *Hotels*, Vol. 36, No. 11, p. 36.

———. 2000. "System for Selecting Management Company," *Hotels*, Vol. 34, No. 11, p. 38.

———. 1999. "Structuring Management Contracts," *Hotels*, Vol. 33, No. 5, p. 36.

Rushmore, Stephen, Dana Michael Ciraldo, and John Tarras. 2001. "Hotel Management Contracts and Related Documents," in *Hotel Investments Handbook—2001*. New York: West Group.

7

Managing the Manager: The Owner–Management Company Relationship

By Bruce F. Stemerman

***Bruce F. Stemerman** is Executive Vice President—Operations for Capital Hotel Management, LLC (CHM). CHM is a highly specialized asset management firm that provides focused services to upscale hotels and resorts, protecting and enhancing value for owners, investors, and lenders. CHM provides asset management services to owners of 24 hotels with approximately 10,000 rooms and a value in excess of $1 billion.*

Before joining CHM, Mr. Stemerman held various positions over a 15-year span with Marriott International and then Host Marriott Corporation, where he served as Senior Vice President, Asset Management. In that role, he led a group of asset managers responsible for all ownership aspects of Host's portfolio of 125 upscale and luxury hotel properties with nearly 60,000 rooms.

Mr. Stemerman is the immediate past president of the Hospitality Asset Managers Association (HAMA) and a long-term member of HAMA's board. In addition, he serves on the Advisory Board of Madison Hotel Opportunity Partners, LLC, a fund focused on financing and acquisition opportunities within the full-service segment of the hospitality industry. He also serves on the Board of Co-Owners of Camelback Inn, Scottsdale, Arizona. Before joining Marriott in 1989, Mr. Stemerman was with Price Waterhouse in their New York and Washington, DC, offices. He graduated from Rochester Institute of Technology and is a Certified Public Accountant.

REAL ESTATE is one of the most dynamic and enticing businesses in our capitalistic society. Much of the great wealth accumulated in this country has its origins in the development, ownership, and management of real estate. While the office, retail, and residential segments all have their challenges and rewards, most view lodging as the most diverse, complex, and multi-dimensional of real estate asset classes.

Our inventory—the guestroom—is perishable, expiring on a daily basis, and therefore must be actively and even scientifically managed to yield the best possible results. Full-service hotels offer food and-beverage outlets, banquet services, fitness facilities, retail outlets, and, in some cases, spas, golf courses, and much more. Economic and competitive cycles create an ever-changing dynamic that must be proactively managed. It is this diversity and complexity that have drawn an increasing number of professional lodging asset managers to this business, and promise to continue to do so. To be successful in this environment, today's lodging asset manager must possess a well equipped toolbox of varied skills.

Today's Lodging Asset Manager

Within the asset management arena, the interest in and demand for skilled asset managers are increasing. As the nature of the hotel owner has evolved over the last two decades from a passive investor (e.g., institutions and real estate limited partnerships) to an active owner (e.g., public companies, including real estate investment trusts, and private equity funds), the importance of the lodging asset management function has grown considerably. Professional lodging asset managers are viewed as integral to an owner's efforts to maximize the value of lodging real estate. The focus on asset management has become more intense during the recent difficult economic times, as hotel owners have become even more determined to maximize returns and enhance the value of their hotels.

For most practicing asset managers in the profession, a substantial portion of their time and effort is spent dealing with the manager ownership has engaged to operate the hotel on a day-to-day basis. Even in the model where the entity owning lodging assets also manages those assets, companies have established an internal asset management function. These enterprises recognize the value of an independent asset management function and appreciate the alternative perspective and value enhancement focus that a professional lodging asset manager brings to the dynamics of the owner-manager relationship.

The relationship between a hotel owner and the hotel manager is typically defined by the management agreement. As management contracts are discussed elsewhere in this book (see Chapters 5 and 6), it is sufficient to note here that they establish the fundamental terms of the relationship between the parties involved. The management agreement addresses the rights and obligations of the parties, compensation, services to be provided, the duration of the agreement, owner approval rights over capital investment and operating budgets, and a multitude of other terms and conditions. From both the owner's and the manager's perspectives, the management agreement is the key document setting forth each party's respective rights and responsibilities. Nothing in this chapter is intended to detract from the critical importance of the underlying document; however, in building an effective owner-manager relationship, the provisions of the management agreement are merely a starting point.

Managing the Owner-Manager Relationship

Building an effective relationship with the third-party manager of an owned hotel is essential to maximizing the value of the asset. The first step in building such a relationship is to align the interests of both parties. While this principle should be obvious, it bears emphasis: a key ingredient to any effective business relationship is a mutual understanding of how success is to be defined and measured. The parties must agree on the goals and objectives to be achieved if the venture is to be successful. Given the complexities of the lodging industry and, at times, the divergent interests of the owner and the manager, achieving a successful owner-manager relationship can be an endeavor fraught with challenges.

A Foundation for Success

The best relationships, in the business world as in our personal lives, are those that involve timely, honest, and open communication between the partners. Mutual respect, a clear understanding of objectives, and open lines of communication characterize an ideal relationship. This type of relationship has the greatest potential for success because everyone's efforts are focused and aligned to accomplish the same goals and objectives.

Fortunately, the goals and objectives of a hotel owner and a hotel manager are relatively well aligned from the start. Both parties want the hotel to be a commercial success. Since success in the business world is typically measured in dollars, this means that a hotel that maximizes the return on investment will be more highly valued. All other measures of success emanate from or contribute to the basic objective of maximizing return on investment. Both parties generally want the hotel to be successful compared with its competitive set—the half-dozen or so properties that it competes against most directly. Both want their guests to feel good about their experience in the hotel so they will not only return but will share their positive impressions with others so that they, too, will patronize the hotel. This natural alignment of interests provides a substantial foundation for potential success.

Often, the compensation of the hotel manager is designed to align the interests of the owner and the manager. In the typical management agreement, a portion of the manager's compensation is based on the hotel's gross revenues, while another, often significant, portion is determined as a share of the profits generated. Profits are "where the rubber hits the road" for owners. To the extent that the manager can generate meaningful fees from producing incremental profits, it is more likely that both parties' interests will be well aligned, moving along a common path.

The Strategic Plan

It is difficult—impossible, actually—to choose a path to follow if you do not know your destination. It seems simple, yet the misalignment of goals and objectives is a common reason for owner-manager relationships to go awry. An effective way to align interests is to develop a strategic plan for the hotel. This should be a collaborative effort between the asset manager and the hotel's property-management team, although the asset manager should lead the way. The strategic plan may take many forms but generally involves an assessment of the current state of the hotel and an identification of the hotel's strengths, weaknesses, opportunities, and threats—commonly referred to as a SWOT analysis. It cannot be emphasized enough that the asset manager should work collaboratively with the hotel management team in developing the SWOT analysis. This is the footing for the overall strategic plan. It is a critical opportunity for all of the stakeholders to focus on the hotel's problem areas, capital-investment needs, and competitive challenges. The strategic plan will identify strengths and opportunities that can be exploited to achieve greater success at the hotel. It also identifies weaknesses that ultimately will need to be overcome to maximize the hotel's value.

The strategic plan should also address the owner's intentions with respect to the hotel: Does ownership expect to hold the hotel indefinitely, or is there a plan to sell the asset in, say, the next three to five years? The ultimate disposition plan for the hotel is one of the most critical objectives for ownership, as it will want to position the hotel to yield the highest possible sales price. From the manager's point of view, a change in ownership can be daunting, for a number of reasons. The management contract may terminate upon a change in ownership, but even if the acquiring entity is locked into the contract or chooses to retain the current property-management company, it may have different views on adherence to brand standards or capital improvements at the hotel.

A strategic plan for a hotel asset that ownership intends to sell in a relatively short time (within less than five years) may create tension between the manager and the owner because the owner's priorities for value creation opportunities will likely differ from the manager's objectives. For example, the owner might be more interested in extending the life of the guestroom furnishings, allocating funds instead to repairing the façade of the building. It is crucial that the asset manager work these differences out collaboratively and cooperatively with the manager, finding some middle ground that both parties can live with. At the end of the day, ownership needs the manager's "buy-in" to the strategic plan.

Once developed and documented, the strategic plan should be referred to regularly and adjusted based on changes in the economy and the competitive environment. As in the creation of the strategic plan, it is just as important that revisions be developed collaboratively to avoid future disagreements between the asset manager and the hotel manager. The strategic plan should be viewed as a living document that needs regular attention and nurturing.

Action plans for the accomplishment of the goals set forth in the strategic plan must be developed with specific milestones, and these action plans must be periodically reviewed, assessed, and updated. Keep in mind that while the objectives set out in the strategic plan should be aggressive, they should also be viewed as being achievable. It will be difficult to keep the parties involved focused on objectives that are considered impossible to achieve.

Challenges and Opportunities

While the asset manager is focused exclusively on economics, the manager might have competing motivations. For first-tier, branded managers (as opposed to independent managers), the interests of the brand may also come into play. For example, brand standards might require certain capital expenditures that the owner would not otherwise consider productive investments. A similar conflict arises if the brand has an interest in developing additional product in the same market area where an owner's property is located. The owner may view the new product as adversely affecting the operating results of its existing hotel.

The preceding situations are only two of many examples where the owner and the manager might have different perspectives that may lead to conflict. There are no easy answers for resolving such differences, but it is important that the asset manager understand the manager's perspective and motivations. With regard to brand standards, for example, the manager should always be motivated by the desire to gain preference for the flag's product among customers, but she must also be able to demonstrate clearly to ownership the economic or competitive benefits of each initiative proposed. It is the asset manager's responsibility to require an economics-driven business case that supports any initiative proposed by the manager. If a cogent business case is consistently required, the manager will ultimately provide one automatically with every proposal submitted. In many cases, the asset manager should participate in and guide the preparation of the business case so the needs of ownership are met.

Many of the best value-additive opportunities originate from the hotel's property-management team. An effective asset manager encourages the general manager and the property-management team to suggest opportunities frequently. By creating a collaborative environment where new and creative ideas and opportunities are welcomed—even expected—the asset manager can considerably advance the sense of partnership with the property-management team. It is also likely that many of the opportunities that the general manager or other members of the executive committee propose will yield meaningful results. The asset manager who discourages or dismisses such proposals will not only foreclose potential opportunities, but will also foster an environment of disengagement among the hotel executive team.

Communicating More

It is also crucial for the asset manager to ensure that the general manager knows all of ownership's expectations. The critical expectations will have been set forth in the strategic plan. But beyond that, the asset manager should clearly communicate the owner's desires regarding the frequency and content of communications, the level of detail to be contained in financial analyses, the manager's role at periodic owner-manager meetings, and all of the other expectations and nuances that will contribute to an effective ongoing relationship. Making the general manager aware of what the asset manager expects reduces the chances of disappointment and can greatly contribute to a solid working relationship.

Communication of expectations applies equally to the general manager, so the asset manager should solicit the general manager's views on his expectations from the relationship, and strive to accommodate them. Many of today's management-contract companies, particularly the largest ones, have varying chains of command. Therefore, it is crucial for the asset manager to understand any limits that might apply to the general manager's authority. If the asset manager is to achieve his objectives, it is likely that, in some instances, he will need to establish relationships beyond those at the property level.

As with all relationships, balance and an appropriate sharing of the rewards of success are critical for the long-term well-being of the relationship. If one party is viewed as reaping more than its fair share of the rewards, then the other party will ultimately seek to revise or end the relationship. Equity in a relationship is difficult to define. It is not surprising, therefore, that we have witnessed a power shift in recent years as owners have more aggressively and publicly exercised their rights, achieving a relationship they feel is more equitable. In the opinion of many, this shift has resulted in a more balanced sharing of rights between the owner and the manager. In light of the more active involvement of professional lodging asset managers, it is not surprising that owners have demanded and achieved greater influence regarding all aspects of the hotels they own. Some management companies have contributed to this power shift by being less than forthright in disclosing certain details of their stewardship. These instances have been well documented in the press and, as a result, most managers have adopted a much more open and transparent approach, sharing with their owners previously undisclosed information. Although this is a very positive development in the evolution of the owner-manager relationship, it is difficult to predict all of the consequences that this power shift may bring. Like all relationships, balance is important, and too great a shift in favor of ownership could yield a whole new set of challenges.

As the vignette presented in Exhibit 1 illustrates, practitioners in our profession employ quite disparate techniques in their efforts to enhance the value of their hotels. Aggressiveness, dedication, passion, and knowledge of the lodging business are attributes of a successful asset manager, but some employ more contentious and belligerent methods in their asset management efforts. This approach involves berating, belittling, and disparaging the general manager and his team, constantly invoking the lurking threat of litigation. Although this type of behavior can occasionally be effective, it is rarely successful over an extended period of time. More often, an overly aggressive and adversarial approach to the owner-manager relationship will lead to a misalignment between ownership's and management's goals and objectives for the property. A relationship in which there is a misalignment of interests will lack trust, and the inevitable disagreements will often escalate, becoming more serious problems that can be resolved only through litigation. Regrettably, there are times when litigation becomes a necessary course for a party, but it is also a clear sign of failure in the relationship and usually is not a productive path. It often causes harm to the hotel as financial resources and time are diverted to defending positions rather than to enhancing the value of the asset. The hotel's management team should view an effective asset manager as a partner, not as the enemy.

The Ideal General Manager

At the property level, the professional lodging asset manager's key point of contact with the management company is normally the general manager. (The title "general manager" is intended to refer to the most senior-level employee of the management company at the hotel, although the person in this role may in fact hold an alternative title such as "managing director.") The general manager is the person who can most influence the day-to-day results achieved by the hotel. In a perfect world, the management agreement would provide the hotel owner with approval rights over the hiring of the general manager, as well as the authority to remove the general manager for unacceptable performance. Among the many rights an owner might negotiate in a management agreement, the ability to hire or dismiss the general manager, even though rarely exercised, may be one of the most

Exhibit 1 A Tale of Two Asset Managers

Presented below are two very different approaches to setting up the annual budget-review process at comparable hotels.

The annual budget-review process for both the **First Class Resort** and the **Upscale Resort** will occur in the next month. Both hotels are full-service luxury resorts located in the United States. Both have approximately 500 guestrooms, four food-and-beverage outlets, multiple retail outlets, a full-service spa, and an 18-hole championship golf course. Both are typically ranked among the top 50 resorts in the country and both enjoy premium market share when compared with their competitive sets. Both hotels have performed well in recent years, but have been adversely affected recently by a general downturn in the economy.

The hotels are owned by an institutional owner of a multi-billion-dollar portfolio of real estate that includes, among other asset classes, more than 20 hotels. The owner has assigned new asset managers to these hotels. **Carl Collaborative** is responsible for the First Class Resort and **Allan Adversarial** is the asset manager for the Upscale Resort.

Several weeks in advance of the budget-review process for the First Class Resort, Mr. Collaborative calls the hotel to introduce himself to the general manager. In the call, he expresses his enthusiasm for becoming involved with the hotel and working with the general manager and his team. He provides the GM with the timetable for the budget review and suggests several alternative dates for the review session, which he anticipates will take two days and will involve members of the GM's executive team for portions of that time. He comments on some of the challenges facing the hotel in the upcoming year and stresses the need to work together in setting specific outcomes for the budget review. He gives the GM some overall objectives that the owner has for the hotel's economic performance in the next year and acknowledges that they will be difficult to achieve but that "we need to work together to accomplish these financial objectives." He provides the GM with a detailed proposed agenda for the meeting, seeks the GM's input and suggestions for other topics that should be covered, and solicits the GM's desired outcomes for the meeting. He also suggests that the meeting be used to update the hotel's strategic plan in light of current economic difficulties. He offers to spend some time at the beginning of the meeting to help the hotel management team better understand the owner's business strategy and perspective. Finally, he stresses the importance of working together during these difficult times, pointing out the critical role that the GM and his team will play in the continuing success of the First Class Resort. Both agree to speak at least weekly during the period leading up to the budget-review meeting to continue the planning process and avoid any unanticipated events.

Several weeks in advance of the budget-review process for the Upscale Resort, Mr. Adversarial calls the hotel to introduce himself to the general manager. He tells the GM that things need to change, that the GM and his team are not focused on the right things and need to do a much better job managing the hotel or there will be consequences. "There's a new sheriff in town and things are going to change from now on." He instructs the GM to block one week for the budget-review process and to clear his schedule and his executive team's schedule for the entire week. In response to the GM's request to discuss some critical capital-expenditure needs during the meeting, Mr. Adversarial responds that he will set the agenda and

(continued)

Exhibit 1 *(continued)*

does not need input from the GM or anyone else. He reminds the GM who owns the hotel. He provides the GM with a voluminous list of minutiae and analyses to be prepared in advance of the meeting. When the GM indicates that existing reports in slightly different formats will provide the requested information, Mr. Adversarial demands that new reports be prepared in the format he prefers. The GM also expresses his concern that, in light of the current volume of business at the hotel, it may be challenging to assemble all the requested information before the meeting. Mr. Adversarial informs him that "if you can't get it done, I'll find someone who can." He reminds the GM that he has the contractual right to have the GM fired, and that he will not hesitate to do so if the GM does not do everything he asks. In closing, Mr. Adversarial tells the GM to make sure the hotel limousine picks him up at the airport and that the Presidential Suite be reserved for his stay.

These are two very different approaches to performing the asset management role. If you were the GM of the Upscale Hotel, would Mr. Adversarial and his approach motivate you to achieve success?

powerful toward ensuring that the owner's and the manager's goals and objectives are aligned. It is encouraging to note that some of the more progressive management companies seek input from the asset manager in evaluating the general manager's performance.

Characteristics of the Ideal General Manager

There are certain characteristics the ideal general manager should possess, and it is important that the asset manager be aware of these characteristics in order to seek them out in a general manager. The characteristics of the ideal general manager generally fall into five categories: market expertise, operating results, capital expenditures, employee and community relations, and communication. It would be rare for any general manager to have achieved highly developed skills in all of these areas, but an effective asset manager should understand the strengths and weaknesses of the general manager. In this way, the asset manager can more appropriately focus attention where it will supplement the general manager's talents and add the most value.

Market Expertise. The ideal general manager understands the key demand drivers in the property's market. She knows who her customers are, who her competitors' customers are, and who her potential customers are. Marketing plans are developed to retain existing customers, obtain new customers, and attract customers from the competition. She is the consummate salesperson. The ideal general manager develops an effective marketing plan based on market conditions and motivates the property's sales team by setting specific goals. She understands and, more important, anticipates trends and changes in her market, and she reacts to these shifts before anyone else is even aware of them. The ideal general manager demonstrates great flexibility in reacting to market shifts and achieving balance among the various market segments served (group vs. transient, for example). She is able to identify new business opportunities and to create demand during slack periods in the business cycle. The ideal general manager knows the hotels in her competitive set as well as she does her own. She knows how to compensate for her hotel's weaknesses, how to leverage her hotel's strengths, and how to exploit the competition's weaknesses. The ideal general manager prepares for new competition by aggressively solidifying existing business and even more aggressively seeking new business. She has an attentive, meaningful relationship with all her major customers and is eager to interact with hotel guests and to exceed their expectations regularly.

Operating Results. The ideal general manager budgets aggressively and continually strives to exceed budgeted performance. He is focused on adding long-term value to the hotel; he does not pursue short-term performance and engage in "window dressing" to the detriment of creating value over the long term. He is constantly striving to find new and creative opportunities to generate incremental revenues and profits in every operating department of the hotel.

The ideal general manager is focused on profits, not just revenues, and never submits a proposal to the asset manager without assessing what it means for the bottom line. He understands the profitability of the hotel both by its component businesses (rooms versus food and beverage, for example) and by source (i.e., which customers are truly profitable). He realizes that a manager cannot compensate for a product sold at a loss per unit by increasing volume. He eagerly utilizes technology to maximize profits generated. He reacts quickly and effectively to economic downturns through aggressive cost management. The ideal general manager understands the owner's financial hurdles and objectives. He recognizes that he and the asset manager are financial partners and embraces the asset manager's financial objectives as his own.

Capital Expenditures. The ideal general manager spends the owner's money parsimoniously, as if it were coming out of her own pocket. She maintains a clean hotel, not only the areas of the hotel the guest sees, but also those parts that the guest does not see. She supports a proactive preventive maintenance program and recognizes the importance of maintaining an effective life-safety system and procedures. The ideal general manager prioritizes capital spending in a manner consistent with the strategic plan. She manages the furniture, fixtures, and equipment reserve with a long-term view and proposes capital expenditures that will provide the greatest value enhancement for the hotel at the lowest cost. She seeks any and all opportunities to extend the useful life of the hotel's capital assets. The ideal general manager is acutely aware of the appropriate positioning of her hotel to maximize results, and avoids making any aesthetic changes to the hotel without the involvement of ownership.

Employees and Community. The ideal general manager maintains superb interpersonal relationships with his employees and strives to minimize staff turnover and associated costs. He has the ability to attract, motivate, and develop a talented and effective executive team. He enjoys a positive rapport with both employees and members of the community. He treats employees fairly, counsels those in need of improvement, and deals decisively with those who fail to improve. The ideal general manager plays an active role in the community, particularly in those areas that will ultimately benefit the value of the hotel. He is, for example, an active board member of the local convention and visitors bureau. The ideal general manager is widely regarded throughout the community as a great corporate citizen.

Communication. The ideal general manager takes charge of the relationship with the hotel's asset manager. She communicates in a proactive, timely, and transparent manner, never withholding important information. She ensures the integrity and accuracy of all financial data provided to the asset manager. The ideal general manager keeps the asset manager informed of all significant issues and avoids surprises. She has the highest ethical standards and recognizes and believes that an effective business relationship begins with outstanding communications.

The preceding overview of the ideal general manager is intended to highlight those skills that a lodging asset manager should seek in the person charged with day-to-day responsibility for the success of the hotel. It is not comprehensive, but it emphasizes the important skills an effective general manager should possess—and therefore the areas where the asset manager must focus his or her efforts in the quest for value enhancement.

Conclusion

It is difficult to predict how the owner-manager relationship will evolve in the future. (See Chapter 5 for a discussion of this topic.) It appears likely that there will be further growth in the number of hotels managed using the owner-operator model, where ownership and management come together under one entity, because owners will continue to seek greater control over the hotels in their portfolios. Hotel managers are likely to continue to focus on improving the profitability of operations while simultaneously achieving great customer satisfaction and preference. Hotel management companies will continue to enhance the usefulness and transparency of information provided to ownership. There will continue to be high demand for talented lodging asset managers who are passionate about practicing their profession and enhancing the value of hotels.

Success in this and any business relies to a great extent on the ability to communicate and collaborate effectively with others. The lodging business, almost by definition, attracts people who enjoy and are motivated by the prospect of dealing with others. The range of skills needed to be a successful lodging asset manager is nearly endless. Today's talented lodging asset manager needs to be a world-class hotelier, a skilled engineer, an energetic salesperson, a brilliant attorney, a shrewd businessperson, a creative interior designer, a proficient project manager, and an ingenious real estate professional. Even with this toolbox of experience and talent, to be truly successful the lodging asset manager must also have the interpersonal skills necessary to create a cooperative, collaborative relationship with hotel management, so that owners and managers work as partners in achieving ownership's goals and objectives. This ability to build effective relationships is the most important attribute an asset manager can possess; those who develop and deploy their ability in this area will move readily down the path to success.

8

Evaluating Franchise and Chain Affiliation Programs

By John McCarthy and Lori E. Raleigh

John McCarthy *is President of Liberty Hospitality Group. Mr. McCarthy, who has over 25 years of experience in the hospitality industry, joined Liberty in 1989. During his tenure with Liberty, he has managed Liberty's hotel investments, including a world-class hotel in Florida and a large portfolio of Residence Inn by Marriott (RIBM) hotels. He also participated in numerous real estate transactions, including the acquisition of a substantial portfolio of Resolution Trust Corporation assets.*

Mr. McCarthy currently oversees all aspects of Liberty's investment in Sanibel Harbour Resort and Spa, a four-star, four-diamond destination resort in southwest Florida. Mr. McCarthy completed Marriott's Management Training Program in 1984 and has held various management positions at hotels throughout the United States. He is a former Chairman of RIBM's National System Marketing Fund Committee and a former member of The Residence Inn Association's Board of Directors. From 1998 to 2001, he served on the board of directors of the Hospitality Asset Managers Association (HAMA) and continues to be an active member. Mr. McCarthy is a graduate of Ithaca College.

Lori E. Raleigh *is President of The Travers Group, a hotel investment and asset management advisory firm, and currently serves as the Executive Director of the International Society of Hospitality Consultants. Before founding The Travers Group, Ms. Raleigh was Vice President of Asset Management for the Liberty Real Estate Group, where she headed up the hotel department from its establishment in 1987. Ms. Raleigh also served as Director of the Loan Management Branch of the U.S. Department of Housing and Urban Development.*

Ms. Raleigh has lectured at numerous industry conferences and her work has appeared in many prominent hotel, financial, and real estate publications. She currently serves on the board of directors of the American Hotel & Lodging Association, the New York University Preston Robert Tisch Center for Hospitality, the Tourism and Travel Administration Advisory Board, and the New England Real Estate Journal *Advisory Board. A member and past President of the Hospitality Asset Managers Association (HAMA), she has also served on the board of directors of ISHC, Residence Inn by Marriott, and the Network of Executive Women in Hospitality. A member of the Urban Land Institute and the Association of Hospitality Financial Management Education, Ms. Raleigh is a graduate of Emmanuel College and holds an MBA from Boston College.*

In light of the dollars involved in purchasing, implementing, and maintaining a franchise or affiliation, the decision to be a franchise or chain-affiliated property is one of the most critical decisions affecting the value of a hotel investment. With the cost of a typical franchise or chain affiliation program representing seven to nine percent of revenue, and given that the hotel industry in general is bringing approximately 18 to 20 cents of the average revenue dollar to the net operating income line, franchise and affiliation fees can potentially account for the equivalent of 35 to 40 percent of a hotel's bottom line.

In the United States today, approximately 55 percent of all hotels, or some 25,000 out of just under 46,000 properties, and 67 percent of the guestroom inventory, or 2.9 million out of approximately 4.4 million rooms, are affiliated.[1] For many hotels, affiliation can represent the difference between financial viability and failure. However, affiliation does not ensure successful investment performance. Moreover, certain types of hotels, depending upon their market positioning and segments served, perform much better as independents.

In the past, affiliation decisions were often driven by factors such as the ability to obtain financing. Lenders and institutional investors stressed the importance of a property's access to a reservation system and the need for many hotels to tie into national marketing and promotional programs. Since these services were not readily available on a stand-alone basis, a franchise or affiliation was often routinely required as a prerequisite for financing. Today, however, there are numerous cost-effective options available for purchasing reservation system support, direct sales and trade show representation services, advertising and public relations expertise, and other services. Additionally, in recent years the Internet has had a tremendous impact on both the marketing of hotels and the manner in which hotel rooms are booked. In 2002, U.S. online bookings reached $6.3 billion, representing nine percent of total hotel revenue. By 2005, online bookings are forecasted to grow to $15.2 billion, representing 20 percent of all hotel revenue.[2]

Evaluating Franchise and Affiliation Alternatives

Complicating the decision to become a franchise or chain-affiliated hotel is the sheer number of alternatives and the variety of specific programs available. Franchise or affiliation alternatives include:

- Standard franchise agreements.
- Management contracts with branded operators.
- Management contracts with unbranded operators, coupled with franchise agreements.
- Licensing agreements.
- Strategic marketing alliances.

Within these five categories, there are estimated to be over 100 different programs available to an owner, with each one offering various brand identification, marketing, promotional, and distribution opportunities. It is important to keep in mind that different affiliation programs have the potential to generate greatly varying types and volumes of business. The cost of a franchise or affiliation can also vary substantially, depending on the scope of services and benefits provided. Costs for various programs may range from approximately 1.5 percent to well over 10 percent of revenue.

Although there are some rules of thumb to consider, essentially there is no single best approach or established criteria for evaluating affiliation alternatives. Affiliation options should be evaluated on the basis of the specific marketing needs and the strategic objectives of a given hotel. As described in the sections that follow, investors can evaluate affiliation alternatives by:

- Analyzing the business mix.
- Assessing the potential benefits of affiliation.
- Determining the costs of affiliation.
- Evaluating the costs versus the benefits of affiliation.
- Evaluating potential conflicts of interest.

Analyzing the Business Mix

Evaluating the merits of a franchise or affiliation should begin with an in-depth analysis of both the existing and potential market segmentation for the subject hotel. Hotels do not compete with all other hotels for all types of business. Rather, a particular hotel competes with certain hotels for specific types of business. The size, location, level and scope of services, ambiance or character, physical characteristics, and condition of a hotel will dictate the market segments the hotel may potentially attract. Different market segments require very different marketing strategies, as well as different sales and promotional programs.

For example, an extended-stay hotel generally captures 70 to 80 percent of its business from demand generators located within a 10- to 15-mile radius. At the opposite extreme, a destination resort will typically realize only a small percentage of its business from within the local community. A typical extended-stay hotel uses only a few property-level sales managers in a direct sales campaign targeting local companies. In the case of a destination resort, the sales and marketing efforts are broad-based and require many sources for distribution, including a much larger property-level sales force, and regional, national, and international sales representation. In addition to this more complex sales structure, destination resorts also require dedicated marketing, public relations, and advertising campaigns at the local, regional, national, and international levels.

Moreover, some types of business can be significantly more profitable for a hotel than others. Accordingly, given the specific attributes and positioning of a particular hotel, there may be a more desirable business mix for optimizing the property's financial performance. This strategic business mix will determine the marketing and promotional programs and distribution systems needed for an individual hotel. An analysis of a property's business mix should begin with answers to fundamental questions, such as:

- What type of business is the hotel targeting?

- Why are guests staying at the hotel?
- Where is the business coming from?
- Who is booking the business?
- How is the business booked?
- When does the business travel?

What Type of Business Is the Hotel Targeting? A variety of market segments generate demand for a hotel. Business travelers represent a large percentage of the patronage for airport, suburban, and downtown hotels. Group business and leisure travelers are the predominant market segments attracted to convention hotels and resorts. Some franchises and affiliations are better at promoting certain types of business than others. Understanding what type of business a hotel is best positioned to capture and which mix or combination of business from the various segments is potentially the most profitable is essential to evaluating the ability for a franchise or affiliation to meet the specific marketing, sales, and promotional objectives of a hotel.

Why Are Guests Staying at the Hotel? While seemingly a very simple and straightforward question, this is one of the most difficult questions to answer. Are current guests attracted to the property because of its location, service, reputation, cleanliness, price-value relationship, or other factors? Why are they staying at this particular hotel and not at a competitor's property? To what extent is the brand name or affiliation of the hotel a factor in the guest's decision?

There have been many studies conducted over the years on hotel selection criteria—always with interesting results. Exhibit 1 summarizes the business traveler and meeting planner hotel selection criteria from two recent studies, one conducted by the Hotel Sales and Marketing Association International (HSMAI) Foundation and one performed by *Meetings & Conventions* in compiling its "Meetings Market Report 2002." Of the top ten most important selection criteria for business travelers, only one—i.e., frequent hotel stay/airline points—relates directly to the specific franchise or chain affiliation of a hotel. All of the other top-ten criteria such as location, room rate, value, in-room amenities, and so forth are factors that are potentially property-specific versus affiliation-based. That is, a property does not necessarily require an affiliation to deliver on the respondents' key decision criteria. As the right-hand panel of Exhibit 1 shows, similar results are reflected in the parallel survey conducted by *Meetings and Conventions* magazine on the most important selection criteria for association meetings.

Where Is the Business Coming From? Different market segments have different origination patterns. Understanding where the business comes from and identifying the distribution channels that provide the best opportunities and the most cost-effective means of capturing a particular type of clientele are fundamental to evaluating the merits of various franchise and affiliation programs. In addition to evaluating where the business is coming from, as market dynamics shift, it is equally important to assess where the business could *otherwise* be coming from. The source of today's business may not necessarily be the source of future

Exhibit 1 Selection Criteria of Business Travelers and Association Meeting Planners

BUSINESS TRAVELERS*	ASSOCIATION MEETING PLANNERS**
1- Location	1- Number, size, and quality of meeting rooms
2- Room rate	2- Negotiable F&B
3- Previous experience	3- Cost of facility
4- Value for the price	4- Quality of food
5- Reputation of hotel/chain	5- Number, size, and quality of sleeping rooms
6- In-room amenities	6- Assignment of one staff person
7- Recommendations (friends/associates)	7- Efficiency of billing procedures
8- Special promotions	8- Meeting support services & equipment
9- Frequent hotel stay/airline points	9- Efficiency of check-in/out
10- Ability to make reservation via Internet (tied with #9)	10- Previous experience with facility and staff

* Edward Watkins, "How Guests Choose Hotels," *Lodging Hospitality*, February 2003, p. 36. Article based on HSMAI Foundation research on "Defining Value Drivers for Hotel Customers."
** "Meetings Market Report 2002," edited by Sarah J. F. Braley, *Meetings & Conventions*, August 2002, p. 42.

business. Reviewing and analyzing the various lodging outlook reports and demand trends for the market in which a hotel competes can help determine the best strategic direction.

For example, local business is often best captured through direct sales programs, grass-roots networking, and memberships or contacts with local professional organizations. Accordingly, a hotel does not necessarily require an affiliation or brand name to generate local business. Similarly, some properties are well positioned to capture international business because of their location, prominence, distinctive amenities, or because of the working relationships their on-site staff enjoys with key wholesalers and tour operators. However, for other hotels, the volume of international business can be greatly influenced by the contacts and relationships that a franchisor or chain organization has with international travel agents, wholesalers, and tour operators. The franchisor's or chain's international reputation or global presence might also be a contributing factor.

Who Is Booking the Business? An analysis of a property's business mix will also determine how much business is booked directly by on-site staff and how much is booked by the regional or national staff of the franchise or chain organization. It is important to determine whether the business booked by the regional or national staff could have been booked directly—and potentially at less cost—by on-site staff. If business is booked through intermediaries, such as travel agents or wholesalers, it is important to understand if the travel agent and wholesaler relationships are property-based or franchise-based.

How Is the Business Booked? It is also important to identify and understand how the business is booked because the cost to the hotel of different alternatives varies significantly. The analysis should determine the room nights and dollar volume of business booked through the Internet, with further segmentation by at least three separate electronic channels: directly via the hotel's web site, via the brand's web site, or through third-party web sites (e.g., Expedia, Hotels.com, Travelocity). The analysis should also reveal the volume of business booked through the franchisor's or chain's central reservation system (CRS) and above all attempt to answer an important question: Does the business coming through the CRS represent incremental volume? Similarly, the amount of business booked through Global Distribution Systems (e.g., Sabre, Amadeus, Worldspan) should be charted. Finally, the analysis should determine how much business is being booked directly by the hotel through the property's sales staff or through an on-site "800" (toll-free) number.

When Does the Business Travel? Although there are many market segments that travel extensively throughout the year, there are some types of business that will travel only during selected times of the year. For example, a large segment of leisure business consists of families traveling on vacation. School vacation schedules have a direct effect on this segment's demand pattern.

It is also important to note that some group business will travel only at certain times of the year. Groups with tighter budgetary constraints typically opt to travel during shoulder periods or the off-season, when hotels may be more willing to negotiate price to secure occupancy. Other types of groups, whether corporate or association in nature, may travel only during times when a meeting or conference does not interfere with other core business responsibilities. Moreover, many groups avoid scheduling meetings during holiday periods, when traditional vacation schedules or family commitments could adversely affect attendance.

It is important to assess seasonal demand patterns to evaluate whether an affiliation can positively influence capture. Ideally, this analysis will determine which affiliation, if any, can stabilize the potentially dramatic ebb and flow of such "consistently inconsistent" demand patterns.

Assessing the Potential Benefits of Affiliation

Most franchise or chain affiliations offer reservations, sales, marketing, and promotional programs. Many also offer additional services, including training, purchasing programs, technical assistance (for design and development), financing programs, operating policies and procedures, revenue management systems, and inspection and quality assurance programs.

Once the hotel has developed an understanding of its current business, the next step in evaluating the merits of a franchise or affiliation is to assess the potential of a particular system to generate room nights from the segments (e.g., association, incentive, leisure, international) the hotel is targeting to meet its strategic business-mix objectives. Here one needs to evaluate the potential of a particular brand or affiliation to generate incremental business—business the hotel could not otherwise capture, or business the hotel might capture at a higher average rate or more cost effectively. It is also important for the hotel to evaluate the cost-effectiveness of a particular franchise or affiliation program in comparison with other options, such as remaining independent and purchasing various services on a stand-alone basis.

Exhibit 2 details various potential sources of business and distribution channels for generating different types of business. Promotional programs and distribution channels typically available through a franchise or chain affiliation are highlighted.

As demonstrated by the exhibit, there are many different sources of business and potential distribution channel alternatives for generating different types of business. For example, potential sources to generate group business include direct sales programs, advertising, directory listings, public relations, trade shows, word-of-mouth referrals, etc. Although most franchises and affiliations offer certain key programs to promote group business (e.g., national sales programs, advertising, public relations), it is important to note that there are also numerous alternatives available to a hotel to generate group business on its own (e.g., on-site sales staff, representation firms, trade show attendance).

Determining the Cost of Affiliation

After determining which types of business a hotel should target and after assessing the potential of a franchise or affiliation program to generate those types of business, the next step is to determine the likely costs of acquiring, implementing, and maintaining the franchise or brand affiliation.

Traditionally, the cost of a franchise or affiliation has been thought of as comprising four components: initial, royalty, marketing, and reservation fees. However, the expenses involved in implementing and maintaining the affiliation (e.g., signage, upgrading to comply with system standards, providing amenities), promoting the affiliation (e.g., honored or frequent guest programs), and meeting technology standards should also be accounted for in estimating the total costs.

The cost of a franchise or affiliation can vary substantially, depending upon the perceived value of the brand and the scope of services and programs provided. While the overall cost of most franchise and affiliation programs currently offered is between seven and nine percent of revenue, the total cost can be substantially more if the component fees discussed below are at the higher end of their respective ranges and if there is a multiplication of fees as services and programs are added to the franchisor's offering.

Initial Fees. Most franchisors charge an initial or "up-front" fee as the price of admission to their systems. Initial fees may be established as a minimum dollar amount, as a variable payment based on the property's room count, or as a fixed payment coupled with a per-room assessment. In recent years, some franchisors have considered waiving or reducing their initial fees to secure more business.

Exhibit 2 Business Segmentation and Source of Business/Distribution Channel Alternatives

XYZ Hotel/Resort

Group

- Direct Sales (via on-site staff) Program
- Representation Firms
- Alliance Partners
- Franchise/Affiliation Company
  - regional sales staff
  - national sales staff
- Advertising
  - property-specific/generated
  - franchise/affiliation-based
- Public Relations
  - property-specific/generated
  - chain/franchise program
- Trade Shows
- Directory Listings
- Direct Mail
- Word-of-Mouth Referral
- Repeat Business

Social

- 800#
  - franchise/affiliation
  - on site
  - independent reservation service
- Travel Agent
  - direct sales
  - via 800# (franchise/
  - affiliation)
  - via 800# (on site)
  - via 800# (independent service)
  - incentive/reward programs
- Advertising
  - property-specific/generated
  - franchise/affiliation-based
- Public Relations
  - property-specific/generated
  - affiliation-based
- Walk In/Drive By
- Directory Listings
- Direct Mail
- Word-of-Mouth Referral
- Repeat Business
- Brochure Fulfillment
  - Tourism Development Councils
  - Chamber of Commerce
  - 800# (franchise/affiliation)
  - 800# (on site)
  - 800# (independent service)

Corporate

- 800#
  - franchise/affiliation
  - on site
  - independent service
- Travel Agent
  - 800# booking (via franchise/affiliation)
  - 800# booking (via independent service)
  - direct booking
- Direct Sales
- Recognition/Reward Programs
  - franchise/affiliation
  - property-specific
- Directory Listing
  - individual property
  - franchise/affiliation
- Direct Mail
- Word-of-Mouth Referral
- Repeat Business
- Advertising
  - property-specific/generated
  - franchise/affiliation-based
- Public Relations
  - property-specific/generated
  - franchise/affiliation-based

Wholesale

- Direct Sales to Intermediaries
  - wholesalers
  - tour operators
  - via on-site staff
  - independent representatives
  - franchise/affiliation
- Trade Shows
- Directory/Publication Listings
- Advertising
  - property-specific/generated
  - franchise/affiliation-based
- Direct Mail
- Public Relations
  - property-specific/generated
  - franchise/affiliation-based

Discount Programs

- Direct Sales
- Direct Mail
- Industry/Target Audience Publication Listings
- Advertising
  - property-specific/generated
  - franchise/affiliation-based
- Public Relations
  - property-specific/generated
  - franchise/affiliation-based
- Word-of-Mouth Referral
- Repeat Business

Royalty Fees. Royalty fees reflect the ongoing charge by a franchisor for the right to use the brand and to participate in the system. Nearly all current royalty fees are based on a percentage of revenue, ranging from approximately 1.0 to 6.5 percent.

Management Fees. Major branded hotel operators incorporate into their management contract agreements the right to use their name and to access their chain marketing and promotional services. The fee structure for this arrangement differs significantly from that of the traditional franchise relationship. The cost associated with the right to use the name and the chain's system is effectively built into the management fee structure. (For a more complete discussion of management contracts and fee structures, see Chapters 5 and 6.)

License Fees. For affiliations, the license fee is the equivalent of the franchise system's royalty fee. Members of an affiliation or "voluntary chain" (e.g., Best Western, Leading Hotels of the World, Relais et Châteaux) gain the right to use a brand name but also retain the character and identity of their individual properties.

Marketing and Promotional Fees. Many franchisors and chain organizations assess properties in their systems for marketing and advertising services. Fees for these services currently range from less than one to more than four percent of revenues.

Sales Representation Fees. These fees support regional, national, and international direct sales programs. In some franchise systems, the costs associated with direct sales programs are covered by assessments for marketing and promotional services. In other systems, affiliated properties may be charged an additional amount, based on the actual volume of bookings generated by a franchisor's or chain's direct sales programs.

Reservations Fees. Although some franchises and affiliations provide for the cost of reservation services in their marketing fees, most chains charge a separate reservations fee. Methods of charging for reservation services include a fee per reservation, a fixed percentage of rooms revenue, and a fixed amount per room plus a fee per reservation booked.

Termination Fees and Liquidated Damages. The fees payable on termination of a contract with a brand can vary substantially among the different franchise and affiliation programs. From an owner's perspective, an exit strategy from a hotel asset is as important as the acquisition decision, so a clearly defined and reasonable termination provision is a critical component of a franchise or affiliation agreement. However, because such provisions can be costly, they must be evaluated on a case-by-case basis.

Other Cost Considerations. The ideal franchise or affiliation is a growing, evolving system. Participants in successful systems incur expenses to promote the system and meet emerging standards (and guest expectations). However, some of these expenses might not be of measurable benefit to an individual hotel in the system and would be incurred only because of the requirements of the franchise or affiliation relationship. Two frequently encountered examples of this conflict include the cost of complying with system standards and the cost of honored or frequent guest programs.

Complying with system standards. In evaluating the costs of affiliation, a hotel owner must weigh the expense of complying with system-wide standards. Franchisors and chain organizations implement programs and impose standards that meet system needs and make economic sense at a national level. However, national programs and standards may not always meet the needs or make economic sense for an individual property in the system. For example, food-and-beverage requirements (e.g., hours of operation, availability of room service, menu offerings) or levels of service (e.g., high-speed Internet access, turn-down service, amenity offerings, etc.) may not be necessary given a particular hotel's positioning, customer profile, or competitive market.

Honored or frequent guest programs. Many hotel chains have implemented honored or frequent guest programs to promote brand loyalty. Offerings range from basic recognition programs in which a frequent guest receives upgraded accommodations, a welcome gift, or other premium to complex reward programs that permit customers to earn points and mileage redeemable for hotel room nights, airline travel, car rentals, and myriad other products and services. The cost of honored or frequent guest programs can vary dramatically from less than one percent to as much as five or six percent of rooms revenue. Therefore, it is very important to assess the potential costs versus benefits of the guest recognition and reward programs offered by different franchise or chain organizations. It is also important to note that some hotels within a franchise system may experience a disproportionate amount of redemption of such rewards, which may potentially increase associated costs.

Evaluating the Costs versus the Benefits of Affiliation

It is very difficult to conduct a cost-benefit analysis for a franchise or affiliation because there is no single approach or standard set of criteria by which to evaluate the overall economics. Not only is it difficult to evaluate the merits of an individual franchise or affiliation, it is also extremely difficult to evaluate consistently the merits and performance of one franchise or affiliation program over another.

Traditionally, one of the fundamental metrics for evaluating a franchisor's or chain's performance has been the volume or percentage of business generated by the brand's reservation system. Various franchisors and chain organizations indicate that their reservation systems are the source of anywhere from 15 percent to just under 40 percent of a property's business. However, it is difficult to make performance comparisons between affiliation alternatives because franchisors and chain organizations have different ways of accounting for reservation activity—including, for example, call volume, conversions, cancellations, gross versus net bookings, etc. Also, it is often very difficult to determine the total cost of generating reservations. For example, the total cost might include expenditures associated with frequent or honored guest programs, brochures, advertising, and other promotional costs, plus the direct costs involved in generating business through a central reservations system.

It is often a challenge to determine whether business generated through the franchise's or chain's reservation system truly represents incremental business or bookings that a hotel could generate on its own. For example, group business represents a major market segment for many hotels. Although group meeting business is booked directly by the on-site hotel sales staff, reservations for meeting attendees are frequently included in brand reservation-system counts, especially in situations where attendees are responsible for making their own reservations (the typical case for association group business).

In light of the difficulties inherent in evaluating a franchisor's or chain's reservations performance, it is critical to identify alternative ways of evaluating the costs versus the benefits of the available franchises and affiliations. Alternative approaches include:

- Assessing the bottom-line versus the top-line impact of franchise or affiliation fees.
- Estimating the net effective cost of business generated by a franchise or affiliation.
- Estimating a breakeven point that suggests the volume of business needed to support the cost of a specific franchise or affiliation.

Assessing Bottom-Line Versus Top-Line Impact. The cost of a franchise or affiliation has traditionally been measured in terms of its top-line impact expressed as a percentage of revenue. While this ratio is a reasonable approach for comparing the nominal costs of one franchise or affiliation program to another, it does not take into account the fact that the profitability of different types of hotels can vary significantly. Thus, the impact of franchise or affiliation fees shifts dramatically when fees are evaluated from a bottom-line perspective.

Although the effect of operating leverage can cause significant swings in profitability, on average, hotels yield 18 to 20 cents of every revenue dollar as net operating income (before debt service and reserve for replacement). This yield, however, varies significantly on a property-by-property basis, depending upon the economics of running a particular hotel. The potential net operating income (NOI) of a hotel can vary substantially, depending upon the revenue per available room (RevPAR) generated, the mix of total revenues (e.g., rooms revenue versus food-and-beverage revenue), and the degree of operating leverage, or the ratio of fixed to variable costs. Although there are hotels at one end of the spectrum that are losing money, some types of hotels enjoy impressive profitability, yielding as much as 45 cents on the average revenue dollar at the NOI line.

Exhibit 3 presents a comparative matrix highlighting the relationship between fees as a percentage of top-line revenue and the impact on bottom-line profits. The leftmost column in the matrix lists levels of franchise or affiliation fees, ranging from one to ten percent of revenue. The topmost row lists alternative levels of NOI expressed as a percentage of revenue. The remaining cells of the matrix show the percentage of NOI represented by the franchise or affiliation fee. For purposes of illustration, seven percent of revenue is highlighted as a representative cost for a franchise or affiliation. In this case, the ratio of franchise or affiliation fees to

Exhibit 3 Franchise/Affiliation Fees and Bottom-Line Versus Top-Line Impact

Cost of Franchise/Affiliation (as % of Revenue)	Net Operating Income Percentage							
	10.0%	**15.0%**	**20.0%**	**25.0%**	**30.0%**	**35.0%**	**40.0%**	**45.0%**
1.0%	10.0%	6.7%	5.0%	4.0%	3.3%	2.9%	2.5%	2.2%
2.0%	20.0%	13.3%	10.0%	8.0%	6.7%	5.7%	5.0%	4.4%
3.0%	30.0%	20.0%	15.0%	12.0%	10.0%	8.6%	7.5%	6.7%
4.0%	40.0%	26.7%	20.0%	16.0%	13.3%	11.4%	10.0%	8.9%
5.0%	50.0%	33.3%	25.0%	20.0%	16.7%	14.3%	12.5%	11.1%
6.0%	60.0%	40.0%	30.0%	24.0%	20.0%	17.1%	15.0%	13.3%
7.0%	**70.0%**	46.7%	35.0%	28.0%	23.3%	20.0%	17.5%	**15.6%**
8.0%	80.0%	53.3%	40.0%	32.0%	26.7%	22.9%	20.0%	17.8%
9.0%	90.0%	60.0%	45.0%	36.0%	30.0%	25.7%	22.5%	20.0%
10.0%	100.0%	66.7%	50.0%	40.0%	33.3%	28.5%	25.0%	22.2%

bottom-line performance could potentially range from 15.6 percent for a hotel with a healthy 45 percent NOI to 70 percent for a hotel with a 10 percent NOI.

Estimating Net Effective Cost. Another method of evaluating the costs versus the benefits of a franchise or affiliation program is to determine the net effective cost of business generated by the franchise or chain organization. Net effective cost can be defined as the ratio of franchise fees to the percentage or volume of business generated though the franchise or affiliation. This analysis assumes that reservations are the primary or only franchise- or chain-generated source of business for the hotel. As stated earlier, most franchisors and chain organizations indicate that their respective central reservation systems (CRSs) are the source of between 15 to just under 40 percent of a member property's business.

Exhibit 4 highlights net effective cost by showing the ratios of franchise or affiliation fees, expressed as a percentage of revenue, to the percentages of business generated through the franchise or chain reservation system. For purposes of illustration, seven percent of revenue is again highlighted as a representative cost for a franchise or affiliation. In this case, the net effective cost of the room nights generated through a reservation system would range from 17.5 percent of the franchise or affiliation fees paid when 40 percent of the hotel's business comes through the CRS to 46.7 percent of the cost if only 15 percent of the hotel's business comes through the CRS.

Estimating a Breakeven Point. Another useful tool for evaluating the financial contribution of a franchise or affiliation program is to estimate the incremental volume of business needed to break even, or just cover the cost of a franchise or affiliation. To determine the additional volume of business necessary, the estimated cost of the franchise or affiliation should be divided by the anticipated departmental

Exhibit 4 Net Effective Cost of Business Generated by a Franchise or Affiliation

Franchise/Affiliation Fees (as % of Revenue)	Percentage of Business Generated via Franchise or Affiliation					
	15.0%	**20.0%**	**25.0%**	**30.0%**	**35.0%**	**40.0%**
1.0%	6.7%	5.0%	4.0%	3.3%	2.9%	2.5%
2.0%	13.3%	10.0%	8.0%	6.7%	5.7%	5.0%
3.0%	20.0%	15.0%	12.0%	10.0%	8.6%	7.5%
4.0%	26.7%	20.0%	16.0%	13.3%	11.4%	10.0%
5.0%	33.3%	25.0%	20.0%	16.7%	14.3%	12.5%
6.0%	40.0%	30.0%	24.0%	20.0%	17.1%	15.0%
7.0%	46.7%	35.0%	28.0%	23.3%	20.0%	17.5%
8.0%	53.3%	40.0%	32.0%	26.7%	22.9%	20.0%
9.0%	60.0%	45.0%	36.0%	30.0%	25.7%	22.5%
10.0%	66.7%	50.0%	40.0%	33.3%	28.5%	25.0%

profit per room sold. For example, assume that the annual cost of a franchise or affiliation would be $200,000 for a hotel of 120 rooms. Assume further that the average daily rate for the hotel is $80 and the departmental profit from rooms is 75 percent. It would require over 3,300 additional room nights ($200,000/$60 contribution margin per room sold) specifically attributable to the franchise or affiliation to reach the breakeven point. This equates to an additional 7.5 occupancy points required to cover the costs of the franchise or affiliation (365 × 120 = 43,800 annual available room nights; 3,300/43,800= 7.5 percent incremental occupancy).

Evaluating Potential Conflicts of Interest

In making the decision to become a franchisee or chain-affiliated property, the investor must take into consideration potential conflicts of interest between the licensee and a franchisor or chain. Conflicts might arise between competing properties bearing the same brand or among properties of different brands within systems with multiple brands.

The interests of the brand and its affiliates are not always aligned. The brand's room count, revenue, and profit growth objectives are not necessarily in harmony with the best interests of an existing affiliate. Thus, it is not surprising that licensees have mounted several lawsuits in recent years charging adverse impact and the impairment of value because of a franchisor's decision to grow a brand within an existing licensee's competitive market. There have also been cases where a franchisee has claimed that a franchisor did not act in good faith—i.e., in the best economic interests of the franchisee.

Brands will inevitably seek growth. Therefore, it is important that an investor understand a franchise or chain system's growth strategy, attempting to deduce how anticipated system growth will affect the future performance of the investor's asset(s). It is also very beneficial to evaluate past practices to determine the likelihood of a licensor's resolving such conflicts reasonably, should they emerge.

Potential Conflicts of Interest within a Brand. Conflicts within a specific brand include those that might arise from radius-clause or impact issues, regional and national sales programs, national marketing and promotional programs, and quality control and image concerns.

Radius-clause or impact issues. Because of the current emphasis from franchise and chain systems on pursuing conversions to achieve growth, radius-clause or impact issues have received increased attention. Radius-clause and impact conflicts typically arise when there is overlap in competitive market(s) or in potential customers for which two or more hotels with the same brand or affiliation compete. When evaluating the potential for conflicts in this area, it is important to define clearly the market segments the subject hotel competes for, the market areas its customer base is drawn from, and the competitor properties that vie with the subject hotel for specific types of business.

Regional and national sales programs. While the primary objective of regional and national sales programs is to generate as much business as possible for properties within the system, the degree to which an individual hotel might actually benefit from these programs can vary dramatically. Regional and national sales programs must be evaluated in relation to the specific needs and objectives of a hotel. The hotel investor should also ensure that there are no conflicts of interest in the way the programs are administered. Factors to consider include how leads are generated, how bookings are handled (for example, how does the sales staff determine the business allocated to properties within the system?), what types of information are exchanged with other properties, and how the sales staff is compensated.

National marketing and promotional programs. Although national marketing and promotional programs can be expected to enhance the overall performance of a franchise or chain system, it is very difficult for a brand to develop strategies and programs to meet the specific needs of *all* properties within the system. National programs tend to address the broad goals and objectives of the overall system, such as increasing weekend occupancy or promoting family business. The benefits of these programs for an individual hotel in the system may vary substantially.

In some instances, national programs may in fact undermine the objectives of a specific property. For example, one chain's special airline mileage promotion offered triple bonus miles and generated significant incremental business for some hotels in the system. However, the same program adversely affected the financial performance of other hotels. Because they were in the midst of their peak seasons, at least some resort properties in the chain would have been at 100 percent occupancy without incurring the additional cost of underwriting the award of triple mileage points.

Quality control and image concerns. A guest's favorable experience at one hotel can very positively influence that customer's perception of other hotels within the brand. Conversely, a guest's unsatisfactory experience at another hotel within the system can negatively influence that individual's overall perception of the brand and indirectly affect the image of other properties in the system. When selecting a franchise or affiliation, it is important to review the system's quality assurance and control requirements, as well as its compliance policies and procedures to ensure consistency in the quality and standards across the properties within the system.

Potential Conflicts of Interest among Brands. When chains have more than one brand, the licensee should ensure that there are no conflicts in the way that the various brands are marketed and promoted. Potential problem areas include positioning conflicts among brands in the marketplace, multi-brand sales and promotional programs, and multi-brand joint reservation systems.

Positioning conflicts. As the number of brands has proliferated, the demarcation lines separating brands have blurred for many hotel product types. As a result, it is often difficult for a franchisor or chain organization to position one brand without overlapping with its other brands. Moreover, on the consumer side, the reality is that frequently there is overlap in the customer base of different brands in a multi-brand chain. To minimize the potential conflict in this area, it is important for the prospective licensee to identify early in the decision process the likely overlap in customer bases among the licensor's various brands and to try to quantify the impact on the licensee's hotel.

Multi-brand sales programs. The primary objective of multi-brand sales programs is to maximize overall revenues for all properties within the chain. However, the extent to which such programs affect different brands in a company's array of flags and specific hotels in the system can vary greatly. These programs should be closely monitored and evaluated to ensure that they contribute to—rather than undermine—the financial performance of a hotel.

Multi-brand joint reservation systems. Reservation agents can significantly affect bookings for an individual brand versus another, as well as for one particular hotel within a brand segment versus another. In instances where a franchisor's or chain's reservations center sells more than one product or hotel brand, it is important to understand and evaluate how the different brands are promoted and sold.

Assessing the Independent Alternative

The decision to align a property with a particular franchise or affiliation is often arrived at by evaluating the merits of one system versus another. However, the decision-making process should also include an evaluation of the merits of various franchise and affiliation programs in comparison with the option of operating as an independent hotel.

An interesting way to think of hotel products is to place them on a continuum. At one end are hotels with little opportunity to differentiate themselves from similar types of properties. At the other extremity are those hotels and resorts that are considered to be one-of-a-kind properties. Affiliation alternatives and the merits of affiliation differ substantially, depending upon where an individual hotel is situated along this continuum.

Certain limited service and highway properties have few ways of differentiating themselves from their competitors. For these hotels, a franchise or brand affiliation often is critical to financial success. For hotels at the other end of the continuum—e.g., specialty properties with unique locations, high-end resorts, five-diamond properties—a franchise or affiliation may not be necessary. In fact, for these hotels a franchise or brand affiliation could potentially be detrimental, undermining their ability to attract certain market segments and clienteles, such as high-end social and corporate business travelers, selected types of group business, and incentive meeting business. Often, these types of guests prefer to stay at a unique property rather than at a franchise or chain-affiliated hotel or resort.

In the past, there have been few opportunities for independent hotels to tie into a global reservations system or into national or international marketing, sales, and promotional programs. Programs that were available tended to be expensive when sold on a stand-alone basis, making it more cost-effective to purchase sales, marketing, and reservation support services through a franchise or chain affiliation.

In recent years, however, many firms have specialized in providing services in these areas. Today, there are numerous options available for purchasing reservation system support, direct sales and trade show representation services, advertising and public relations expertise, etc. Depending upon the specific needs of an individual hotel, the cost of purchasing such services on a stand-alone basis may be significantly less than the cost associated with a franchise or chain affiliation. Additionally, the Internet has had a dramatic impact on the marketing and promotion of hotels. Although brand web sites offer potential advantages over hotel-specific web sites—in particular their greater customer reach—one can also argue that the Internet has substantially leveled the playing field for independent hotels.

It is very difficult for chains to develop and implement national positioning, pricing, and promotional strategies and programs that meet the specific needs of all properties within their systems. The absence of a brand can afford an owner greater flexibility in positioning a specific hotel against its competition. As an independent hotel, the property has the opportunity to explore its strengths and special points of differentiation from the competition, especially in terms of location, size, character, ambiance, and level of service.

Independent positioning also allows for greater flexibility in establishing rates and more control over rate integrity. As a member of a chain, a hotel must use a pricing strategy consistent with the overall positioning and perception of the chain. It is very difficult for franchisors or chain organizations, especially those having more than one brand, to develop national pricing strategies that address the needs and objectives of all hotels within their systems. Rate integrity, inventory control and allocations to intermediaries, and opaque versus transparent pricing have emerged as major issues and challenges, particularly in light of the dramatic increase in online bookings.

The Outlook

Looking to the future, there are several changes and developments in franchise and affiliation systems and their programs that are likely to be seen, including:

- Emergence of new franchise and affiliation fee structures.

- Greater flexibility in franchise and affiliation contracts.
- Standardization of brand performance criteria.
- Expanded role of the Internet.
- Targeted marketing programs.
- New program offerings.
- New hotel prototypes.

Emergence of New Franchise and Affiliation Fee Structures. Currently, the fee structures of nearly all franchise and affiliation systems are based on the revenues achieved by member properties. In the future, we might expect new fee structures to emerge that tie franchise and affiliation expenses more closely to the amount of business generated and the benefits received by individual properties. Also, we might see fees based more on an à la carte approach to services, leaving the hotel owner the option of purchasing only the specific services (e.g., access to a reservation system, international sales representation) needed for an individual property.

Greater Flexibility in Franchise and Affiliation Contracts. Many contracts in effect today are geared to protecting a franchisor's interests and objectives. These contracts often provide little opportunity for a franchisee or affiliation member to address and resolve problems or conflicts should they arise. Going forward, we might expect that contracts will provide for stricter franchisor default covenants and will address some of the conflicts of interest, (e.g., adverse impact, multi-brand conflicts) that have emerged, as well as providing franchisees with more flexible termination provisions. Similarly, we might expect more shorter-term contracts.

Standardization of Brand Performance Criteria. Given the inherent challenges in evaluating brand performance, ideally we will see more transparent, better standardized benchmarks for evaluating brand performance. Better criteria will permit more cogent evaluation of stand-alone brand performance and the performance of one brand versus another.

Expanded Role of the Internet. Over the last decade, access to independent central reservation services and the advent of web-enabled booking capabilities have proved very cost-effective options for independent hotels, providing these properties an alternative to joining a franchise or chain system. Going forward, the Internet can be expected to play an increasingly significant role in the marketing and distribution of hotel accommodations. The precise configuration of this expanded Internet role, however, is less clear: Will more bookings come through individual hotel web sites, brand web sites, or third-party channels?

Targeted Marketing Programs. Traditionally, franchisors and chain organizations have relied heavily on national advertising and promotional programs both to increase brand recognition and to generate business. While such programs can be expected to benefit the performance of the overall chain or franchise system, their impact on specific hotels within the system can vary significantly. In the future, we can expect that franchisors will explore more cost-effective ways, especially online opportunities, to promote properties within their systems and to focus on customized, targeted marketing opportunities rather than mass marketing programs.

New Program Offerings. Several leading franchise companies have launched innovative programs designed to help franchisees improve overall financial performance. Offerings have included yield management programs to improve top-line performance as well as operational support programs to help franchisees achieve savings in operating expenses.

New Hotel Prototypes. New hotel prototypes designed to reduce the capital investment have been launched by major companies. The same prototypes also are designed to reduce day-to-day operating costs, potentially improving franchisees' return on investment.

Conclusion

As hotel franchise and affiliation systems have grown, the largest and most successful have either gone public or been absorbed into publicly traded firms. The inevitable pressure to grow earnings by adding rooms to the system is both beneficial to the individual licensee and a potential source of conflict. However, astute licensees who understand the functioning of their systems and observe the precautions enumerated in this chapter will better protect their individual interests and reap greater benefit from their franchises and affiliations.

Endnotes

1. Smith Travel Research, "Property and Portfolio Research," *Hotel & Motel Management*, Vol. 218, No. 7 (2003): 24.
2. William J. Carroll, *Hotel and Lodging Commerce 2002–2005: Distribution Strategies and Market Forecasts* (Sherman, Conn.: PhocusWright, 2002), p. 3.3.

Part III

The Asset Manager's Analytical Tool Box

9

Benchmarking and Financial Analysis

By Michelle Russo and Tracy Cooper

***Michelle Russo, MAI, CHA,** founder and President of Hotel Asset Value Enhancement, LLC (hotelAVE), is a leader in the hotel asset management arena. Ms. Russo previously managed a $500 million portfolio for John Hancock Mutual Life Insurance Company, where she improved the profitability of the portfolio and achieved 20-percent cash-on-cash returns. She is well-known for initiating legal action in the 2660 Woodley Road case, involving the Sheraton Washington Hotel, in which Hancock was awarded $52 million. In addition, Ms. Russo was responsible for replacing the property's management and overseeing a $70 million repositioning and renovation of the 1,500-room convention hotel. She has also served as a two-term president and a five-year board member of the Hospitality Asset Managers Association (HAMA).*

Before her asset management experience, Ms. Russo spent ten years conducting real estate appraisals and feasibility studies for more than 500 hotels throughout the United States. Ms. Russo has appeared as an industry expert on CNN and CNBC and authored the widely followed "Top 15 Urban Market Report" while a Wall Street analyst at Deutsche Bank. She has also published in The Real Estate Finance Journal *and* Real Estate Review. *Ms. Russo is a graduate of Cornell University's School of Hotel Administration, where she is a frequent guest lecturer.*

***Tracy Cooper** has ten years' experience in the hospitality industry, including hospitality consulting and hotel underwriting. She is currently Vice President at Hotel Asset Value Enhancement, LLC (hotelAVE), a third-party hotel asset management company. Previously, Ms. Cooper worked as an underwriter for a boutique investment banking firm, where she was responsible for underwriting hotel mezzanine and first mortgage loans for high-yield investment funds.*

Ms. Cooper's professional experience also includes underwriting for Wyndham International, where she was responsible for corporate hotel development, acquisition, and disposition analyses. Her core responsibilities at Wyndham included market analysis, fieldwork, financial analysis, pro forma projections, and investment analysis. Ms. Cooper's early career was steeped in feasibility, appraisal, market, and financial analysis for hotel assets while at Pinnacle Advisory Group of Boston. Her consulting experience includes assignments nationwide for a variety of property types. Ms. Cooper earned her Bachelor of Science degree from the School of Hotel Administration at Cornell University.

THE ULTIMATE GOAL OF ANY savvy asset manager is to enhance an asset's market value, which is generally a function of a property's profitability. To improve a hotel property's profitability, the asset manager must assess the property's performance and work with the hotel's management staff to develop strategies for revenue enhancement and expense reduction that are consistent with the quality and market orientation of the asset. Essentially, this includes:

- Identifying a property's competitive strengths and weaknesses.
- Developing and implementing strategies for increasing market penetration.
- Reviewing expense control measures and increasing profitability levels.

Determining what revenue and expense levels are reasonable and achievable can be a difficult task because many factors affect a hotel's ability to generate revenue and manage expenses. How can an asset manager determine whether the hotel is properly positioned in the marketplace? How can an asset manager determine what revenue and expense levels are reasonable? What profitability ratios indicate an efficient operation versus one that needs improvement?

Fortunately for asset managers, lodging has evolved to become a particularly data-heavy industry. Daily, weekly, monthly, and annual reports are available. There are myriad industry benchmarks designed to assist asset managers to understand the relative current performance of a hotel asset and its potential upside.

This chapter outlines useful revenue and expense benchmarking tools available to asset managers in the hospitality industry today. These tools, used in tandem, can provide the basis for an asset manager to analyze a hotel's performance. The chapter concludes with lists of specific questions that an asset manager might pose to property management to identify opportunities for increasing the property's profitability and value.

Framework for Analysis of Hotel Performance

The goal of the hotel owner is to increase the value of his asset. The asset manager can contribute to this goal by completing two fundamental exercises:

- Determining a hotel's proper market position, based on *external, market-based factors.*
- Increasing the hotel's net income, including uncovering opportunities for gaining incremental revenue and improving expense control, based on *internal, property-specific factors.*

To accomplish the above objectives, the asset manager employs two complementary analytical techniques, *comparative analysis* and *variance analysis*. Comparative analysis evaluates the subject hotel's performance relative to other comparable hotels or the subject's local market using industry data or standards. For example, an asset manager might compare the subject hotel's occupancy in October 2004 against that of its competitive set during the same month. Variance analysis is longitudinal, involving a comparison of the subject hotel's performance

Exhibit 1 Calculations for Revenue Analysis

$$\text{Average Occupancy Percentage} = \frac{\text{Total occupied rooms}}{\text{Total available rooms over a given time period}}$$

$$\text{Average Daily Rate (ADR)} = \frac{\text{Total rooms revenue}}{\text{Total occupied rooms over a given time period}}$$

$$\text{Revenue Per Available Room (RevPAR)} = \text{ADR} \times \text{Average occupancy percentage}$$

or

$$\frac{\text{Total rooms revenue}}{\text{Total available rooms over a given time period}}$$

to its own performance in a preceding period. For example, an asset manager might compare a hotel's October 2004 marketing expense to the marketing expenditure for the same property in October 2003.

A hotel's performance may be benchmarked against other properties in either its regional area or on an industry-wide basis. Generally speaking, a hotel's *revenue* performance is benchmarked against those hotels in its competitive set or within its regional area, while *expense* items are compared against industry-wide norms. There are exceptions to this rule of thumb, however. Sometimes it is reasonable, for example, to compare a hotel's individual revenue performance to the average revenues achieved across all hotels within the same brand. Similarly, it is not uncommon to compare one extended-stay hotel's revenue performance to extended-stay hotels' average revenue performance nationwide. Whenever possible, utilizing revenue comparables from the local area is preferable, because it will reflect the actual supply and demand trends in the subject market.

Benchmarking Revenue

A hotel and its comparables are generally analyzed using three metrics: average occupancy percentage, average daily rate (ADR), and revenue per available room (RevPAR). The formulas for calculating these three metrics appear in Exhibit 1. The purpose of revenue benchmarking is to determine a hotel's appropriate occupancy and average rate potential, as indicated by comparing the hotel's performance relative to its competitive market.

The Competitive Set

A critical component of benchmarking the subject hotel's revenue is defining a set of competitive properties whose performance serves as a standard of comparison. The importance of selecting the appropriate competitive set cannot be overstated, as it will provide the basis of analysis for the asset manager. The asset manager should review data from:

- Management personnel at the subject property.
- Recent marketing plans for the subject property.
- Primary market research, including the asset manager's tours of competing properties and local operator and demand-generator interviews.
- Existing feasibility studies, appraisals, and internally-generated market reports for the subject property.

The competitive set, as identified by the subject hotel's management, is a good starting point for the asset manager's analysis. Reviewing the most recent and prior year's marketing plan for the subject property should provide the asset manager with an overview of the hotel's positioning, market strategy, and the relative strengths and weaknesses of the hotel and its competition, as understood by the management team.

Whenever possible, the asset manager should complete initial primary market research, including interviews with local operators, as well as a tour of the local market to understand the property's proximity to demand generators and the ease or difficulty of access to the subject property from the demand generators.

To determine what hotels compete most directly with the subject property, the asset manager should collect and evaluate the following data relative to the subject hotel.

- Physical characteristics: year built, condition, most recent renovation
- Franchise affiliation
- Ratio of meeting space per guestroom
- Amenities: indoor/outdoor pool, gift shop, health club, business center, etc.
- Location: proximity to major demand generators
- Prior operating history (occupancy and ADR statistics)
- Market segmentation (commercial, group, leisure)
- Management: ownership, operator

Generally, hotels having similar physical attributes, in proximity to the same demand generators, and serving a similar mix of market segments will form the subject hotel's competitive set.

The asset manager should also collect information from local planning or zoning offices regarding any planned or proposed hotels in the competitive lodging market. This information is often disclosed in a hotel's marketing plan or is known by local-market hotel consultants or appraisers. The impact of a new hotel in the market and the degree to which it will compete with the subject property should be estimated by the standard supply-and-demand analysis techniques used in preparing lodging feasibility studies.

In addition to supply research, the asset manager should determine the major demand generators in a market through interviews with the general managers and directors of sales in the competitive market. Direct interviews with personnel at the attractions, businesses, government offices, etc. that are the market area's demand generators will help the asset manager to understand the market's demand characteristics and lead to a proper market positioning for the subject hotel. In general, for each of the major market demand generators, these interviews should reveal:

- Number of annual room-nights generated in the competitive market.
- Seasonality of demand by day of week and month of year.
- Purpose of travel for incoming guests.
- Negotiated corporate rates with area hotels.
- Criteria, by market segment, for selecting a hotel.
- Special leisure rates negotiated with area hotels.
- Preferred or required amenities or services.
- Demand for meeting facilities.

Positioning the Subject Property

Using the preceding data, the asset manager applies judgment and analytical experience, determining which hotels are most competitive to the subject property, estimating how well the subject hotel is positioned to capture demand within its competitive market, and identifying potential opportunities to improve the market positioning of the asset.

This local research should also enable the asset manager to rank the competitive properties' anticipated success based on individual property characteristics. For example, it is likely that a newly renovated hotel would be able to command a higher rate than a tired hotel, and a hotel next door to a major demand generator will capture more of that demand than a hotel located five miles away. Once defined, the hotels in the competitive set will provide the framework for benchmarking the subject hotel's performance.

A property's market positioning is generally gauged by its *penetration ratio,* which compares the property's performance to market performance. A penetration ratio is calculated by dividing the property's performance on a given metric to the same metric for the market. Some standard penetration ratios used by asset managers are presented in Exhibit 2. Penetration ratios are expressed as a percentage; therefore, ratios in excess of 100 percent indicate that the hotel is out-performing the market.

But how does an asset manager determine the appropriate RevPAR position for the subject hotel? In theory, if a hotel's competitive set consists exclusively of purely competitive properties, the hotel should strive resolutely to achieve above 100 percent RevPAR penetration. However, in some cases, lodging markets consist of such a wide array of properties that defining a true competitive set within a local market may not be achievable. For example, consider a subject hotel that is an

Exhibit 2 Penetration Ratio Calculations

$$\textbf{ADR Penetration Index} = \frac{\text{Property ADR}}{\text{Market ADR}}$$

$$\textbf{Occupancy Index} = \frac{\text{Property Occupancy Percentage}}{\text{Market Occupancy Percentage}}$$

$$\textbf{RevPAR Index} = \frac{\text{Property RevPAR}}{\text{Market RevPAR}}$$

$$\textbf{Transient Demand Index} = \frac{\text{Property Transient Demand}}{\text{Market Transient Demand}}$$

independent property in fair condition with no meeting space and serving primarily a transient market. Let's further assume that the properties within the competitive market are in relatively good condition, all contain meeting space, and are all "flagged" with nationally recognized hotel brands. Assuming further that there is a base of group demand in the market seeking branded, good-quality hotel accommodations, it would be rather difficult for the subject hotel to achieve a RevPAR penetration in excess of 100 percent.

It is clearly unreasonable (and mathematically impossible) to expect every hotel to achieve a RevPAR penetration in excess of 100 percent. Moreover, RevPAR positioning is admittedly a subjective matter. But in considering and defining the goals for the hotel, the asset manager should work with the property management to determine:

1. The subject hotel's competitive advantages and disadvantages relative to the hotels in its competitive set.
2. Recent trends in RevPAR at the subject property and in its market, including the subject's historical RevPAR penetration.

Industry Data Sources—Revenues

Once the competitive market and anticipated positioning of the subject hotel are defined, the asset manager should review one of several resources that provide industry-wide or market-specific competitive-set statistics for revenue performance. The authors' firm, for example, uses reports from Smith Travel Research (www.smithtravelresearch.com) and TravelClick, Inc. (www.travelclick.net). In addition to collecting data from national lodging consulting companies and speaking with area hospitality consultants, the asset manager should also collect reports used by the hotel's management team to measure the hotel's performance.

Lodging-industry reports provide abundant and varied data. Smith Travel Research (STR) and TravelCLICK's Hotel*Flash* reports are used to measure a property's occupancy, average rate, and RevPAR relative to the market. TravelCLICK's Hotelligence, PHASER, and RateView reports analyze a hotel's capture of demand generated by global distribution systems (GDSs), such as airline companies and travel agencies.

Smith Travel Research. Smith Travel Research's database includes demand and revenue data for both branded and independent hotels in the United States, Canada, Mexico, and the Caribbean. Within the U.S. domestic market, STR collects data from more than 20,000 properties representing some 2.6 million rooms. STR's reports are based on actual total demand as reported by individual properties, management companies, and major hotel chains. STR's reports include:

- The STAR Report: a monthly report providing performance measurements (occupancy, ADR, RevPAR, and market share) for an individual hotel and the comparative averages for the aggregate market area and one or more user-defined competitive sets.
- STR Weekly DaySTAR Report: e-mailed to participating properties weekly, this report provides daily performance statistics.
- STR DaySTAR PLUS Report: provides competitive performance benchmarking by customer and revenue segments.
- STR Weekday/Weekend Report: measures performance of weekdays versus weekends relative to prior periods.

As the above list suggests, STR provides a participating hotel with a significant quantity of data, including a breakdown of weekday/weekend business and the individual hotel's rank within its competitive set. Most recently, STR has begun to collect demand data by segment (transient, group, contract), permitting the firm to produce segmented demand reports for selected markets. Exhibit 3 provides an example of a typical monthly STAR report for a hotel participating in STR's program. Generally, the asset manager receives the STR Reports from the hotel manager, who receives these reports at no cost so long as the hotel contributes its data to STR.

As illustrated in Exhibit 3, a STAR Report consists of three panels showing the subject property's performance and penetration index on three fundamental metrics—occupancy percentage, ADR, and RevPAR. STAR Reports, available on both a weekly and a monthly basis as shown in Exhibit 3, are useful in that they provide data demonstrating a property's performance relative to the market.

STR also offers a report known as The Historical Trend Report, which reports the monthly occupancy percentage, ADR, room revenue, room supply, and room demand aggregated for a competitive set of hotels. This report does not calculate the penetration data for the subject hotel as compared to its competitors, but the information is available without cost, even to non-participating hotels.

TravelCLICK. TravelCLICK's comprehensive database is the exclusive source of hotel-industry electronic distribution data from the Amadeus, Galileo, Sabre, and Worldspan global distribution systems (GDSs) that, collectively, are used by 98 percent of travel agents worldwide. TravelCLICK's reports are particularly useful

Exhibit 3 Sample STAR Report

Any Contributing Hotel
Address
Any City, Any State ZIP
United States
Telephone: (555) 555-5555

STAR Trend Report - February 2003
Property vs. Competitive Set Excluding Subject Hotel

3/21/2003
e-star_trend
1.01

1 STR #: XXXX
2 Chain ID: 337X8
3 Open Date: 199005
4 MgtCo: None
5 Owner: None
6 Total Rooms: 500
7 Operation: Chain Management
8 Market: New York, Ny
9 Tract: Manhattan - West

		Occupancy						Average Room Rate						RevPar					
		A	B	C	D	E	F	G	H	I	J	K	L	M	N	O	P	Q	R
Year	Month	Property	% Change	Comp Set	% Change	Index	% Change	Property	% Change	Comp Set	% Change	Index	% Change	Property	% Change	Comp Set	% Change	Index	% Change
2001	September	61.9	-31.8	57.9	-31.4	106.9	-0.7	291.68	-17.3	279.75	-21.7	104.3	5.7	180.59	-43.6	162.00	-46.3	111.5	5.1
2001	October	85.1	-1.2	73.0	-12.8	116.6	13.3	277.56	-25.8	251.10	-29.3	110.5	4.9	236.28	-26.6	183.30	-38.3	128.9	19.0
2001	November	87.8	-1.5	78.0	-6.8	112.6	5.7	287.96	-24.5	283.38	-22.1	101.6	-3.1	252.71	-25.7	221.16	-27.4	114.3	2.4
2001	December	84.4	6.0	75.7	2.7	111.5	3.2	292.08	-22.9	297.37	-23.8	98.2	1.1	246.51	-18.3	225.16	-21.7	109.5	4.4
2002	January	79.3	14.8	67.9	8.3	116.8	6.0	258.16	-14.8	249.69	-12.8	103.4	-2.3	204.78	-2.2	169.54	-5.6	120.8	3.5
2002	February	83.7	13.6	76.3	7.6	109.7	5.6	270.79	-17.9	259.13	-12.5	104.5	-6.3	226.58	-6.8	197.62	-5.8	114.7	-1.0
2002	March	84.0	21.7	75.7	1.9	111.0	19.5	286.35	-8.8	254.88	-11.8	112.3	3.4	240.61	11.0	192.95	-10.2	124.7	23.7
2002	April	70.6	-6.6	76.7	3.5	92.0	-9.8	303.83	-3.7	274.52	-7.3	110.7	3.9	214.56	-10.1	210.50	-4.2	101.9	-6.3
2002	May	83.2	4.8	75.3	-3.8	110.5	9.0	301.71	-3.8	283.30	-5.8	106.5	2.1	251.03	0.7	213.37	-9.4	117.7	11.2
2002	June	80.3	-8.4	73.7	-8.6	109.0	0.2	300.79	-2.5	277.38	-8.2	108.4	6.2	241.67	-10.7	204.41	-16.0	118.2	6.4
2002	July	70.6	-9.4	65.1	-8.6	108.4	-0.9	269.72	-0.2	241.55	-5.5	111.7	5.7	190.33	-9.6	157.23	-13.6	121.1	4.6
2002	August	75.5	-4.1	73.9	-0.8	102.2	-3.2	263.14	-2.8	233.74	-8.8	112.6	6.5	198.66	-6.7	172.75	-9.5	115.0	3.1
2002	September	76.7	23.9	76.2	31.6	100.7	-5.8	301.08	3.2	282.28	0.9	106.7	2.3	230.89	27.9	215.05	32.7	107.4	-3.7
2002	October	82.7	-2.8	80.9	10.8	102.2	-12.3	313.53	13.0	297.97	18.7	105.2	-4.8	259.38	9.8	240.99	31.5	107.6	-16.5
2002	November	88.4	0.7	80.9	3.7	109.3	-2.9	319.19	10.8	296.83	4.7	107.5	5.8	282.30	11.7	240.13	8.6	117.6	2.9
2002	December	85.2	0.9	77.1	1.8	110.5	-0.9	336.09	15.1	334.84	12.6	100.4	2.2	286.20	16.1	258.10	14.6	110.9	1.3
2003	January	73.4	-7.4	65.2	-4.0	112.6	-3.6	262.08	1.5	244.24	-2.2	107.3	3.8	192.45	-6.0	159.29	-6.0	120.8	0.0
2003	February	73.2	-12.5	67.0	-12.2	109.3	-0.4	272.58	0.7	248.06	-4.3	109.9	5.2	199.58	-11.9	166.19	-15.9	120.1	4.7
Three Months - Ending February																			
2001		74.2	-10.1	69.0	-7.9	107.5	-2.4	339.45	1.9	327.65	2.4	103.6	-0.5	251.73	-8.4	226.14	-5.7	111.3	-2.9
2002		82.4	11.1	73.2	6.1	112.6	4.7	274.11	-19.2	269.66	-17.7	101.7	-1.8	225.94	-10.2	197.36	-12.7	114.5	2.9
2003		77.4	-6.1	69.9	-4.5	110.7	-1.7	293.20	7.0	279.82	3.8	104.8	3.0	226.94	0.4	195.47	-1.0	116.1	1.4
Year to Date - Ending February																			
2001		71.3	-10.3	66.6	-13.4	107.1	3.6	316.22	1.3	291.25	4.3	108.6	-2.9	225.42	-9.2	193.87	-9.7	116.3	0.6
2002		81.4	14.2	71.9	8.0	113.2	5.7	264.32	-16.4	254.44	-12.6	103.9	-4.3	215.12	-4.6	182.86	-5.7	117.6	1.1
2003		73.3	-10.0	66.1	-8.1	110.9	-2.0	267.06	1.0	246.08	-3.3	108.5	4.4	195.84	-9.0	162.56	-11.1	120.5	2.5
Twelve Months - Ending February																			
2001		85.2	0.4	79.6	0.4	107.0	-0.1	339.20	3.8	320.30	5.3	105.9	-1.4	288.93	4.1	254.86	5.6	113.4	-1.3
2002		79.2	-7.0	73.5	-7.7	107.8	0.7	288.92	-14.8	277.25	-13.4	104.2	-1.6	228.80	-20.8	203.71	-20.1	112.3	-1.0
2003		78.7	-0.6	74.0	0.7	106.4	-1.3	295.37	2.2	273.96	-1.2	107.8	3.5	232.46	1.6	202.72	-0.5	114.7	2.1

Key:

1 STR Property Number assigned by STR
2 Chain ID Code assigned by STR
3 Opening Date
4 Management Company (if known)
5 Ownership Entity (if known)
6 Total Availble Rooms
7 Type of Operation
8 Defined Market Area
9 Defined Market Tract Within Area

A Property Occupancy
B Property Occupancy % change over same period last year
C Comp Set Occupancy
D Comp Set Occupancy % change over same period last year
E Property Occupancy Penetration
F Property Occupancy Penetration % change over same period last year
G Property ADR
H Property ADR % change over same period last year
I Comp Set ADR

J Comp Set ADR % change over same period last year
K Property ADR Penetration
L Property ADR Penetration % change over same period last year
M Property RevPAR
N Property RevPAR % change over same period last year
O Comp Set RevPAR
P Comp Set RevPAR % change over same period last year
Q Property RevPAR Penetration
R Property RevPAR Penetration % change over same period last year

for transient-oriented hotels, while group-based properties are less likely to benefit from these data.

TravelCLICK's data are significantly different from STR's data in that the firm reports only actual demand derived from the GDSs. This demand originates primarily with travel agents, whereas STR reports and TravelCLICK's Hotel*Flash* reports reflect demand from all sources. TravelCLICK also produces a monthly newsletter, *eMonitor,* which reports all hotel bookings made through third-party travel web sites powered by Pegasus Solutions.

Reports available from TravelCLICK include:

- Hotelligence Report: this report measures an individual hotel's penetration of room-night demand captured through GDSs by comparing its performance to the room-nights captured through GDSs by its competitive set.
- Internet Hotelligence Report: similar to the preceding report, except that it measures room-night demand captured through both GDSs and web sites powered by Pegasus Solutions.
- PHASER Complete Access Report: a forward-looking report that summarizes posted GDS and central reservation system (CRS) transient rates for each hotel in a defined competitive set for 30 to 60 days into the future.
- RateVIEW Report: this report works in tandem with the PHASER report, providing rate data for a competitive set from the GDSs and travel-related web sites like Orbitz, Travelocity, and Expedia.

Hotelligence Reports are useful because they allow an asset manager to recognize opportunities to improve GDS and Internet penetration. For example, the Hotelligence Report shown in Exhibit 4 shows the sample property's penetration of GDS demand against its competitive set. The property is capturing well over its fair share from the Worldspan GDS (room-night and revenue penetration of 186 percent and 150.8 percent, respectively) but doing far less well in capturing business from the Amadeus system (room-night and revenue penetration of 32.6 percent and 74.1 percent, respectively). The subject property's failure to capture its fair share (or more) through the Amadeus system is reducing the subject's overall penetration of GDS-generated demand to less than its fair share (88.1 percent penetration of room nights and 96.1percent penetration of revenue). The shortfall in Amadeus-system-generated demand might represent an opportunity for the property to capture additional business from the Amadeus system.

TravelCLICK's PHASER Report is especially useful for future rate positioning, allowing the asset manager to ensure that the subject hotel maximizes its revenue by basing rate decisions on both in-house demand and competitor pricing. The report can also be used as an indicator of future demand strength if the asset manager tracks increases and decreases in the market area's posted room rates.

Summary: Revenue Benchmarking

Hotel revenues can be benchmarked against data available for hotel performance analysis from multiple sources, including Smith Travel Research and TravelCLICK. Defining an appropriate competitive set and market positioning for the

Exhibit 4 Sample Hotelligence Report

The Premiere Hotel | **Performance Summary** | **Reporting Period: July-02**

GDS	Period		Bookings	Room Nights	Revenue in USD	Variance vs Last Year: Room Nights	Variance vs Last Year: Revenue in USD	Market Share: Room Nights	Market Share: Revenue	Market Penetration: Room Nights	Market Penetration: Revenue
ALL	Jul 02	*Subscriber*	6,300	13,253	2,637,780	3,310	1,008,440	27.2%	29.0%	111.3%	118.7%
		Competitive Set Total	15,744	35,537	6,465,917	3,130	1,469,462	72.8%	71.0%	96.3%	93.9%
		Rank						1	1	2	1
	YTD	*Subscriber*	39,456	81,296	18,347,954	17,754	6,261,039	21.5%	23.4%	88.1%	96.1%
		Competitive Set Total	135,563	296,856	59,934,928	29,369	14,279,142	78.5%	76.6%	103.8%	101.3%
		Rank						3	2	4	4
A	Jul 02	*Subscriber*	892	917	169,643	230	54,094	7.9%	18.1%	32.6%	74.1%
		Competitive Set Total	3,951	10,621	768,658	892	159,736	92.1%	81.9%	121.8%	108.4%
		Rank						4	3	5	5
G	Jul 02	*Subscriber*	1,300	2,829	589,576	706	224,559	27.8%	25.5%	114.1%	104.5%
		Competitive Set Total	3,489	7,335	1,723,696	713	466,435	72.2%	74.5%	95.5%	98.6%
		Rank						1	2	2	3
S	Jul 02	*Subscriber*	2,637	6,409	1,423,649	1,601	570,945	31.6%	30.8%	129.6%	126.4%
		Competitive Set Total	6,516	13,853	3,192,439	1,184	843,291	68.4%	69.2%	90.4%	91.5%
		Rank						1	1	1	1
W	Jul 02	*Subscriber*	1,471	3,098	454,911	773	158,842	45.4%	36.8%	186.0%	150.8%
		Competitive Set Total	1,788	3,728	781,124	341	174,120	54.6%	63.2%	72.2%	83.6%
		Rank						1	1	1	1

The letters on the left of the page represent abbreviations for each GDS (A=Amadeus, G=Galileo/Apollo, S=Sabre/Abacus/Axess/Infini, W=Worldspan). Variance numbers represent change in Room Nights versus the same period during the previous year. Numbers highlighted in red represent Market Shares lower than your hotel's fair share or Market Penetrations less than 100%. **Fair Share: 24.4%**
Competitive Set: LUXURY SUITES, PRESIDENTIAL TOWERS, EXECUTIVE SUITES, CAPITAL TOWERS, THE TOWER, REGAL PLAZA

Source: TravelClick, Inc. ©Copyright 2000

subject hotel, based on the property's competitive strengths and weaknesses, is a critical step to revenue-performance benchmarking.

An asset manager can contribute to the achievement of revenue goals by working with management to employ efficient, targeted marketing. This might include reviewing local demand generators to ensure that important sources of room-nights have not been overlooked, employing best practices regarding Internet advertising and pricing, and, in the case of group-oriented hotels, increasing the property's marketing exposure through contacts with meeting planners, direct marketing efforts, and the use of familiarization (FAM) trips. Further, an asset manager should ensure that the appropriate amount of capital is spent at the property, allowing it to remain competitive in the market.

The asset manager should monitor the property's revenue penetration by conscientiously reviewing the weekly and monthly reports described in the preceding paragraphs. The goal of revenue benchmarking is to have the asset manger review both the historical revenue performance of the hotel and its future rate positioning to suggest strategies for increasing the property's overall revenue.

Benchmarking Expenses

Data permitting the benchmarking of expenses are also abundant, with several reliable sources providing a framework for comparative expense analysis. Typically, the asset manager completes an analysis during budgeting season, comparing a property's performance to comparable hotels or assessing it against aggregate data from reports produced by consulting and investment advisory firms serving the lodging industry. Analysis of the hotel's own performance relative to budgeted or prior year results, known as *variance analysis*, is discussed later in the chapter.

Basis for Comparative Analysis

The asset manager should review the schedules supporting the property's summary profit and loss statement to understand the revenue and expense items included in each line item. Understanding the account coding system of the property's management company is critical to accomplishing an appropriate comparative analysis.

Most hotel management companies follow the ninth revised edition of the *Uniform System of Accounts for the Lodging Industry (USALI)*, published by the American Hotel & Lodging Association (www.ahla.com). To develop a reliable analysis, the asset manager should ensure that the presentation of the financial results under scrutiny conforms to the *USALI* or a similar standard chart of accounts so that the line items being analyzed are truly comparable.

Adjustments to the presentation of the subject hotel's results might be required to maintain comparability. For example, profit and loss statements prepared by some management companies identify credit card commissions as a separate expense, while under the *USALI* format, they are typically included in the administrative and general (A&G) line item. Therefore, for true comparability, the A&G expense in this example must be adjusted to include credit card commissions.

Similarly, independent management companies operating franchised hotels might include all fees associated with the franchise (reservation expense, frequent guest program fees, franchise royalty fees, and national marketing fees) in a property's franchise-fee line item. This would clearly present a significantly higher franchise expense than that reported by other hotels following the more common convention of coding reservation costs as an expense of the rooms department, while frequent-guest-program costs and national marketing fees are coded as marketing expenses. If an asset manager is not cognizant of such financial reporting nuances, the reliability of the comparative analysis may be compromised.

Data Sources

Numerous investment advisory and consulting firms warehouse data and operating statements from various hotels nationwide. These reports include industry-wide survey reports and more focused reports that can be customized to provide data from a selection of hotels defined according to a narrower set of attributes.

Survey Reports. Companies that currently provide industry-wide survey data include Smith Travel Research and the Hospitality Research Group (HRG), a division of PKF Consulting (www.HRGonline.com). STR compiles summary financial operating data from nearly 3,400 full-service and limited-service properties through its Hotel Operating Statistics (HOST) Data Service. Individual hotel data are gathered on revenues, operating expenses, and fixed charges from major chains, management companies, and independent hotels. The *HOST Report* is published annually and offers broad categories of comparability, including a summary report by geographic region, property size (room count), location type (airport, city center, etc.), and rate tier. The annual *HOST Report* is a relatively inexpensive industry resource and sometimes a good starting point for expense analysis.

HRG's annual survey, *Trends in the Hotel Industry,* is derived from a database containing detailed financial statistics for some 6,000 full- and limited-service hotels. The operating statistics presented in the *Trends* report are categorized by property type (full-service, limited-service, all-suite, convention, resorts) and further segmented by geographic region, property size, and rate tier. In addition to the annual *Trends* report, which is available in both printed and electronic form, HRG also publishes a quarterly *Trends* report, as well as monthly regional reports.

HRG's and STR's industry-wide reports are useful for tracking trends on a national and regional basis, but far more useful to the asset manager are customized reports derived from the two companies' data. STR's customized *HOST Report* and HRG's *Benchmarker Report* both present aggregated data, drawn from each company's larger database, for a client-defined set of hotels. The major benefit of using these made-to-order reports is enhanced comparability, because the asset manager defines the competitive set based on relevant attributes such as location, region, property size, and rate tier.

HOST Report. When ordering STR's *HOST Report,* the asset manager selects the desired comparables from STR's database of contributor properties. STR averages the statistics from each of the properties in the defined set, providing a summary profit and loss statement against which the asset manager compares the subject hotel's performance. Exhibit 5 presents an example of a customized *HOST Report*. Note that the summary statement's line items are reported using three measures: (percentage) ratio to sales, dollar amount per available room, and dollar amount per occupied room. These metrics will be explained in further detail later in this chapter.

Benchmarker Reports. HRG offers three types of *Benchmarker Reports* that provide summary statistics derived by averaging data from a comparable set of properties selected by the asset manager. Although STR is planning to expand its data collection efforts to include more detail, as of this writing, STR provides only summary income-statement data. In contrast, HRG is able to provide more detailed data on revenue and expense line items appearing on the summary income statement. Thus HRG's Benchmarker Income Statement report is similar to the *HOST Report* in its level of detail, but the HRG also produces reports of labor costs and other departmental statistics.

Exhibit 6 shows a sample Benchmarker Income Statement report. A distinct advantage of the format of HRG's income statement is that it reports the percentage *variance* from the competitive set's average value for each metric. For example, the subject hotel whose results are depicted in Exhibit 6 achieves a total departmental, or gross, income that is 1.1 percent higher than its competitive set when expressed on per-available-room basis and an 18.1 percent higher net operating income (NOI) when expressed on a per-occupied-room basis.

The Benchmarker Labor Cost report is also a valuable tool, as labor is the largest operating cost of lodging properties. Exhibit 7 shows a sample labor cost report comparing the subject hotel's performance to its competitive set. As can be seen, the report shows the total payroll and related expenses for various revenue and cost centers in the hotel, further categorized into cash wages and benefits and payroll taxes. For example, the subject hotel's labor cost in the rooms department is the same 9.2 percent of revenue reported by the 16 hotels in the subject's competitive set, but it expends more for cash wages and less for benefits and payroll taxes than the average of its competitive set.

Both the HOST and Benchmarker reports are valuable because they offer the asset manager the ability to compare the subject property's performance with the results achieved by a set of similar hotels. There are several reasons why a hotel might operate differently from comparable properties, but looking at a representative sample of similar hotels' performance data can provide a reliable standard, forming a basis for asking important questions about the subject property's overall operation.

Other Sources of Comparable Hotel Data

In addition to using industry-wide databases and custom reports derived from them, to the extent possible, the asset manager should collect individual operating statements from properties similar to the subject hotel. These "comparables" or "comps" may be shared with the asset manager by consultants and other hospitality real estate professionals, or the asset manager may use internal data from a

Exhibit 5 Sample Customized STR HOST Report

	Ratio To Sales	Amount Per Available Room	Amount Per Occupied Room
Occupancy		75.4%	
Average Rate		$78.01	
Revenue			
Rooms	76.00%	$21,622	$78.01
Food	13.4	3814	16.03
Beverage	3.8	1076	4.64
Other Food & Beverage	1.9	544	2.71
Telephone	2.9	820	3.05
Minor Operated Departments	1.5	416	1.71
Rentals & Other Income	0.6	171	0.85
Total Revenue	100.00%	$28,461	$107.00
Departmental Expenses			
Rooms	23.00%	$4,977	$18.16
Food & Beverage	81.5	4429	16.4
Telephone	46.8	384	1.41
Other Departmental Expenses	1.2	336	1.49
Total Departmental Expenses	35.60%	$10,126	$37.46
Departmental Profits			
Rooms	77.00%	$16,645	$59.85
Food & Beverage	18.5	1004	6.98
Telephone	53.2	436	1.64
Other Departmental Profits	0.9	250	1.07
Total Departmental Profit	64.40%	$18,335	$69.54
Undistributed Operating Expenses			
Administrative and General	10.10%	$2,872	$10.60
Marketing	4.8	1375	5.63
Franchise Fee	2.6	737	2.47
Energy	4.2	1198	4.51
Property Operation & Maintenance	4.4	1258	4.85
Total Undistributed Operating Expenses	26.10%	$7,440	$28.06
Gross Operating Profit	38.30%	$10,895	$41.48
Management Fees	3.60%	$1,030	$3.62
Income Before Fixed Charges	34.70%	$9,865	$37.86
Property Taxes	2.7	777	2.7
Insurance	0.4	114	0.44
Reserve For Replacement	0.9	259	1
& Other Fixed Charges	30.70%	$8,715	$34.72
Fixed Charges			
Land & Building Rent	0.70%	196	0.8
Equipment Rental	2.5	717	2.13
Interest	4.2	1204	4.24
Depreciation & Amortization	2.8	803	3.14
Other Fixed Charges	1.3	370	1.11
Total Fixed Charges	14.70%	$4,181	$14.56
Pre-Tax Income	20.00%	$5,684	$23.30
Payroll Analysis			
Rooms	13.90%	$3,010	$10.86
Food & Beverage	39.6	2151	7.97
Telephone	5.9	49	0.23
Other Operated Departments	0.6	168	0.85
Administrative & General	5	1426	5.26
Marketing	2.2	618	2.48
PO&M	2.2	620	2.64
Total Payroll	28.30%	$8,041	$30.29
Food & Beverage Costs			
Cost of Food Sales	31.9	$1,216	$5.07
Cost of Beverage Sales	16.3	175	1
Total Cost of F&B Sales	30.00%	$1,391	$6.07
Number Of Properties	44		
Number Of Rooms	9628		

* Figures above represent average of all hotels
* Totals may not add due to rounding
* Expense Ratios to sales for the Rooms, Food, Beverage & Telephone departments are based on their respective department sales. All other are to Total Sales.

Exhibit 6 Sample *Benchmarker* Income Statement Report

REVENUES AND EXPENSES	VARIANCE - SUBJECT VS. BENCHMARK PROPERTIES (%)			
	Dollars	Ratio To Revenue*	Per Available Room/Year	Per Occupied Room/Day
Revenues				
Rooms	1.8	5.2	0.1	(0.1)
Food	(25.7)	(5.4)	(26.9)	(27.1)
Beverage	(20.5)	(0.8)	(21.8)	(21.9)
Telecommunications	(26.4)	(0.7)	(27.6)	(27.7)
Other Operated Departments	96.2	2.4	93.0	92.6
Rentals and Other Income	(45.5)	(0.7)	(46.4)	(46.5)
Total Revenues	(6.1)	0.0	(7.6)	(7.8)
Departmental Costs and Expenses				
Rooms	(9.1)	(2.6)	(10.6)	(10.7)
Food	(32.8)	(7.8)	(33.9)	(34.0)
Beverage	(1.9)	11.2	(3.5)	(3.7)
Telecommunications	(45.3)	(12.7)	(46.2)	(46.3)
Other Operated Departments	89.5	(2.4)	86.4	86.0
Total Costs and Expenses	(18.5)	(5.5)	(19.8)	(20.0)
Total Operated Departmental Income	2.8	5.5	1.1	0.9
Undistributed Operating Expenses				
Administrative and General	(9.9)	(0.3)	(11.4)	(11.6)
Marketing (Includes Franchise Fees)	0.4	0.5	(1.2)	(1.5)
Property Operation and Maintenance	(10.3)	(0.2)	(11.7)	(11.9)
Utility Costs	13.1	0.8	11.3	11.1
Other Unallocated Operated Departments	(100.0)	(0.1)	(100.0)	(100.0)
Total Undistributed Expenses	(3.4)	0.7	(5.0)	(5.2)
Income Before Fixed Charges	7.1	4.8	5.3	5.1
Management Fees, Property Taxes, and Insurance				
Management Fees	(34.4)	(0.9)	(35.4)	(35.6)
Property Taxes and Other Municipal Charges	(53.6)	(2.0)	(54.4)	(54.5)
Insurance	13.6	0.2	11.8	11.5
Total Management Fees, Taxes and Insurai	(37.4)	(2.6)	(38.4)	(38.5)
Income Before Other Fixed Charges	20.3	7.4	18.3	18.1

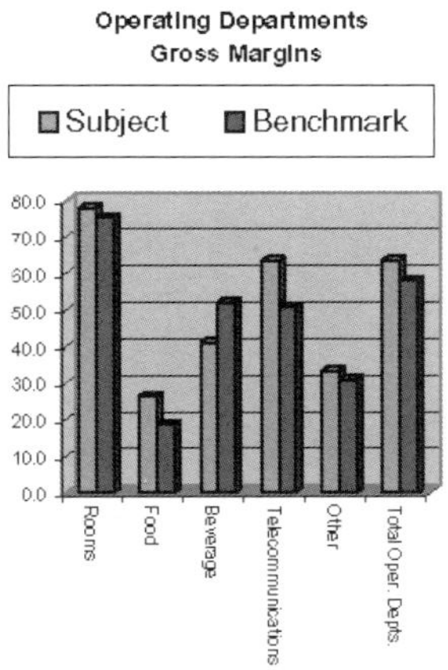

* Expressed as percentage points
NC - Not Computed

Source: The Hospitality Research Group

Exhibit 7 Sample *Benchmarker* Labor Cost Report

EXPENSES	SAMPLE SUBJECT				AVERAGE OF 16 BENCHMARK PROPERTIES			
	1999 ($)	Ratio To Total Revenue (%)	Per Available Room/Year ($)	Per Occupied Room/Day ($)	1999 ($)	Ratio To Total Revenue (%)	Per Available Room/Year ($)	Per Occupied Room/Day ($)
Rooms Department								
Salaries & Wages - Including Vacations	1,386,106	7.1	3,072	11.63	1,395,272	6.7	3,143	11.92
Payroll Costs & Employee Benefits	411,347	2.1	912	3.45	518,488	2.5	1,168	4.43
Total Payroll & Related Expenses	1,797,453	9.2	3,983	15.08	1,913,760	9.2	4,311	16.35
Food and Beverage Department								
Salaries & Wages - Including Vacations	1,622,562	8.3	3,596	13.61	2,013,118	9.7	4,535	17.20
Payroll Costs & Employee Benefits	489,449	2.5	1,085	4.11	724,449	3.5	1,632	6.19
Total Payroll & Related Expenses	2,112,011	10.8	4,681	17.72	2,737,568	13.2	6,167	23.39
Telecommunications Department								
Salaries & Wages - Including Vacations	107,818	0.6	239	0.90	98,263	0.5	221	0.84
Payroll Costs & Employee Benefits	30,781	0.2	68	0.26	32,933	0.2	74	0.23
Total Payroll & Related Expenses	138,599	0.7	307	1.16	131,196	0.6	296	1.12
Other Operated Department								
Salaries & Wages - Including Vacations	0	0.0	0	0.00	71,702	0.3	162	0.61
Payroll Costs & Employee Benefits	0	0.0	0	0.00	22,546	0.1	51	0.19
Total Payroll & Related Expenses	0	0.0	0	0.00	94,248	0.5	212	0.81
Administrative and General Department								
Salaries & Wages - Including Vacations	662,079	3.4	1,467	5.55	638,811	3.1	1,439	5.46
Payroll Costs & Employee Benefits	209,437	1.1	464	1.76	193,582	0.9	436	1.65
Total Payroll & Related Expenses	871,516	4.5	1,931	7.31	832,392	4.0	1,875	7.11
Marketing Department								
Salaries & Wages - Including Vacations	640,046	3.3	1,418	5.37	406,265	2.0	915	3.47
Payroll Costs & Employee Benefits	185,507	1.0	411	1.56	132,772	0.6	299	1.13
Total Payroll & Related Expenses	825,553	4.2	1,830	6.93	539,037	2.6	1,214	4.61
Property Operation and Maintenance Department								
Salaries & Wages - Including Vacations	371,446	1.9	823	3.12	345,946	1.7	779	2.96
Payroll Costs & Employee Benefits	109,177	0.6	242	0.92	121,146	0.6	273	1.04
Total Payroll & Related Expenses	480,623	2.5	1,065	4.03	467,092	2.2	1,052	3.99
All Other Departments								
Salaries & Wages - Including Vacations	0	0.0	0	0.00	11,493	0.1	26	0.10
Payroll Costs & Employee Benefits	0	0.0	0	0.00	2,351	0.0	5	0.02
Total Payroll & Related Expenses	0	0.0	0	0.00	13,844	0.1	31	0.12
Total Overall Payroll & Related Expenses	6,225,755	31.9	13,797	52.23	6,729,137	32.4	15,159	57.50
Average Daily Rooms Available	451				444			
Percentage of Occupancy	72.4%				72.2%			
Average Daily Rate per Occupied Room (Excluding complimentary rooms)	$ 112.07				$ 111.19			
Rooms RevPAR	$79.38				$79.26			

Source: The Hospitality Research Group

Exhibit 8 Metrics for Expressing Line Items

$$\textbf{Dollars Per Occupied Room (POR)} = \frac{\text{Total dollar amount of line item}}{\text{Occupied rooms at hotel for the period}}$$

$$\textbf{Dollars Per Available Room (PAR)} = \frac{\text{Total dollar amount of line item}}{\text{Total rooms available daily at hotel}}$$

$$\textbf{Percentage of Revenue (PER)} = \frac{\text{Total dollar amount of line item}}{\text{Total (or departmental) revenue}}$$

portfolio of managed assets to develop comparable operating statements. The following factors should be considered when selecting comparables, whether from industry-wide databases or from the asset manager's ad hoc sources:

- Number of guestrooms
- Market mix (e.g., proportion of group versus transient business)
- Occupancy percentage and ADR, or RevPAR positioning
- Franchise affiliation
- Amount of meeting space
- Collective bargaining agreements: are employees union or non-union?
- Location within a region

Comparative Analysis Techniques

Because of the possibility of extreme variations in dollar amounts of revenues and expenses from one hotel to the next, or from one reporting period to the next, it is preferable to convert line items from an income statement to more useful metrics that facilitate comparisons. In general, hotel financial statement line items are expressed in terms of three measures: percentage of total sales or applicable departmental revenue (PER), dollars per available room (PAR), and dollars per occupied room (POR). Formulas demonstrating the calculation of the three fundamental metrics commonly used to express hotel operating statistics appear in Exhibit 8.

Certain metrics are more appropriate to the analysis of individual line items, depending on the factors affecting the revenue or expense. For example, line items that are a function of guest use (e.g., telephone revenues, rooms department labor cost) are generally measured on a per-occupied-room-night basis. Line items that are affected primarily by the size of the hotel (e.g., most undistributed operating expenses) are measured on a per-available-room basis. Costs that are mostly variable and dependent on revenue levels—for example, contractual items like base management fees or franchise royalty fees—are measured as a percentage of total revenue.

It is not unusual to mix the metrics used to analyze line items, even within the same department. For example, unless there is significant local demand for a hotel's food and beverage outlet(s), a hotel's food and beverage departmental revenue is generally a function of how many guests are staying at the hotel, so the most meaningful measure of departmental sales performance is expressed as revenue per occupied room-night. Food and beverage expenses, however, are typically a function of departmental revenue, since most of the department's costs vary with sales volume.

Exhibit 9 lists various line items from a standard hotel operating statement. A boldface **X** in a column indicates that the measure is the metric on which the line item is generally analyzed. Secondary metrics employed to evaluate the individual line items are indicated by a check.

Choosing the Right Data

When conducting an analysis of the principal departmental expenses, it is important for the asset manager to rely on data derived from comparables that are similar to the subject hotel in terms of operational characteristics. Thus, when performing an expense analysis, it is less important that the comparables employed be properties in the same competitive market than it would be when determining, say, the most appropriate RevPAR positioning, where choosing comparable properties in the same market is critical.

For example, total rooms department expense at a subject hotel would be affected most by service staffing levels, complexity of guestrooms (e.g., all-suite versus standard room mix), the level of the amenities package, and the overall market orientation of the hotel. Similarly, food-and-beverage total departmental expense will be a function in part of the department's sales mix; higher proportions of beverage and banquet revenues, for example, will typically yield lower costs as a percentage of overall food-and-beverage revenue. Thus for these line items, the asset manager would want to focus attention on comparables that are physically and operationally most like the subject hotel, not necessarily those located in the same competitive market or region.

Alternatively, for some fixed charges, it may be helpful for the asset manager to rely on regional or market-area statistics to determine the most reasonable expense levels. For example, the per-room property tax liability should be relatively comparable for hotels within the same legal jurisdiction. Similarly, a subject hotel's energy expenses should track closely to statistics for local hotels, as factors affecting energy costs will affect all hotels in a competitive market.

Sample Line-Item Comparative Analysis

As previously defined, comparative analysis is a review of how the subject hotel has performed relative to comparable properties. The table presented in Exhibit 10 demonstrates how these data might be organized for a subject hotel when analyzing the energy line item. In this example, the authors utilized data, drawn from an

Exhibit 9 Basis for Analysis of Line Items

Revenue	% of Total Revenue	POR	PAR	% of Rooms Revenue
Rooms		X		
Food		X		
Beverage		X		
Telephone		X		✓
Minor Operated Departments		✓		✓
Rentals & Other Income		✓	X	
Departmental Expenses				
Rooms	✓	X		
Food & Beverage*	✓			
Telephone	✓	X		
Other Departmental Expenses	✓			
Undistributed Operating Expenses				
Administrative and General	✓		X	
Marketing	✓		X	
Franchise Fee	✓			X
Energy	✓	✓	X	
PO&M	✓		X	
Management Fees	✓			
Income Before Fixed Charges				
Property Taxes			✓	
Insurance	✓		X	
Reserve For Replacement	✓			
Fixed Charges				
Land & Building Rent			✓	

*Food and beverage revenue might also be analyzed on a per-cover basis.

Source: hotelAVE, LLC, Tiverton, RI

STR HOST Report, on five hotels (A-E) that we determined to be operationally comparable to the subject property.

As shown in the top panel of the table in Exhibit 10, the subject property's energy expense seems to be in line with the comparables' average expenditure for

Exhibit 10 Sample Line-Item Comparative Analysis

Energy Expense Analysis			
	% revenue	**POR**	**PAR**
Subject Hotel	3.7%	$6.58	1,697
HOST average	3.7%	$6.75	2,000
Comparable Properties	% of revenue	POR	PAR
Hotel A	5.1%	$6.63	1,773
Hotel B	4.8%	$6.18	2,006
Hotel C	3.1%	$3.39	916
Hotel D	3.9%	$6.61	1,285
Hotel E	4.8%	$9.42	2,401

Source: hotelAVE, LLC, Tiverton, RI, and STR

energy. The subject property's energy expense was $1,697 per available room (PAR), which is in the mid-range of the comparable properties, and lower than what is indicated as the average dollar amount PAR from the *HOST Report*. Assuming that the comparables presented are operationally and physically similar to the subject, it is reasonable to conclude that the subject's annualized energy expense is within the industry range. However, two comparable properties are achieving lower energy expenses, indicating that there may be an opportunity to decrease the subject's energy expense. It may in fact be worth evaluating the practices of comparable Hotel C to determine if the subject hotel might achieve similar energy costs per room.

Sample Line-Item Variance Analysis

In addition to the comparative analysis discussed above, the asset manager should also scrutinize the subject property's performance relative to budgeted and prior years' performance. This review, known as *variance analysis*, may be performed on an annual or monthly basis.

A detailed variance analysis of the subject property permits the asset manager to understand recent trends and the impact of operational decisions at the hotel. Asset managers generally complete a variance analysis on a monthly basis, comparing the property's month-over-month performance with the same time period of the preceding year, the current year budget, or the most recent property reforecast. Particular attention should be given to significant variances in the property's year-over-year performance or against budgeted performance.

Exhibit 11 Sample Line-Item Variance Analysis

Historical Financials	% revenue	POR	PAR	% change
1998	3.7%	$6.58	1,697	
1999	3.7%	$6.85	1,647	-2.9%
2000	4.0%	$5.84	1,692	2.7%
2001	4.5%	$6.48	1,951	15.3%
2002	3.9%	$5.12	1,500	-23.1%
Budget 2003	4.0%	$5.00	1,490	-0.7%
YTD 2002	3.6%	$5.11	1,400	
YTD 2003	3.6%	$5.10	1,550	10.7%

Source: hotelAVE, LLC, Tiverton, RI

In Exhibit 11, we present data on energy expense from the same subject hotel discussed in the preceding comparative analysis. However, in this example, we omit data from its comparable set, concentrating instead on historical data for the subject property. As can be seen in Exhibit 11, the subject property's management has budgeted for a modest decrease in energy expenses for 2003, but on a year-to-date basis, expenses have increased by more than 10 percent. Notice, however, that on a percentage-of-revenue basis and on a per-occupied-room basis, there has been insignificant change in year-to-date energy expense. This would indicate that the hotel's occupancy and revenues have increased, accounting for the larger dollar expenditure for energy (reflected in 2003's higher per-available-room energy cost) but also confirming that management's control of energy costs is as effective as in the preceding year.

The asset manager should conduct parallel variance analyses of each line item on a monthly basis to ensure that revenues and expenses are in line with the plan for the period.

Increasing the Property's Efficiency and Profitability

The exercise of completing comparative and variance analyses provides insights into a property's efficiency and profitability, but only by reviewing operational aspects of the hotel can the asset manager uncover opportunities for improvement. Thus, a financial analysis generally results in lengthy list of questions regarding the hotel's operation. The table that appears as the appendix to this chapter presents questions in the left-hand column that asset managers might pose to property managers. In the right-hand column are presented action steps and suggestions to improve the hotel's profitability. The list presented in the appendix is by no means exhaustive, but rather a sampling of questions to ask the management team as the asset manager works to enhance the value of a hotel asset.

Conclusion

There are a several resources available to asset managers for benchmarking the performance of lodging assets. In addition to industry-wide databases, a hotel asset manager can rely on user-defined compilations of data to evaluate a hotel's relative performance. These industry data sources provide powerful tools for understanding a hotel's current performance in comparison to competitors' results and for identifying the hotel's potential.

The asset manager's review of a property's revenue and expense performance must be timely—as a minimum, on a monthly basis. The majority of statistical data are available from the lodging industry's research and advisory firms on a weekly or monthly basis, permitting virtually continuous benchmarking of a property's current performance. Studying a wide range of data and publications provides the asset manager a strong framework for analysis and decision-making.

Variance and comparative analyses of financial performance using reliable industry norms can reveal opportunities to increase operational efficiency and profitability. Improved operating performance validates the asset management function, enhancing a property's market value and protecting the owner's equity interest in the investment.

Appendix:
Asset Management Value-Enhancing Questions

Rooms Division	*Asset Management Suggestions:*
• How many rooms do room attendants clean each day? (Industry standard is 14–16) • How much demand is generated from the national reservations system? • How much does the hotel spend on linen, towels, and in-room guest amenities on a POR basis? • What is the efficiency of the laundry operation? (85 lbs per hour is reasonable)	• Review labor productivity. Consider front-of-house cross-training, implementing incentive programs. • Review travel agent productivity: check pricing of rooms produced by travel agencies versus other distribution sources. • Consider revising amenities package and operating supplies to reduce costs (but not at the expense of guest experience or brand standard).
Food and Beverage Revenue and Expense	***Asset Management Suggestions:***
• What is the breakdown of outlet revenue vs. banquet and catering revenue? Catering tends to be more profitable than outlet revenues. • Is the hotel's banquet service charge at market price? • What is the catering and banquet revenue per occupied group room? • What is the food and beverage capture ratio by meal period? (i.e., how many of the in-house guests are eating meals at the hotel?) In general, breakfast has the highest capture ratio, with dinner the second highest, and lunch the lowest capture ratio. • Are the operation's food, beverage, and labor costs in line with the costs for similar operations in the local market?	• Evaluate pricing and menu mix at restaurants. • Determine catering goals for the sales staff, including group food and beverage requirements. • Brainstorm off-site catering opportunities. • Evaluate possibility of increasing audiovisual profitability by renegotiating the contract. • Evaluate opportunity to increase capture of food and beverage demand from local residents. • Use comparative analysis to check food, beverage, and labor cost percentages. • Evaluate ROI of live entertainment. • Ensure management is regularly bidding its food-and-beverage purchases. • Check pour control mechanisms, beverage mix, and policy on free drinks if beverage cost seems high. • Consider closing one outlet during slower meal periods to reduce labor hours. • Consider decreasing overall complexity or service level of menus and outlets to decrease kitchen labor cost.

Telephone Revenue and Expenses	*Asset Management Suggestions:*
• What is the long-distance mark up? • Who is the hotel's long distance provider and is there a cheaper, local alternative? • Is the hotel charging competitive rates for local, 800 number, and long-distance rates?	• Consider bundling Internet access fees and telephone calls to increase telephone utilization. • Consider "upselling" Internet access at check in. • Review the lease agreement for telephone access lines and consider purchasing access lines from provider.
Other Revenue	***Asset Management Suggestions:***
• What do competitors charge for overnight parking, health spa services, and exercise facility access? • Are guests charged for Internet access capabilities, fax service at the front desk, additional amenities, and mini-bar service at the subject? • What is the hotel's policy on cancellations?	• Consider selling parking to non-guests. • Determine whether the exercise facility is of a caliber that the hotel could solicit monthly memberships. • Study the possibility of an opportunity to lease space at the hotel to a third-party retail tenant.
Administrative and General	***Asset Management Suggestions:***
• Is there an opportunity to reduce management or administrative support positions? • What travel-related and training expenses are being charged to the hotel? • What corporate management charges are being allocated to the property for human resource or financial reporting services and how are they being allocated? • Is accounting done on-site or at corporate offices?	• Review departmental organizational chart to evaluate staffing and opportunity to reduce management or administrative support positions. • Review management agreement; make sure the hotel is receiving services for fees.
Sales and Marketing	***Asset Management Suggestions:***
• Is the current marketing plan consistent with the property's postion in the market? • How are corporate marketing/advertising fees and frequent guest charges fees calculated and allocated?	• Ensure that there are defined revenue goals for each employee in the sales department. • Review employees' salary vs. revenue goals. • Review franchise and management agreements for compliance.

Sales and Marketing *(cont.)* • How does the on-site staff work with the brand's national sales force to generate business? • What is the breakdown of sales department employee responsibility (i.e., are employees allocated by region/market segment? • How is in-house travel and entertainment calculated (i.e., is it zero-based?) and what control mechanisms are in place?	***Asset Management Suggestions:*** • Determine direct ROI of print, direct mail, and Internet advertising. • Determine the ROI of association membership and trade show attendance.
Property Operations and Maintenance • Does the hotel have a scheduled preventive maintenance system for all equipment and guestrooms? • Is aged equipment creating excessive labor or parts expense?	***Asset Management Suggestions:*** • Review all contracts for services and labor, including elevator and trash removal, and bid each contract out upon renewal. • Review preventive maintenance process, including communication with housekeeping.
Energy • Has the hotel taken advantage of energy deregulation? • Does the hotel have an energy management system (EMS)? If so, how effectively is it being used? • Is domestic hot water consistently at 115–120 degrees F?	***Asset Management Suggestions:*** • Consider completing an energy audit to determine opportunities to decrease cost. • Complete ROI analysis of installing an energy management system. • Ensure that the hotel solicits competitive bids for utilities.
Insurance • Does the hotel solicit competitive bids for insurance? Are deductibles reasonable? • What is the hotel's program for ensuring guest and employee safety and thereby reducing accidents? • How are replacement cost and deductibles determined? Do they conform to management contract requirements?	***Asset Management Suggestions:*** • Study reasonableness of increasing deductibles to reduce expense. • Solicit bids on general liability insurance and understand why premiums are at current levels. • Determine property's eligibility for premium discounts based on its management/franchise affiliation, or claims history.

Real Estate and Personal Property Taxes • What is the per-room building assessment of the hotel as compared to other hotels in the same municipality? • Is the assessment income-based? How has the hotel's income changed in recent years? • Does the hotel employ a tax consultant?	***Asset Management Suggestions:*** • Consider contesting the real estate tax assessment.
Management/Franchise Fee • Is the hotel being charged the proper base and incentive management fee? • What are the calculations for the hotel's royalty and other franchise fees?	***Asset Management Suggestions:*** • Review and discuss contracted fees; understand calculations for allocated management and franchise-related costs • Compare fees being charged to management and franchise agreements. Make sure hotel is receiving the negotiated services for the fees.
Labor • Is there an opportunity to cross-train in any of the hotel's departments? • Is there an opportunity to reduce supervisory, middle management staffing, or number of full-time employees per shift? • Are the hotel's employees unionized? • Are the salaries and wages of the hotel's employees competitively priced? • Do employees pay for meals?	***Asset Management Suggestions:*** • Obtain an organizational chart for the hotel. It should include all management positions by department. • Consider replacing overtime hours with contracted labor

Source: hotelAVE, LLC, Tiverton, RI.

10

The Hotel Investment Decision: Buy, Hold, and Sell Analyses

By Craig A. Mason and Richard E. Musgrove

__Craig A. Mason, CHA, CPM,__ is Senior Vice President of Asset Management for Host Marriott Corporation's full-service hotel portfolio. Mr. Mason directly oversees the asset management function for a portfolio of hotels that includes the New York Marriott Marquis, the Orlando World Center Marriott, and the Naples Ritz-Carlton Resort. Before joining Host Marriott, he served as Senior Vice President of the Carey Winston Company, a full-service commercial real estate firm, where he represented numerous institutional clients in the investment, management, and leasing of commercial office and retail properties. He also served as Vice President of Asset Management at The Balcor Company, a real estate subsidiary of American Express Company.

Mr. Mason earned his bachelor of science degree from the School of Hotel Administration at Cornell University. He also holds a master of management degree from the Kellogg Graduate School of Management at Northwestern University. He is a member of the Cornell Hotel Society, the Hospitality Asset Managers Association, and the Institute of Real Estate Management, through which he has attained the Certified Property Manager® designation. He also holds the Certified Hotel Administrator designation from the Educational Institute of the American Hotel & Lodging Association, the Commercial Investment Real Estate Member designation from the CCIM Institute, and the Real Property Administrator designation from the BOMI Institute.

__Richard E. Musgrove, CHA, CPM__ is Vice President of Asset Management for Host Marriott Corporation, with responsibility for a 15-property portfolio comprising more than 5,600 hotel rooms and 210,000 square feet of office space. His portfolio includes Ritz-Carlton hotels, a Swissôtel, full-service Marriott hotels, and class A office projects. Before joining Host Marriott, he served as Senior Asset Manager for the estate of James Campbell, a private real estate trust, where he directed the management and leasing of a $200 million commercial portfolio. He has also served as Financial Manager at The Trammell Crow Company and has an extensive background in the hospitality industry, working in front office, marketing, and food and beverage positions.

Mr. Musgrove earned a bachelor of science degree from Cornell University's School of Hotel Administration and an MBA with a concentration in finance from the University of Chicago's Graduate School of Business. He is a member of the Hospitality Asset Managers Association and the Institute of Real Estate Management, through which he has attained the Certified Property Manager® designation. He has also received the Certified Hotel Administrator designation from the Educational Institute of the AH&LA, the Commercial Investment Real Estate Member designation from the CCIM Institute, and the Real Property Administrator designation from the BOMI Institute. Mr. Musgrove is a member of the Cornell Hotel Society and an institute affiliate of the Greater Washington Commercial Association of Realtors®.

As a freshly minted MBA from a "top-ten" business school, Lou was excited about his new position in asset management with ZZL Realty Corporation. With an undergraduate degree in accounting and several years of solid audit experience, he was confident his background was particularly well suited to the financial orientation of his new post. When his initial portfolio assignment included a 400-room upper-upscale hotel on Michigan Avenue in downtown Chicago, he was overjoyed. Egyptian cotton sheets and gourmet cuisine—what a great assignment this would be!

At his first anniversary on the job, Lou was rethinking his initial assessment. The hotel's performance had deteriorated dramatically. The engineering department had unionized, and management was concerned that the rest of the staff was not far behind. As the economy softened, transient room-nights had declined sharply, as had cover counts at both restaurants. House profit had dropped from 37 percent to below 35 percent, reducing net cash flow to ownership by nearly one quarter. With two new full-service hotels under construction in the market, Lou feared that things would get much worse before they started getting better. Reluctantly, he convinced the senior management of ZZL to put his prize asset on the block. Within three months, the hotel was purchased by White Rock Partners for $60 million, and Lou was relieved ZZL had found a "greater fool."

Two years later, while skimming a trade periodical, Lou read that White Rock had sold his former property to Urban Life Insurance Company for $90 million. Lou was floored. How could he have been so far off-base? He had been through the numbers backwards and forwards. What did White Rock know that he had not?

As he dug further into the article, Lou read that White Rock had invested $10 million to convert the specialty restaurant into a junior ballroom, a move that improved the property's ability to increase its group base while eliminating a marginally profitable food-and-beverage outlet. The investment had improved the meeting-space-to-guest-room ratio enough that White Rock had been able to negotiate a new franchise agreement, significantly improving distribution. In short, White Rock had not based its purchase decision on what the hotel was; it had identified beforehand what the asset could and should become.

AVOIDING LOU'S EARLY-CAREER GAFFE is not a matter of luck or clairvoyance, but careful analysis. This chapter will discuss the investment-decision process for hotel owners. Although the universe of factors to consider in evaluating the purchase, redevelopment, repositioning, and sale of lodging assets could fill many volumes, the following pages will establish the basic framework for thoughtful evaluation.

The Hotel Acquisition Decision

Investors in real estate are motivated by a variety of factors. The benefits of owning hotel assets may include one, some, or all of the following:

- Positive cash flow from operations
- Deferred taxation, providing enhanced cash flow
- Hedge against inflation
- Appreciation in property value
- Diversification from other investments offering different risk profiles
- Ability to apply positive financial leverage, enhancing equity returns
- Psychological benefits (e.g., pride in owning a distinctive physical asset)

The first step in making any investment decision is establishing goals and objectives for that investment. In the case of hotel investments, determining the most appropriate path to ownership—developing new hotels, acquiring existing hotels of various performance profiles (e.g., stabilized, under-performing, repositioning candidates), or converting buildings from other uses—is merely one element an investor must contemplate. Other considerations include hotel type, size, cost, and location. Above all, the required return and anticipated hold period for the investment must be established at the outset.

Once an investor has addressed these issues, an exit strategy should also be constructed. For a long-term investor whose emphasis is on the cash throw-off from a lodging property, valuations at appropriate intervals may be prudent to ensure that returns are on target. For shorter-term investments, where the emphasis is on property appreciation, selling the asset at the targeted price is critical to generating the desired return. Faced with a narrower window of opportunity and greater variability in potential returns, investors with shorter intended holding periods must recognize that their exit strategy is as important as their entry strategy. Maintaining a disciplined investment strategy is the key to meeting acquisition goals and objectives. To this end, the critical (and invariably linked) factors—selecting the appropriate holding period and identifying viable acquirers—must be carefully studied and definitively established before the acquisition trigger is pulled.

An example of the goals and objectives for a hotel investor might be the following set:

- Acquire domestic luxury and upscale full-service hotels of over 300 rooms in growth markets with high barriers to entry.
- Targeted hotels must be located in one of the top 30 Metropolitan Statistical Areas (MSAs) having a hotel supply of at least 5,000 rooms.
- Hotel acquisition price should be at or below replacement cost, and the investment must provide ownership an internal rate of return (IRR) in excess of 14 percent, assuming no leverage and a 10-year investment horizon.

- Hotels to be targeted must have the potential for removal of existing management contract and franchise agreements.

Acquisition Due Diligence

Once the investment criteria and the broad parameters of the target markets sought are established, a number of steps must be undertaken before the transaction is completed. These steps, which concentrate on the investment decision, are necessary if a successful transaction is to be completed. They are:

- Identify hotel acquisition criteria and preferred markets.
- Develop a list of potential targets, either through primary research in a market or through the use of intermediaries such as brokers and the asset manager's network of lodging-industry contacts.
- Based on acquisition criteria, screen potential candidates and select target assets.
- Conduct a preliminary site visit to establish parameters for creating the framework for a strategic plan.
- Develop pricing for the asset.
- Develop a letter of intent that formulates the fundamentals of the transaction.
- Perform detailed market feasibility analysis and property due diligence.
- Reassess whether the deal still fits the investment criteria.
- Negotiate final terms and close the transaction.

The key to a successful investment is having realistic goals and objectives. Once the investment criteria are established, detailed research of potential acquisitions will ensure that new assets fit the corporate strategy. The property analysis is accomplished through a comprehensive due-diligence process that identifies the many investment risks and opportunities before the transaction closes. An acquisition team of experts (either internal or third-party representatives) should be assembled to carry out the research and negotiations. This team should include an acquisitions officer, a feasibility expert, an asset manager, accounting support, tax and insurance support, legal support, design and architecture support, engineering support, and potentially a broker and representatives from a prospective management company. A series of checklists showing the various tasks to be accomplished and the assignments of key participants in the due-diligence process appears in the appendix to this chapter.

The primary function of the due-diligence process is to conduct a complete investigation of any factors that may influence the return on investment and value of the asset. Those factors will include market considerations, product evaluation, risks-and-opportunities assessments, contractual considerations, and a financial review.

As investors set goals and objectives for their lodging investments, they need to recognize that defining their strategy necessarily creates limitations on the available assets that meet their criteria. For example, the criterion that prospective acquisitions must be located in the top 30 MSAs will eliminate many hotel investment opportunities, but honoring the constraint will simultaneously enable the investor to more quickly identify potential acquisition targets. Again, maintaining a disciplined approach is key. In this instance, an asset that satisfies the top-30-MSA requirement carries the benefit of more restrictive barriers to entry (e.g., less available buildable land) and improved liquidity in a disposition because a larger pool of prospective buyers yields more efficient market pricing.

Evaluate Market Considerations

Regardless of investment criteria, the first step in an acquisition decision is analyzing the potential upside for a market, which is based on the supply of and demand for lodging products. The possible overall market characteristics that may yield opportunities for hotel acquisitions include:

- Demand growth rates that are expected to exceed regional or national averages.
- Existing restrictions on supply growth.
- Costs of new development that exceed market valuations for similar existing supply.
- A wide base of economic activity (e.g., finance, technology, defense, medical, etc.), thus limiting the impact of upturns and downturns in any one sector and reducing demand volatility.
- Assuming there is an expectation of recovery, bottoming demand cycles that may offer significant upside if the acquirer buys into a depressed market.

Assessing Market-Wide Hotel Supply and Demand. Evaluating historical and future supply and demand growth is critical in determining the prospects of any potential acquisition. It is also extremely important to understand the equilibrium or disequilibrium of the supply-demand relationship in the market to predict reliably the upside potential for an acquisition candidate.

The evaluation of market trends should begin with a review of historical market-wide supply and demand statistics. Smith Travel Research (STR) is the standard data source underpinning this more global analysis. STR provides useful data for a selected geographic market—supply (total available room nights), demand (total room nights sold), and hotel room pricing as expressed by a market-wide average daily rate, or ADR (total room sales divided by total room nights sold). Studying the historical trends and seasonal patterns of occupancy and ADR will help an investor better understand how a market reacts to excess supply or tight supply. RevPAR, or revenue-per-available-room, statistics (occupancy percentage times ADR) provide a smoother trend line that tracks overall rooms revenues in the market.

It is important to first understand the dynamics of the larger market before drilling down to the various segments. A more detailed analysis that focuses on the subsets within the market will reveal opportunities and challenges (e.g., continued growth in demand or stalled growth due to new supply) in individual segments. When dissecting a market, one can also look for segments that are underserved to identify opportunities for investment.

Determining the Competitive Set. The first step in analyzing the supply component of a market is to establish the acquisition target's competitive set. Identifying the hotels that compete directly with the target hotel will help clarify the asset's potential upside. If a property is performing below its fair share in occupancy or rate, the acquisition team can then evaluate the property's location, physical attributes, brand affiliation, and management team to determine if adjustments are appropriate to improve the subject hotel's competitive position.

To evaluate the property's relative performance, a detailed competitive analysis is an absolute necessity. Once completed, the competitive analysis also serves as a basis for formulating a business plan to achieve investment goals. A thorough SWOT (strengths, weaknesses, opportunities, and threats) analysis should be completed for each competitor, including a property-by-property evaluation of market penetration for each demand segment. The metrics of the SWOT analysis should include service quality, physical-plant quality, scope of amenities, brand affiliation, management company strength, ownership strength, rate structure by segment, mix of business, and occupancy patterns on both a weekday versus weekend and seasonal basis. The analysis reveals competitor hotels' principal sources of demand and the key property characteristics that drive their respective success. If one competitor is dominating the market, can the target property exploit weaknesses or mitigate particular strengths by making changes? Without this information, it will be difficult to create a business strategy that will position the acquisition target against the competition effectively.

As part of the competitive analysis, future competition must be evaluated. Considerations include new properties entering the market, as well as hotels that are potentially changing their competitive positioning by upgrading, renovating, or expanding their properties (e.g., adding a ballroom, signature restaurant, spa, or new room tower) or changing affiliations by selecting a new management company or franchisor.

Analyzing Market Dynamics of Demand Sources. After thoroughly evaluating the changes in supply that might affect the market and the acquisition candidate, potential buyers must consider the demand component by studying the market dynamics of demand sources. A demand analysis might consist of a study of the local economy for a transient market or a review of feeder markets for a destination market. It is important to review the historical growth of demand in the market as a first step. But to estimate effectively the future demand, the analyst must also look at growth in various sectors of the local economy to evaluate the correlation between those indicators and changes in lodging demand. Some of the demographic and other statistics to study include:

- Population growth and characteristics.
- Household income growth.
- Employment growth.

- Office building supply and demand growth.
- Airport passenger traffic statistics.
- Convention center growth (e.g., meetings, city-wide conferences and conventions, future expansion plans for the existing facility, etc.).
- Area attractions' growth (parks, museums, sports teams, festivals).
- Retail sales statistics.
- Highway and rail traffic statistics.

To evaluate market demand further, potential buyers must understand the diversity within the marketplace. Is the economy driven by manufacturing or by financial services? Since certain industries generally create more lodging demand than others, it is imperative to understand workforce characteristics and future prospects for various segments of the market. Understanding this relationship will help determine the level of risk for an investment. For example, a hotel that is located in a high tech corridor may have experienced substantial growth during the technology boom, but the lack of diversification in the economic base means greater volatility in demand. The fortunes of a property in a sector-dependent market follow a feast-or-famine cycle compared to a hotel located in a market that enjoys broadly diversified demand.

When evaluating potential demand in the marketplace, feasibility experts will also evaluate two other types of demand—*unaccommodated demand* resulting from a lack of supply or product type and *induced demand*, which may be generated by a new area attraction, an expanded convention center, aggressive marketing, or new brand representation in the market.

Determining Future Demand. After the data influencing the demand for each broad lodging segment—business, leisure, and group—are collected, they are used to forecast future demand for hotel room nights. For example, if the convention center is expected to book ten percent more business over the next three years, it is probably safe to assume that group business in the market will increase (although the analyst should also evaluate the extent of the market's dependency on the convention center to generate group business). Similarly, projected growth in theme parks and other area attractions would be a reliable indicator of future leisure demand. It should be noted that the forecasting of both supply and demand becomes less accurate as the projection horizon increases, since many other influences outside of the market area, such as the state of overall economy, can affect its future prospects.

Projecting Performance. After a thorough supply and demand analysis has been completed for the market, prospective buyers can evaluate the acquisition candidate's potential performance by applying historical penetration rates to future projections of market-wide occupancy. Typically, ADR levels track closely the supply and demand relationship and inflation. While not a hard-and-fast rule, when supply growth exceeds demand growth, ADR growth will generally be less than inflation; when supply growth is equal to demand growth, increases in ADRs will more or less coincide with inflation rates; and when demand growth exceeds supply growth, ADR increases can be expected to exceed inflation.

Current occupancy levels in the market can be a good indicator of future growth potential. For example, a market with 53-percent market-wide occupancy may experience stronger demand growth than supply growth yet achieve only minimal gains in ADR. Conversely, a market enjoying an occupancy rate in the high-80-percent range may be able to sustain growth in ADR greater than the inflation rate, despite supply increases in excess of the growth in demand. In evaluating future ADR growth, buyers must investigate the specific market segments a hotel is competing in and determine if supply constraints will allow aggressive pricing. Once expectations for the overall market are formulated, the acquisition target's rate potential can be estimated based on its competitive positioning as measured by such factors as its physical plant, brand affiliation, management strength, etc. Proposed changes to these attributes will influence the forecasted penetration and yield assumed in the financial underwriting of the investment.

Evaluate the Lodging Asset

Once the acquisition target has been identified and research confirms the market in which it is located meets the investment criteria, the hotel asset must be evaluated to determine its current value, opportunities, and investment risks. This analysis will lead to developing a price to be included in a letter of intent to purchase.

Location and Site Characteristics. The first step in understanding the hotel product requires an evaluation of the property's location relative to major demand generators, its visibility and accessibility, and other physical site characteristics. "Location, location, location" is a familiar real estate mantra, with good reason. Location is the primary determinant of success in any real estate investment. Hotels whose locations provide a significant advantage over similar products in the market will often outperform their competition.

Other characteristics of a hotel site should be compared to the same advantages or disadvantages of competitive properties in the market. For example, ease of ingress and egress and other traffic patterns are important factors to consider. If the visibility of the product is poor, would added signage (provided this is permitted by local zoning regulations) improve the situation? Are there changes to the neighborhood that will affect future demand? An effective way to evaluate a site is to compile a map that displays the location of supply, both existing and proposed, and major demand generators. The map provides a visual explanation of how the acquisition target's location compares to the locations of other hotels in the market and may indicate new demand sources for the hotel.

Regulatory and Legal Restrictions. Another aspect of site evaluation is a thorough review of regulatory and legal restrictions, including height restrictions, setback requirements, zoning requirements (including grandfather clauses), land-use restrictions (imposed by ground leases, the Federal Aviation Administration, covenants, conditions, and restrictions [CC&Rs] contained in deeds, etc.), permit and licensing requirements, parking requirements, and floor area ratio (FAR) utilization. Is the property fee simple or subject to a ground lease? If the property is subject to a ground lease, what are the rights and responsibilities of the lessee with respect to maintenance, change of use, and additions or deletions to the property? Are any public works programs planned that may cause a condemnation of part of the property or potentially change the traffic patterns to or from the property? A comprehensive legal and regulatory review of the site should be performed to include a complete analysis of the above-mentioned items, as well as any deed restrictions, permit or code violations, air rights, easements, flood plain location, title search, and any planned changes in zoning or land use for the neighborhood. These questions are critical to understanding the potential value of any real estate asset.

Neighborhood Characteristics. Along with the site analysis, an investor must fully understand the subject property's neighborhood characteristics. Potential purchasers should understand the land uses of all properties located adjacent to or in proximity to the subject property. The details to unearth as part of this analysis include the occupancy of nearby buildings and the likely duration of tenancy, the size and condition of the buildings, proposed changes to their use or structure, and the availability of vacant land for future development. An understanding is also necessary of the history of the neighborhood, potential changes in land use, the age of buildings and their image in the community, crime rates, trends in real estate pricing, and the economic and demographic profile of residents of the neighborhood or those who patronize the businesses in the neighborhood. The analyst must develop a sense of the trends affecting the neighborhood and the likely consequences for the subject property. Is the neighborhood growing and becoming more affluent, or is it beginning to decline? How does the neighborhood influence the demand for the hotel? Are there nearby restaurants and tourist attractions that serve as demand generators? Do transportation systems facilitate access to the hotel? An understanding of all the characteristics of the neighborhood is necessary to evaluate fully the risks and opportunities the investment presents.

Physical Plant. The evaluation of the subject property's physical plant is often a critical juncture in the analytical process, determining whether the prospective purchaser goes forward with the acquisition or moves on to other opportunities. The first area that must be reviewed is the environmental condition of the site and improvements. A licensed environmental engineer should perform a complete audit, thoroughly reviewing the property's history as well as its current condition. This investigation typically includes testing for the presence of asbestos, PCBs (polychlorinated biphenyls), mold, or other substances affecting indoor air quality, as well as the existence of dry cleaning facilities and underground storage tanks (USTs). If any of these issues affect the property, an operations and maintenance plan must be in place and employees must be certified to work with the applicable hazardous materials. If USTs have been removed, related concerns, such as spills on the site and resulting contamination, must be identified and their impact evaluated. A soil test should also be performed as part of the due-diligence process.

Evaluation of the hotel's physical plant starts with a complete inventory of the property's facilities, including an evaluation of the age, condition, and other characteristics of the following features:

- *Parking*—stand-alone or attached structure, surface, excess capacity, paid or free parking for guests, valet services, operator (managed, leased, or in-house)
- *Lobby*—layout, traffic flow, security
- *Guestrooms*—number, size, bathroom layout and number of fixtures, mix of suites, kings, double-doubles, amenities, style, balconies, HVAC (heating, ventilation, air conditioning) system
- *Food and beverage facilities*—description of each outlet, including style, décor, number of seats, hours of operation, managed or leased, pricing
- *Meeting space*—total square footage, pre-function space, number and types of rooms, largest venue, flexibility of space, outdoor venues, technology in meeting rooms, ratio of meeting space to room count, and comparison to market
- *Amenities*—retail services and management (third-party, in-house, or leased); transportation services; description of other possible services offered and their size or extent, including swimming pool(s), health club, spa, beach facilities, children's centers, game rooms, business centers, concièrge services, concièrge lounges, golf courses, marinas, stables, etc.
- *Building design*—style, functionality, materials, fit with surrounding land use, "curb appeal"
- *Handicap accessibility*—compliance/non-compliance with federal Americans with Disabilities Act (ADA) and state and local requirements for handicap accessibility and accommodations
- *Systems*—façade, roof, HVAC systems, plumbing systems, electrical systems, fire- and life-safety systems, kitchen and banquet equipment and facilities, structural systems, grounds/landscaping materials

The property review should be conducted by many members of the acquisition team, including the acquisition officer, asset manager, architect, interior designer, engineers, feasibility analyst, and one or more representatives of the prospective property management company. Each member should observe the condition of the property, identifying any physical deficiencies and functional or economic obsolescence. This evaluation, along with myriad other inputs, contributes to the due-diligence report assessing the opportunities and risks associated with the prospective investment.

Identify Upside Potential

When evaluating the upside potential for an asset, prospective buyers should start with a thorough financial and operational review. This review should include a detailed analysis of historical operating statements to reveal operational patterns and recent trends, as well as a comparison with comparable properties to uncover areas where the hotel is underperforming. When comparing the subject hotel to comparable properties, the broad metrics helpful in identifying potential opportunities are departmental margins and sales and costs per occupied room (POR) and per available room (PAR). Other factors that affect upside potential include the physical layout of the facilities; the current local labor market; the condition of the asset; and its location, brand, and management team capabilities.

Some of the areas where the asset manager may identify upside opportunities include:

- An *operations audit* that identifies departmental efficiencies and opportunities, such as:
  - Staffing levels and services offered by each department in comparison to competitors.
  - Potential consolidation of management with a sister property.
  - Food-and-beverage margins, menu engineering changes, hours of operation, and closure or repositioning of outlets.
  - Procurement—energy, food and beverage, and other supplies.
  - Leases—at market rates? Opportunities to renegotiate or outsource?
  - Service-contract renegotiations.
  - Warranty enforcement.
  - Inventory adjustments.
  - New revenue potential—parking, new retail shops, and off-site catering.
  - Appropriate room mix? Is there opportunity for increasing key count or adding premium rooms?
  - Guest satisfaction surveys to help identify product and service deficiencies.
- A *sales audit* that evaluates opportunities regarding:
  - Product positioning.
  - Sales strategy and implementation.
  - Effectiveness of the sales team in light of product attributes (physical plant, service, brand, location) in comparison to competitors.
  - Future booked business and rate structure.
  - Corporate and travel company discounts.
  - Transient, group, and leisure focus and strategy.
  - Availability of meeting space appropriate to market positioning.
  - Meeting planner satisfaction surveys to help identify product and service deficiencies.
- A *labor audit* that includes:
  - An evaluation of wage schedules by department and a comparison to wage surveys in the local market.
  - A benefits survey.
  - A turnover history.

  - A union activity or contract review.
  - Opportunities to consolidate positions.
  - Opportunities to cross-train for positions.
  - Opportunities to outsource or benefit from internal transfers.
  - Productivity measures.
  - Employee satisfaction surveys
- A *systems audit* that includes:
  - An inventory of appropriate computer systems available to achieve staffing efficiencies.
  - An energy audit to identify retrofits that are available to reduce costs and improve investment returns.
  - A building systems repairs-and-maintenance audit to determine if any individual system is absorbing an inordinate proportion of the property operations and maintenance budget.

Asset managers must also look for opportunities to add revenue-producing space, such as additional guestrooms or meeting facilities. Opportunities might include adding a restaurant, retail pad, or condominium tower on the site, or converting an existing use to another that generates more cash flow. Examples of the latter might include converting a restaurant to meeting space, converting a gift shop to a board room, or merely improving the flexibility of an existing space, which might be accomplished by changing the air-wall system in meeting space or transforming restaurant space into private dining rooms that double as small meeting rooms.

There may be an opportunity to reposition the asset by upgrading the guest rooms and other facilities to gain greater market share or target a more lucrative segment of the market. This level of investment must be in line with the market potential and be supported by a thorough competitive and demand analysis. It is quite easy to over invest in a property with the expectation that a superior product will drive ADR. Since expectations do not always materialize, it is imperative to understand the true potential of the market.

A combination of operational changes and capital improvements may yield a return on investment greater than the targeted return for the acquisition, thus enhancing the overall investment return. This in turn could justify paying a price for the asset in excess of a price based solely on historical operating performance.

Identify Downside Risks

Potential downside risks must be identified to evaluate accurately a property's current value and future growth potential. With planned dispositions, it is not uncommon for owners to cut operating costs to improve cash flow and justify a higher asking price. Operationally, these cuts might include:

- Reducing staffing to levels below the brand standard, likely resulting in poor guest-service scores. Low staffing levels may also lead to employee dissatisfaction, potentially motivating employees to organize in order to be heard by management.

- Offering wage scales significantly below market, which also gives rise to employee dissatisfaction and turnover.
- Cutting supervision and training of employees, which may increase turnover costs and increase employee dissatisfaction.
- Reducing inventory levels of food and beverage, laundry, and other operating supplies. Adequate inventory levels may need to be restored on acquisition, adding to costs. However, depleted inventories may also be identified as an opportunity for longer-term cost containment if inadequate inventories are affecting operating efficiencies at the property.
- Reducing levels of maintenance and eliminating service contracts, thus shortening asset lifecycles and increasing future expenditures for furniture, fixtures, equipment, and other capital items.
- A poor sales effort as the sales team learns a property will be traded. A good indicator of this possibility is a weak booking-pace report.
- Reducing insurance coverage.
- Failing to pay appropriate occupancy and use taxes.

As regards the physical aspects of the property, risks should be identified by the due-diligence team. Some of the areas requiring specific attention include:

- Evaluating the fire- and life-safety systems for code compliance and remaining useful lives.
- Determining any existing building code or zoning violations.
- Assessing the quality of the guest environment—guestrooms, food and beverage facilities, meeting space, lobby and other public areas.
- Evaluating the building envelope—condition and appearance of façade and roof, etc.
- Evaluating the condition of HVAC equipment and adequacy to heat and cool the building
- Evaluating the vertical transportation system's condition and adequacy to meet guest needs.
- Inspecting the grounds and site.

Each risk identified should be quantified to the extent possible and included in the investment analysis. Qualitative, less tangible risks, such as guest rooms smaller than competitors', can be identified and factored into the analysis when determining the appropriate growth rate for the property's RevPAR. The identification of all possible risks arms the asset manager for the give-and-take of negotiations and is beneficial in arriving at a favorable final price for the hotel. Moreover, understanding the property's operational and physical-plant opportunities and risks leads to the development of a comprehensive asset strategy that fully unlocks the value of the real estate.

Evaluate Contractual and Legal Obligations

Numerous legal documents must be reviewed before potential buyers can properly forecast the operating results of a hotel investment. Each contract should undergo a legal review, with an abstract prepared for the acquisition team. The asset manager should also read all legal documents to understand fully the rights and obligations of the property ownership group. A list of some of the essential documents and clauses to review when preparing the underwriting analysis includes:

- A *management agreement* covering base management fees, incentive management fees, approval rights, termination and default provisions, property improvement plan (PIP) requirements on sale, trade-area restrictions, capital expenditure requirements, priority returns to ownership on additional invested capital, sales, marketing, and reservation fees, employee relocation fees, employee dismissal rights, chain services fees and caps, loyalty programs, procurement requirements, and brand standards.
- A *franchise agreement* covering fees, loyalty programs, procurement requirements, and brand standards.
- *Ground leases* covering control provisions; lease term; renewal options; cost; approval rights on property changes of use, appearance, or expansion; maintenance clauses; and other restrictions.
- *Labor contracts* covering renewal term, escalation clauses, dispute resolutions, and termination of employees.
- *Other leases and maintenance contracts* describing term, costs, and termination rights.
- Any *pending litigation.*

Understanding these documents and accurately reflecting the terms of these agreements in the financial analysis are critical steps in determining the value of the asset. Contracts that can be renegotiated or terminated should be reflected in the acquisition pro forma by using the market terms that the acquisition team believes it can negotiate in the future. Assumptions should include the timing of the implementation of the new terms as well as any other costs that may result from entering a new contract. For example, if a management contract with a major brand is terminable and a new brand is to be introduced to the property, all costs of the conversion and remarketing of the asset should be included in the analysis. Assumptions may also include the loss of revenue when some or all of the property's services are unavailable during a renovation.

Evaluate Financial Information

As suggested in our discussion of techniques for identifying upside potential, a thorough review of the property's financial statements must be undertaken. This financial analysis is a critical aspect of the due-diligence process and should include a complete independent audit of the operating statements and balance sheets for the property. While a seller may offer audited statements, it is up to the buyer to understand fully the quality of the financial information presented. The buyer can further protect himself by requiring the seller to provide appropriate representations and warranties in the purchase and sales contract. A summary of the documents and areas to investigate as part of a thorough financial review includes:

- A *profit and loss statement*—review historical operating statements, including trend analysis; current operating statements, including variance analysis comparing actual to budget; and future year forecasts or pro forma budgets.
- A *balance sheet*—review of all assets and liabilities.
- A statement of *working capital*—develop a history to determine if current management has maintained too much or too little working capital to operate the hotel effectively.
- *Accounts receivable*—review aging of existing receivables; determine party (buyer or seller) responsible for collection.
- *Accounts payable*: determine history and timeliness of payments to vendors; determine if any litigation or contract disputes are outstanding; investigate if overpayments have occurred.
- A statement of *capital expenditures and escrow status*—review thoroughly the history of expenditures for the property to determine if repairs and maintenance (R&M) expenses are being paid from the escrow fund or, conversely, if capital items are being expensed to the R&M category; evaluate the adequacy of the escrow account to fund future projects, determining if additional owner's capital is required above current escrow contributions from the operating cash flow.
- *Property tax and insurance report*—employ property-tax and insurance specialists to evaluate the impact the sale will have on future costs, including changes in insurance coverage if they will differ from the previous owner's requirements.
- *Capital-structure evaluation*—review various considerations if creating a new capital structure or adjusting the existing capital structure, including target debt-to-equity ratio, cross-collateralized assets, lender requirements and covenants, terms of existing debt (assumable? above or below market rates?), etc.

Pulling the Acquisition Trigger

Once all of the areas identified in the preceding sections have been evaluated, it is time for the acquisition team to develop an acquisition pro forma, a capital expenditure plan, and an appropriate asset strategy so that the investment valuation can be determined. This valuation should include the costs of any property improvement plan (PIP) required by the franchisor or management company and should specify the desired exit strategy. Depending on their attendant risks, the valuation may or may not quantify the value of opportunities identified in the due-diligence process. Including some opportunities that appear readily achievable may be appropriate if there is a strong level of interest from other potential buyers. If the acquisition pro forma indicates a value greater than the asking price of the seller, then the buyer is expecting returns from the investment to exceed his investment underwriting criteria. If the asking price exceeds the valuation, the acquisition team should either try to negotiate a reduced price or abandon the potential acquisition.

A potential buyer's determination to make the acquisition will sometimes affect how strictly that buyer adheres to previously defined underwriting criteria. Investors must be careful not to "push the envelope" when the acquisition valuation falls below the asking price. Absent a strong financial basis for making the investment at the asking price, acquisition teams may justify the purchase by resorting to a non-financial rationale, such as arguing the purchase is appropriate as a strategic move, or by adjusting the pro forma to reflect more potential upside in the investment. These instances should be rare, however, if a buyer is intellectually honest in the acquisition due-diligence process.

The Hold-Versus-Sell Decision

As with the initial purchase decision, the critical first step for an asset manager evaluating the options for an existing property is to understand ownership's goals and objectives thoroughly. Strategic plans evolve over time, and the prudent asset manager should not assume that the original investment criteria remain valid. Key factors affecting owners' objectives may include the holding entity's structure, the targeted "sunset" time frame (for trust investments), capital structure, capital availability, risk tolerance, and investment-product preferences. To the extent any of these factors or others have changed since the time of acquisition, reevaluation of the investment plan is appropriate and necessary.

The "As-Is" Scenario

Upon confirmation of ownership's goals and objectives, the next task in the investment-decision process is to develop an "as-is" scenario. The as-is scenario will serve as the base case against which other options are measured. It may also be a proxy for market value, establishing for ownership the property's potential disposition proceeds. In developing an as-is valuation, asset managers must first determine if maintaining the status quo is even an option. In many cases, a hotel will require some amount of remedial investment to stabilize performance. In developing a valuation for useful comparison to alternative strategies, the as-is analysis should factor in any capital required to address the property's deferred maintenance needs.

Redevelopment Scenarios

After the as-is scenario has been explored and an appropriate baseline valuation established, the next step is to consider potential redevelopment scenarios.

Redevelopment opportunities can be divided into two general classifications: (1) complete or "ground-up" redevelopment and (2) partial redevelopment or adaptive reuse. The primary difference between the two is the extent of preservation of existing improvements. Although complete redevelopment tends to require greater investment, this is not always the case; conversion or expansion of an older facility can be extremely costly. Regardless of the scenario, however, the redevelopment process starts with the most basic real estate question: "What is the highest and best use of the property?"

Market Potential. To determine highest and best use, the first element to be considered is the long-term market potential of the location. A good indicator of market potential is recent real estate development and transaction activity in the area. For example, if office projects are sprouting up around the subject property, hotel and office are likely to be attractive future uses for the subject asset. Another important source of information is demographic data for the subject property's locale. A scenario of heavy population growth, accompanied by few new jobs in the area, may indicate that residential or retail use is most appropriate. A significant increase in the median age of the local population could signal opportunity for conversion to a senior living facility. Typically, evaluation of overall market conditions will reveal several potential uses for the site and existing improvements.

Physical Aspects. A second element to consider in evaluating the subject property's highest and best use is the physical aspects of the site and any improvements. Unusual topographical features, natural barriers to ingress and egress, and geotechnical conditions are examples of physical attributes of land that could influence redevelopment alternatives. Floor-plate size, ceiling heights, bay dimensions, structural design, and mechanical-plant design can similarly affect the practical or economic feasibility of reuse alternatives for existing facilities.

Entitlement Issues. A third element to consider in analyzing redevelopment options is the entitlement environment. The entitlement environment includes all of the statutory, regulatory, and private guidelines that govern or restrict land use, the most significant of which is zoning. Zoning ordinances will typically specify the allowed uses for a site, as well as maximum height, acceptable site density as determined by floor area ratios (FARs), minimum setbacks, acceptable signage, and other criteria. Zoning regulations alone may dictate the highest and best use for a property, especially because the flexibility to obtain variances or modify existing zoning requirements varies widely by jurisdiction.

Other factors that may affect redevelopment feasibility and property use are building codes, easements, shoreline or special-use-area restrictions, and private covenants, conditions and restrictions (CC&Rs) that may run with the land. Due to the wide array of possible factors, it is generally advisable to engage legal counsel to assess the entitlement environment fully.

Contractual Obligations. A fourth element to consider in evaluating redevelopment alternatives is the existence of contractual obligations. If the property is subject to a ground lease rather than being held as a fee simple interest, a change of use may be precluded outright. If a change is not directly prohibited, onerous conversion provisions or a short remaining lease term could render any significant change or incremental investment economically infeasible.

Similar issues arise when management contracts and franchise agreements are in place. While most contracts are terminable at some cost, if the remaining term of an agreement is lengthy, termination may be prohibitively expensive. Other contracts that could affect the economics of redevelopment or reuse include space leases, concession agreements, rooftop leases or license agreements, service contracts, equipment leases, and advance booking contracts.

Capital Structure and Availability. A final element to consider in evaluating redevelopment alternatives is capital structure and availability. The ability to pursue alternative directions for properties is often dependent on debt covenants in place under existing financing. Joint venture or partnership agreements can similarly constrain options. Even if the existing capital or entity structure is not an impediment to redeveloping an asset, a lack of available investment capital may pose an insurmountable obstacle.

When all of the potentially feasible redevelopment and reuse alternatives have been identified, the various scenarios must be quantified for comparison to the as-is scenario. It may be desirable to use varying discount rates and exit capitalization rates to adjust for the relative complexity and inherent risks of the various scenarios. Even though analyzing the array of opportunities for redevelopment is appropriate, complete redevelopment of income-producing assets is typically very difficult to justify when the analysis is based purely on pecuniary factors—i.e., the "numbers." Strategic factors or other non-financial rationales generally figure in the decision to redevelop.

As with acquisition decisions, major redevelopment should entail a comprehensive investment plan and exit strategy consistent with ownership's underlying goals and objectives.

Repositioning Scenarios

Once the as-is and feasible-redevelopment scenarios have been developed and quantified, the next step in the owner's investment decision process is to identify any potential repositioning scenarios.

At this juncture, a point of clarification is necessary. Although the term "repositioning" is sometimes used to refer to all capital-improvement programs, in the authors' view such usage is incorrect. Repositioning implies a significant change in marketing direction. While such change usually is accompanied by significant capital investment, it need not be. Capital investment without a change in marketing strategy is simply renovation, the costs of which should be incorporated into the as-is scenario for purposes of analysis.

SWOT Analysis. To identify desirable repositioning alternatives, it is first necessary to perform a SWOT analysis to establish the existing property's strengths, weaknesses, opportunities, and threats. The primary focus in this effort should be on identifying the weaknesses and opportunities of the hotel and potential solutions to address them. For example, poorly performing food and beverage outlets could be outsourced or converted to an alternative use. To allow repositioning to more of a group house, a full-service property with a poor meeting-space-to-guestroom ratio might convert less productive space to additional meeting space. Conversely, to reposition a hotel with an excess of meeting space, ownership might consider a guestroom expansion or conversion of a portion of its meeting space to retail or spa use. It is worth noting that some deficiencies, such as location or poor access, can be difficult or impossible to address. If the asset manager and owner are creative in their thinking, however, most weaknesses can be mitigated significantly.

Market Trends. A second step in the repositioning process is to evaluate market trends. To gauge opportunities accurately, the asset manager must be aware of future supply additions, changes in market demand, and evolving guest expectations and preferences. In the last example of the preceding paragraph, investment in additional guestrooms is unlikely to be profitable if market demand is insufficient or declining. A spa or additional retail space will be successful only if the feature is consistent with guests' preferences and spending patterns (or those of potential local patrons). Although it is possible to uncover latent demand in a market or to shift demand from other markets, such strategies are not for the risk-averse or those with a short-term time frame. Careful market research and a thorough familiarity with the demographics of the target market are recommended to mitigate the risk of overestimating potential demand.

Entitlement Environment. After completing the SWOT analysis and evaluating market trends, the next step in the repositioning process is to clarify the entitlement environment. As with the redevelopment process, the entitlement environment can often preclude certain repositioning options. Returning to our hotel expansion example, zoning restrictions typically limit the number of possible keys, either explicitly or indirectly though site-density constraints. Rezoning the property or obtaining a zoning variance may be possible, although the probability of winning relief and the time required for the process vary widely. As previously noted, engagement of local legal counsel with land-planning and development experience is highly recommended if the asset manager is to understand fully all entitlement issues.

Contractual Obligations. The next step in identifying repositioning alternatives is to study existing contractual obligations. If the property is held under a fee simple estate, this generally does not pose impediments to most repositioning options, but provisions in ground leases may positively or negatively affect the economics of various options. Changes in the property's revenue mix, for example, will likely affect ground rent because most ground leases contain variable rent clauses. Some ground leases also include extension options or other terms favoring the lessee who undertakes major discretionary investment in the improvements. For ground leases with short remaining terms, the ability to extend is likely to create enormous value. To avoid surprises, owners and asset managers should always have a strong understanding of all the financial and control provisions contained in ground leases.

Another category of contractual obligations affecting repositioning alternatives is management and franchise agreements. Not only do the contracts affect the economic aspects of repositioning, replacement of the contracts themselves represents the most common repositioning strategy pursued by owners. The most critical provisions relate to control of operations, fees, and contract termination.

Other contract considerations pertinent to evaluating repositioning options are common to those for redevelopment decisions, including collective bargaining agreements, space and rooftop leases, and concession agreements. While generally less relevant to repositioning decisions than management contracts or ground leases, labor agreements may present insurmountable obstacles to the flexibility required to outsource particular operations.

Capital Structure and Availability. As with potential redevelopment scenarios, the final factor to consider in evaluating repositioning strategies is capital structure and availability. Current debt covenants and partnership agreements may require consents from other stakeholders before moving forward with major repositionings. More important, if capital is unavailable for reinvestment into the asset, many repositioning options will not be viable for the current owner. Since other potential investors may not have similar capital constraints, restrictive capital structures and lack of investment capital may result in a higher potential disposition value than the current owner's as-is value.

When all viable repositioning alternatives have been identified and quantified, the owner and asset manager should be able to compare the various options to the previously developed as-is and redevelopment scenarios. As noted earlier, risk-adjusted discount rates may be appropriate when comparing scenarios with substantially different risk profiles. As a practical matter, repositioning pro formas developed by current or potential management companies should be evaluated critically. Operators generally take their fiduciary relationship with ownership seriously, but many operating company executives charged with the responsibility of developing pro forma analyses are not accustomed to looking at investment decisions from the owner's perspective. It is therefore the responsibility of the asset manager to ensure that assumptions are reasonable and that projections account for all costs, including "below-the-line" items such as replacement reserves, corporate overhead charges, and incentive management fees.

The Disposition Decision

The final step in the owner's investment-decision process is to evaluate the sale scenario. The as-is scenario and the sale scenario are closely linked, since the as-is valuation generally sets the baseline for potential proceeds on disposition. Whether the owner should entertain a sale depends on the degree to which the subject property continues to meet all of the goals and objectives of ownership. Put simply, if the owner would not purchase the asset again at the as-is valuation, a recommendation for disposition is warranted.

An existing asset may fail to meet an owner's hold criteria for a number of different reasons. Anticipated operating cash flows or property appreciation may not meet current investment standards, and ownership may have identified superior reinvestment alternatives. The owner's portfolio strategy may have changed, and the asset may no longer fit geographic or product parameters. Some owners, including especially certain types of investment funds, have specific investment horizons and may need to liquidate a portfolio. Others may simply need to raise cash to meet other operating needs. Still others may want to achieve a desired tax event (gain or loss). While a disposition to avoid taxes may be a valid objective, deferring the sale of a property solely to avoid tax gain usually is not. Rather than continuing to hold an undesirable asset, owners should pursue other options, such as UPREITs (Umbrella Partnership Real Estate Investment Trusts) or Section 1031 tax-deferred exchanges. Regardless of the motivation for disposition, owners need to ensure that the analysis of disposition proceeds and corresponding reinvestment basis reflects all transaction costs resulting from the sale.

The Post Audit

As a wise individual once noted, "It's hard to know if you are winning if you don't keep score." The truth in this observation notwithstanding, it is surprising how few owners bother to calculate the success or failure of their investment decisions over time. While nearly all owners calculate yield on total investment at disposition, many do not track the ongoing yields from individual ROI-driven investments or larger redevelopment or repositioning projects.

To a certain extent, omitting the post-audit function is understandable. Tracking a large number of projects can become time-consuming and tedious. If managed appropriately, however, the post audit can be a very effective tool in fine-tuning the underwriting process. By regularly comparing actual results to pro forma projections, asset managers can validate their assumptions—an important plus toward establishing credibility for future recommendations. Moreover, building and documenting a base of experience improves the reliability of future projections, decreasing the forecast risk—and potentially the hurdle rates—associated with subsequent projects.

Assessing Costs and Benefits. As with the original pro forma, development of the post-audit analysis requires two frequently challenging steps: (1) assessing all of the benefits of the investment and (2) assessing the true costs. Determining the costs is typically the easier of the two requirements.

Elements of investment cost can generally be categorized as direct expenditures, indirect expenditures, and avoided expenditures. Direct expenditures are relatively straightforward and (ideally) relate closely to the original project budget. Indirect expenditures are costs incurred as a result of pursuing the subject investment but absorbed into operations or other projects. Examples of indirect costs are additional housekeeping labor, contract cleaning, or repairs and maintenance expenses. It is worth noting that no in-house resources should be considered "free" contributions to the project, with the arguable exception of management overtime. If their cost is not allocated to a specific project, hourly staff should be performing other necessary functions or their hours should be reduced.

The third cost classification, avoided expenditure, reduces rather than increases the net investment allocable to a project. Although this category has the potential for manipulation, it is nonetheless valid for consideration in assessing project return. The basis for reducing direct and indirect expenditures by avoided expenditures is the recognition that certain expenditures may be necessary only if a project does *not* occur. An example of avoided costs is the impending renovation of a dated food-and-beverage outlet that is converted instead to leased space. The cost of tenant improvements and any leasing commissions are direct expenditures, but the costs of the refurbishment *avoided* reduce the net project cost when performing the yield calculation.

Assessing all of the benefits of an investment tends to get more difficult as the complexity of the project increases. For an energy-saving ROI-driven project such as a lighting retrofit or the addition of a plate-and-frame heat exchanger, calculation of the benefits can be as simple as quantifying reduced electrical costs and useful life extensions of equipment. For the conversion of a restaurant to meeting space, however, the incremental benefits may include some or all of the following: meeting room rentals, catering revenue, guestroom sales, and minor-operated-department revenues related to increased occupancy. Additionally, for purposes of calculating the net benefits of the project, cash flow generated by the meeting space should be reduced by projected cash flows *lost* from restaurant operations. Invariably, some assumptions will be necessary in analyzing complicated projects. Those assumptions are most defensible if based on historical numbers. For example, assumed incremental telephone revenue for the preceding meeting room example should reflect incremental guestrooms occupied multiplied by the historical telephone revenue per occupied room.

One final point on post-audit technique is worthy of mention. For the post-audit analysis to be useful, it must reflect all expenses and deductions associated with the subject project, as well as the revenues. As when underwriting the initial pro forma, asset managers need to verify that the information reported by the property for the post-audit analysis includes all costs to the owner. Failure to account for the indirect costs of a project—such as incremental repairs and maintenance expenses, revenue-based chain service allocations, and "below-the-line" items like ground rent and incentive management fees—will materially overstate the actual results.

When to Question (or Look Past) the Numbers

With good reason, this chapter has focused on quantifiable processes and techniques to support the investment decision. In the vast majority of cases, poor investment decisions are the result of insufficient or faulty underwriting. Before concluding, however, we must point out that, in some situations, analysis of historical data can be pointless or even misleading.

Evolving Markets. In evaluating investments, it is sometimes difficult to anticipate the effect of changing guest preferences and the evolution of lodging products. Fifty years ago, only a few visionaries foresaw the impact on the lodging industry of the development of our interstate highway system. The situation was similar twenty years ago, when product segmentation was in its infancy. The typical impact of evolving guest preferences and changing lodging products is to accelerate economic and functional obsolescence. However, in some circumstances, changing markets can unexpectedly benefit an investment. An example of unanticipated benefit might be a thirty-year-old airport hotel with significant leaseable office space. As recently as the year 2000, potential investors would very likely have been reluctant to attribute much value to the office component, given that airport office space has historically enjoyed only limited marketability. The recent creation of the federal Transportation Security Administration, however, has created a new (and high-credit) tenant for the product.

Changing Technology. As with evolving markets, rapid technological advancement can unexpectedly shorten the life of many investments. For example, audiovisual equipment with a projected 30-percent annual yield may appear an attractive investment, but the payback may not materialize if most customers are providing their own equipment two years from now. Asset managers should be conservative in projecting useful lives or holding periods for any investments featuring a heavy technological component and therefore potentially rapid obsolescence.

Non-Comparability. Despite the best efforts to identify comparables, some investment opportunities are unique. The principal problem with any pro forma is its inherent reliance on assumptions. When one-of-a-kind investments require pro formas for which there are no established and quantifiable frames of reference, reliance on assumptions can become excessive to the point of losing relevance.

To some extent, the concerns raised by one-off investments can be mitigated through increased risk premiums (typically reflected in higher discount and hurdle rates), reduced holding periods, and diversification. Sensitivity modeling can also be a useful tool. Continued tweaking of assumptions, however, has been known to lead to "analysis paralysis" in which opportunities are lost due to fear of making a decision. As with many things in life, investment decisions are sometimes not clear cut. A decision not to buy or not to reinvest in an asset may appear to be the safer choice, but it fails to create value for ownership. Ultimately, the investment decision must be made based on the professional judgment of the asset manager and the team he or she has assembled, consistent with the strategic goals and risk-tolerance profile of ownership.

Conclusion

The choice to buy, sell, redevelop, or reposition a property is the fundamental decision of real estate investment. Unlike other real estate forms, however, the hotel investment decision is complicated by an array of factors involved in operating the business. While no amount of analysis can eliminate investment risk, a thorough understanding of ownership's objectives and consistent analytical processes can greatly reduce risk and render it manageable. The alternative—investing without a thoughtful plan and an exit strategy—is little different from rolling the dice. It may be exciting and even profitable in the short term, but over time the odds are against you.

References

Baltin, Bruce, James R. Butler, Jr., and Peter Bernudiz. 1997. "The Hotel Acquisition Process." *Hotel Online—Ideas and Trends.* (March). http://hotel-online.com/Trends.

Commercial Investment Real Estate Institute. 1999. *Investment Analysis for Commercial Investment Real Estate.* Chicago: Commercial Investment Real Estate Institute.

Raleigh, Lori E., and Rachel J. Roginsky, eds. 1999. *Hotel Investments: Issues and Perspectives.* 2nd ed. Lansing, Mich.: Educational Institute of the American Hotel & Lodging Association.

Rushmore, Stephen. 1992. *Hotel Investments: A Guide for Lenders and Owners.* Boston: Research Institute of America.

Chapter Appendix

The following appendix presents checklists used to guide the due-diligence process for the acquisition of a hotel asset. The five checklists are organized to present the principal responsibilities of five key components of the overall team: the acquisition department, legal counsel, the feasibility department (or, alternatively, a third-party feasibility-analysis firm), the asset manager, and third-party consultants specializing in various aspects of the review of the subject hotel's physical plant and technical systems.

Acquisition Department Checklist

	Responsible Party						
	A	L	F	AM	C	Due Date	Date Completed
Unannounced cold/blind shop	x						
Write due-diligence memo addressing issues and opportunities	x						
Third-party valuation	x						
Name of hotel contact for site visits	x						
Description of public space, including capacities	x						
Description of amenities	x						
Brochure and meeting planner kit	x						
Copies of any disposition marketing brochures	x						
Insurance inspection	x						
Monthly financial statements for current and past year	x						
Prior three years' detailed profit and loss statements	x						
Prior five years' occupancy and ADR	x						
Prior two years' written monthly reports by manager and/or asset manager	x						
Current and next year operating budgets	x						
Prior three years' real and personal property tax information	x						
Prior three years' sales and use tax information	x						
Prior three years' balance sheets	x						
Federal depreciation schedules, with accompanying worksheets	x						
Detailed asset listings (digital if possible)	x						
All existing loan documents for hotel	x						
Summary and dates of renovations	x						
Current escrow balance	x						
Prior five years' capital budgets	x						

(continued)

Prior five years' actual capital expenditures	x							
Five-year capital expenditure projection	x							
Deferred maintenance items	x							
Franchise inspection report	x							
Reservations activity report	x							
Competitive market information	x							
Latest STR report	x							
Current and next year marketing/business plans	x							
Day-by-day occupancies	x							
Details of any room contracts for more than 6 months or 500 rooms (rooms/rate/terms)	x							
Trade out agreements	x							
Contact regarding how hotel competes in its market	x							
Recent changes in market supply	x							
Recent changes in market demand	x							
Proposed hotels	x							
Details of competitive hotels	x							
Ten largest customer accounts	x							
Five largest area room night generators	x							
Economic market information	x							
Prior three years' market segmentation with ADR	x							
Proposed rates for next three years	x							
Group bookings pace report	x							
Prior two years' weekday/weekend occupancy and ADR	x							
Special corporate rate details	x							
Past feasibility or appraisal reports	x							
Organization chart	x							

Shaded area indicates shared responsibility
A=Acquisition Department L=Outside Legal Counsel F=Feasibility Department AM=Asset Manager C=Third-Party Consultants

Outside Legal Counsel Checklist

	Responsible Party							
	A	L	F	AM	C		Due Date	Date Completed
Write due-diligence memo addressing issues and opportunities		x						
Title report and preliminary title commitment		x						
Survey—site plan and legal description		x						
Zoning		x						
CC&Rs and encumbrances		x						
Master plans		x						
Flood plain information		x						
Environmental studies—phases I & II (if necessary)		x						
Documents for past or present remediation work		x						
City building inspector reports with status of any violations		x						
Summary of existing violations of laws and ordinances		x						
Summary of licenses and permits with expiration dates		x						
Life and safety—detail of fire protection system		x						
All existing building, engineering, environment, & ADA reports		x						
Age of hotel		x						
Architectural drawings and floor plans		x						
All available photography (including aerials)		x						
Liquor license		x						
Lawsuits		x						
Insurance loss runs		x						
Management agreement		x						
Ground lease		x						
Commercial leases		x						

(continued)

Equipment leases—FF&E		x					
Service agreements		x					
Major system/component warranties, including expiration, coverage, and transferability		x					
Summary of insurance		x					
Ownership, partnership, joint venture, shareholder, or other ownership agreements		x					
Abstract purchase and sale agreement and all other contracts		x					
Franchise agreement		x					
Collective bargaining agreement		x					
Employment agreements		x					
Obligations regarding accrued wages, benefits, incentive payments, sick pay, vacation pay, deferred compensation, pension, profit sharing, stock option, employee stock purchase, retirement, or other employee benefit plan.		x					
Vacation schedule		x					
Workers' compensation claims		x					
Summary of all legal claims filed by employees against hotel		x					

Shaded area indicates shared responsibility
A=Acquisition Department L=Outside Legal Counsel F=Feasibility Department AM=Asset Manager C=Third-Party Consultants

Feasibility Department Checklist

	Responsible Party						
	A	L	F	AM	C	Due Date	Date Completed
Write due-diligence memo addressing issues and opportunities		x					

Shaded area indicates shared responsibility
A=Acquisition Department L=Outside Legal Counsel F=Feasibility Department AM=Asset Manager C=Third-Party Consultants

Asset Manager Checklist

	Responsible Party						
	A	L	F	AM	C	Due Date	Date Completed
Unannounced cold/blind shop				x			
Monthly financial statements for current and past year				x			
Prior three years' detailed profit and loss statements				x			
Prior five years' occupancy and ADR				x			
Prior two years' written monthly reports by manager and/or asset manager				x			
Current and next year operating budgets				x			
Prior three years' real and personal property tax information				x			
Prior three years' balance sheet				x			
All existing loan documents for hotel				x			
Summary and dates of renovations				x			
Current escrow balance				x			
Prior five years' capital budgets				x			
Prior five years' actual capital expenditures				x			
Five-year capital expenditure projection				x			
Deferred maintenance items				x			
Franchise inspection report				x			
Reservations activity report				x			
Competitive market information				x			
Latest STR report				x			
Current and next year marketing/business plans				x			
Day-by-day occupancies				x			
Details of any room contracts for more than 6 months or 500 rooms (rooms/rate/terms)				x			
Trade out agreements				x			

(continued)

Contact regarding how hotel competes in its market				x				
Recent changes in market supply				x				
Recent changes in market demand				x				
Proposed hotels				x				
Details of competitive hotels				x				
Ten largest customer accounts				x				
Five largest area room night generators				x				
Economic market information				x				
Prior three years' market segmentation with ADR				x				
Proposed rates for next three years				x				
Group bookings pace report				x				
Prior two years' weekday/weekend occupancy and ADR				x				
Special corporate rate details				x				
Past feasibility or appraisal reports				x				
Insurance loss runs				x				
Write due-diligence memo addressing issues and opportunities				x				
Write strategic plan				x				
Create a SWOT analysis				x				
Guestroom count and room type breakdown				x				
Rooms location map				x				
Personal property inventory				x				
Consumable and operating supply inventory, including average monthly level for each				x				
Salary schedule of key employees				x				
Number of full-time and part-time employees by department				x				
Current week's work schedules of each department				x				
Current employee handbook				x				
Review acquisition memo from acquisition officer				x				
Study tax implications of price/asset allocation				x				

Review franchise brand deficiency checklist				x				
Ensure acquisition CEP and escrow agreements are implemented				x				
Post-closing reconciliation of accounts by accounting firm				x				
Set up reporting packages and requirements				x				
Verify property is following CEP and operations budget				x				
Set up property files and binder				x				
Verify due-diligence memo Items are being carried out				x				

Shaded area indicates shared responsibility
A=Acquisition Department   L=Outside Legal Counsel   F=Feasibility Department   AM=Asset Manager   C=Third-Party Consultants

Third-Party Consultants

	Responsible Party						
	A	L	F	AM	C	Due Date	Date Completed
Summary and dates of renovations					x		
Environmental studies—phases I & II (if necessary)					x		
Documents for past or present remediation work					x		
City building inspector reports with status of any violations					x		
Summary of existing violations of laws and ordinances					x		
Summary of licenses and permits with expiration dates					x		
Life and safety—detail of fire protection system					x		
All existing building, engineering, environment, & ADA reports					x		
Architectural drawings and floor plans					x		
All available photography (including aerials)					x		
Major system/component warranties, including expiration, coverage, and transferability					x		
Guestroom count and room type breakdown					x		
Property construction details, including: structure; roof; fire protection; HVAC; # and types of elevators; emergency generator; hot water and plumbing.					x		
Rooms layout (location of furnishings)					x		
Schematics/renderings for expansion					x		
Square footage of rooms, public space, total hotel					x		
Systems inventory (PMS, ECR, YMS, EMS, reservations)					x		

Shaded area indicates shared responsibility
A=Acquisition Department L=Outside Legal Counsel F=Feasibility Department AM=Asset Manager C=Third-Party Consultants

11

Planning and Managing Capital Expenditures

By Greg Denton and Deno Yiankes

Greg Denton, MAI, *is Vice President of Finance and Asset Management for The Gencom Group, with responsibilities for asset management and financial and acquisition analysis for various hospitality-related investments of The Gencom Group and its affiliates. Gencom is a private developer and owner of hotels and luxury resorts throughout the United States, Canada, and Mexico. Gencom's owned and asset-managed portfolio currently includes properties operated under the Ritz-Carlton, Renaissance, Wyndham, Radisson, and Holiday Inn affiliations.*

Before joining The Gencom Group, Mr. Denton served as Director of Portfolio Management for CNL Hospitality Group, a real estate investment trust located in Orlando, Florida. In this capacity, he oversaw aspects of acquisition and asset management for a $600 million portfolio of owned hotels throughout the United States. From 1996 to 1999, Mr. Denton served as Vice President of Asset Management for White Lodging Services Corporation, a private developer, owner, and operator of hotel properties.

He has lectured frequently and published several articles on hotel real estate finance and asset management and serves as an adjunct professor in the Hospitality Management program at Florida International University. Mr. Denton earned his bachelor's and master's degrees from the Cornell University School of Hotel Administration. In addition, he has earned the MAI designation from the Appraisal Institute. He currently serves as a member of the board of directors of the Hospitality Asset Managers Association (HAMA).

Deno Yiankes *serves as President and Chief Operating Officer of the Development and Asset Management Division of White Lodging Services Corporation (WLS). Established in 1985, WLS is a fully integrated hotel development, ownership, and management company that specializes in Marriott and other leading brands on a nationwide basis. Maintaining ownership in approximately 85 percent of its managed portfolio, WLS has successfully developed and opened more than 75 Marriott-affiliated hotels in the last decade.*

Mr. Yiankes is currently President of the Hospitality Asset Managers Association (HAMA) and a member of the Board of the SpringHill Suites by Marriott Franchise Advisory Council, where he serves as Chairman of the Marketing Committee. He received the bachelor of science degree in Restaurant, Hotel, and Institutional Management from Purdue University Calumet. Before joining WLS in 1990, Mr. Yiankes was employed by HVS International and previously worked in numerous front- and back-of-the-house operational capacities within the hospitality industry.

As THE HOTEL ASSET MANAGEMENT FUNCTION has evolved over the past two decades, the various tasks and responsibilities of asset managers have similarly grown and evolved. However, the participation by asset managers in the capital expenditure, or CapEx, process has remained comparatively steady. Hotel asset managers have consistently been involved in the CapEx budgeting, monitoring, and planning processes, regardless of whether ownership is institutional or entrepreneurial, or has a short-term or long-term investment horizon.

Although the tools, technologies, and research data available to assist in managing capital expenditures have improved, the basic responsibilities—managing ownership's investment dollars, maximizing value, providing the necessary information to make sound strategic decisions—have remained constant. We believe that the reason for this consistency is that the CapEx process has long been a source of frustration and pitfalls for owners, and thus requires the detailed attention, specialized knowledge, and application of strategic planning that dedicated asset managers provide.

Defining Capital Expenditures

Much has been written on the lack of clear definitions and thresholds used in categorizing items as capital expenditures, but little progress has been made in arriving at a uniform standard for defining what is and is not a capital expenditure. Part of this ambiguity is attributed to the vague definition of capital expenditures as "expenditures that increase the value or useful life of an asset," which is subjective in nature and allows a wide degree of interpretation.

Contributing to (or fostering) this ambiguity is the fact that owners see capital expenditures as tax inefficient because the costs of capital items must be depreciated over the useful life of the asset rather than expensed (which would allow realization of the income tax advantages in the year of the expenditure). Operators, as discussed below, typically view capital expenditures as "fee efficient" in that monies expended for CapEx typically do not reduce house profit or affect incentive fees.

Common industry standards are that an item must be a significant expenditure (often defined as $1,000 in cost) and have a minimum life expectancy (often defined as five years) to be considered a capital item. Thus, while replacing a roof would clearly be considered a capital expenditure, making repairs to a roof would not be a capital item unless the repairs were expected to extend the useful life of the roof by at least five years. Similarly, replacing six-year-old carpet would clearly be a capital item, but replacing the same carpet after three years would not be construed as a capital item because the expenditure is not expected to extend the useful life of the existing carpet by the minimum length of time.

This blurring of the line between normal property maintenance and long-term investment is exacerbated by the different objectives of owners and operators. For the most part, owners see both capital expenditures and operating expenses, particularly when they are not effectively managed, as detracting from their financial returns. Operators, on the other hand, are typically held accountable only for operating expenses, and often do not have the same level of motivation or discipline in controlling capital expenditures. Management bonuses, incentive property-management fees, performance thresholds, and other benchmarks are routinely based upon house profit or net operating income, both of which are calculated after deduction of maintenance expenses but not capital expenditures. Therefore, when judgment is required to determine if an expenditure should be classified as either a maintenance expense or a capital item, the operator would normally prefer to capitalize the expenditure rather than have it appear on the income statement, whereas the owner would prefer to have the expense included on the income statement to reap the immediate tax advantages.

The practice of capitalizing normal maintenance expenditures has three negative outcomes for ownership. First, the owner's income tax liabilities are accelerated by the deferral of the expense. Second, the operator may steer the owner toward making low-priority renovations and replacements rather than conserving monies in the CapEx reserve for the major, essential improvements for which the reserve is intended (the "use it or lose it" approach). Finally, with an inattentive (or generous) owner, the manager may be tempted to boost short-term annual profits by cutting corners on preventive maintenance or deferring maintenance until the expense becomes so large that it must be capitalized. For example, replacing one broken $300 mirror would not be considered a capital expenditure, but replacing ten broken mirrors for $3,000 *does* qualify as a capital expenditure. This deferral ultimately costs the owner more money and is also likely to have a negative impact on guest satisfaction, reducing the hotel's mid- to long-term profitability.

The Asset Manager's Role in the CapEx Process

Asset managers add value to ownership by bringing discipline, control, and foresight to the CapEx planning and management processes and by creating a higher level of alignment and communication between owners and operators. Ownership's principal frustrations regarding capital expenditures are that operators often take (or lose!) control of the process, to the detriment of ownership, and that there are too many surprises and unanticipated expenditures that arise. Similarly, operators may easily be frustrated and dissatisfied by a CapEx process that is inconsistent or not communicated effectively, as well as by one that fails to provide them with the funds needed to undertake renovations at critical junctures in the life cycle of a property.

Asset managers facilitate the CapEx process through four critical activities: (1) monitoring and directing property maintenance to maintain or extend the useful life of the assets; (2) exercising oversight over capital budgeting and expenditures to ensure that ownership's funds are expended judiciously; (3) creating an effective system (the capital expenditure plan) for monitoring and anticipating capital expenditures, enabling ownership to plan for future expenditures and thus allocate financial resources appropriately; and (4) assisting in strategic decision-making when ownership faces upcoming capital expenditures, whether required or discretionary.

Property Maintenance

It is incumbent upon the asset manager to understand and facilitate the property's day-to-day maintenance programs, thus ensuring that the capital assets are maintained properly and that their useful lives are not shortened due to inattention. This involves creating and implementing a set of best practices at the property to ensure that repairs are made effectively and that equipment and systems are tuned up, lubricated, cleaned, and otherwise serviced in order to extend their useful lives. The implementation of basic management and time-management tools (such as work order tracking systems, maintenance calendars, and preventive maintenance schedules) can have a profound impact on the effectiveness of a property's maintenance department.

One highly effective and proactive measure is for property management to create and implement a comprehensive program of preventive maintenance (PM) into its operational routine. A number of the items that maintenance workers spend much of their time on can be anticipated and scheduled in advance, making the employee's working hours more efficient, preventing damage or deterioration of the asset, and forestalling a reduction in guest satisfaction levels.

The purpose of the PM program is to intercept and remedy potential problems before they occur, thereby extending the useful life of the property's furnishings, fixtures, and equipment. The welcome benefits of such a program are that proactive maintenance is a much more efficient use of time and money than reactive maintenance (i.e., repairing or replacing items) and that inconvenient, often expensive equipment failures are avoided.

Moreover, the economic impact on ownership can be substantial if an effective preventive maintenance program enables the assets' useful lives to be extended. For example, if guestroom carpeting costs $500 per room to replace and has an average useful life of five years, then the owner of a 300-room hotel can expect to spend $150,000 every five years on carpeting, or an average of $30,000 per year ($150,000/5). However, if a simple PM program extends the life of the carpeting to seven years, ownership's annual expenditure on carpeting is reduced to $21,430 per year ($150,000/7), yielding a savings of 28.6 percent, or nearly $43,000 in every five-year budget cycle.

Presented in Exhibit 1 is a sampling of maintenance "absolutes" that have proven to be critical components of an effective PM program.

In addition to extending the useful lives of capital equipment and mechanical systems, a rigorous PM program creates a high level of efficiency and a proactive mentality among a property's maintenance technicians. For example, the writers' experience has demonstrated that a tactic as simple as requiring maintenance technicians to bring their service carts with them on all repair calls and checking the room for other needed repairs or replacements saves a significant amount of time and reduces the need for repeat visits to guestrooms. If a typical repair trip involves 10 minutes to arrive at the room, 10 minutes to resolve the problem, and ten minutes to return to the maintenance office, then 30 minutes of labor time are expended to complete a 10-minute task. If the technician is called to repair a leaking faucet but also uses that opportunity to change a burned-out light bulb and

Exhibit 1 Preventive Maintenance (PM) Program Guidelines

Guestrooms

- ✓ Perform comprehensive guestroom deep clean/maintenance (three times per year).
- ✓ Clean grout, tub bottoms, and toilet rim with steamer.
- ✓ Change out or clean filters in HVAC system with approved cleaner solution.
- ✓ Rotate mattresses quarterly.
- ✓ Change light bulbs as needed.
- ✓ Verify that all equipment is in good working order.
- ✓ Change out batteries in television remote control during PM.
- ✓ Change batteries in door lock annually.
- ✓ Ensure that all PM carts have vacuum, plus approved cleaning products for carpet and upholstery.
- ✓ Have maintenance follow up with housekeeping daily on work orders.

clean the PTAC (pass-through air conditioner) filter, the worker will have completed three 30-minute tasks in one 40–50 minute visit, thereby leveraging the employee's time and greatly increasing productivity.

Annual Budgeting for CapEx

The asset manager's role in the annual CapEx budgeting process is to serve as the central source of information for both the owner and the operator. The asset manager communicates to the owner regarding the property's general condition, the life-cycle position of major capital items, the anticipated short- and long-term capital expenditure needs, and the resources currently and prospectively available to meet CapEx requirements. In turn, the asset manager communicates ownership's expectations and priorities to the operator. Additionally, the asset manager acts as a filter and a sounding board to ensure that the requests made of ownership are reasonable, contain an appropriate amount of research and detailed support, and are consistent with ownership's objectives.

Exhibit 2 summarizes the CapEx budget process, the tasks involved, and the role the asset manager typically plays. Throughout the process, it is important for the asset manager to recognize and reflect the specific objectives of the property's owner(s), as well as the property's position within its investment horizon. The approach taken to annual capital expenditures will differ dramatically between an institutional owner with a 20-year investment horizon and an entrepreneurial owner who intends to sell the property in the next one to two years. The former will look more favorably upon a request to replace guestroom case goods or major equipment, for example, whereas the latter is often in the mindset of positioning the property for sale and would be extremely reluctant to make long-term investments in the property.

Exhibit 2 The Hotel Asset Manager's Role in the Annual CapEx Budgeting Process

Step 1 **Review Property and Portfolio Objectives with Ownership.**
- Gain alignment on overall plan for property(ies).
- Review long-term capital requirements and resources.
- Gain understanding of any additional owner issues.
- Decide on format and timing for presentation of budgets for approval.

Step 2 **Communicate Expectations to Operators.**
- Share ownership expectations and property and portfolio objectives to gain alignment.
- Review format and timing for budget submissions to ownership.
- Ensure that competitive bids (minimum: three) are obtained.

Step 3 **Review and Revise Proposed Budgets.**
- Conduct physical inspection and walk-through of property.
- Review submitted items for consistency with owner expectations.
- Review projected payback and return-on-investment projections as appropriate.
- Recommend changes, deletions, and additions as appropriate.

Step 4 **Present Final Proposed Budgets to Ownership for Approval.**
- Present management's requests and justifications to ownership.
- Present expected near-term (three to five years) and long-term (five to ten years) capital needs.
- Reconcile requested CapEx budgets with ownership objectives.

Step 5 **Present Approved Budgets to Operations for Implementation.**
- Discuss changes, additions, and deletions made by ownership.
- Prepare implementation plan with timetable and assigned responsibilities.
- Establish a process for monitoring implementation and reporting to ownership.

Also, in a given year, the amount of capital available for an individual property may be subject to outside factors that must be considered. For example, economic conditions may limit ownership's available capital, other properties may be in more urgent need of critical renovation dollars, alternative investment opportunities may compete for limited resources, etc. Such factors need to be considered at the outset of the CapEx budgeting process. In addition, it is important to communicate these considerations to the property managers serving ownership so that they can better understand the planning-and-approval process, thus avoiding dissatisfaction and confusion on the part of operators.

Exhibit 3 CapEx Project Status Report

Item/job #	Budget	Spent to Date	Anticipated Remaining	Total Expense	Variance to Budget	Date to be Completed
Lobby Carpet	$ 25,000	$ 10,000	$ 14,000	$ 24,000	($ 1,000)	Sept 1
Parking Lot	$ 10,000	$ 12,512	$ ---	$ 12,512	$ 2,512	Done Apr 6
Pool Deck	$ 8,500	$ 4,200	$ 4,200	$ 8,400	($ 100)	May 20

Monitoring Capital Expenditures

Once budgets are established, the asset manager must monitor capital expenditures. The asset manager's level of involvement in the oversight of CapEx spending varies depending upon a number of factors. The size of the property (which usually dictates the staffing level and skill set of a property's engineering department), the complexity of the particular activity(ies), and the asset manager's familiarity with maintenance and purchasing processes all affect the extensiveness of the monitoring process. Additionally, the amount and scope of corporate resources available to the property from the management company (e.g., centralized project management, regional engineers) must be taken into consideration, as well as ownership's expectations.

Budgeted Expenditures

After a CapEx budget is established, each expenditure or project is typically assigned a job number and delegated to a person who has ultimate responsibility for completion of the work. Straightforward, routine projects are usually assigned to members of the property management team to undertake at their discretion. Control over more complicated projects might be passed to a regional engineer designated by the management company, whereas major renovations may be assigned to a project manager or an outside, third-party contractor or project management firm. Timetables are established for each project, specifying start and completion dates that take into account such factors as the seasonality of demand and the timing of the property's cash flows. Planning in this way minimizes the impact of renovations on guests, allows the completion of property upgrades in advance of peak demand times (thus maximizing the initial financial upside), and permits the asset manager to time expenditures to match operating cash flows and, where necessary, ownership contributions.

Once project responsibilities have been assigned and timetables established, the process of monitoring can be consolidated into monthly or quarterly reporting schedules whereby the person assigned responsibility for the project reports on the project status, using a format similar to the one shown in Exhibit 3. The report depicted in Exhibit 3 is often accompanied by detailed narrative for each job, outlining both the scope of the task, the specific steps required, and milestones that must be met. Complications that arise in the process (e.g., bids coming in over budget, construction-permit bottlenecks, etc.) are communicated in the narrative, and the items worthy of ownership's attention can then be addressed appropriately.

In the unforeseen event a project bid comes in over the previously budgeted amount (due to a scope change, incorrect calculations, etc.), the operator should submit a budget-overage request to the asset manager for approval, indicating the specific reasons for the cost overrun and supporting the request with appropriate documentation. The form requires the asset manager's or owner's approval before the over-budget aspect of the project may commence. Appendix 1 at the end of this chapter illustrates a sample Request for CapEx Budget Overage form.

Dealing with Unbudgeted CapEx Items

Regardless of how thorough the capital planning and budgeting processes are, unanticipated or unbudgeted capital items *do* occur on a regular basis. An equipment breakdown is a common precursor to an unbudgeted CapEx requirement, and one that usually gives operators little time to react. When such an event occurs, a system must be in place to provide a rapid response to the operator's needs without compromising the oversight role of the asset manager.

A number of ownership entities address the challenge of unbudgeted capital expenditures by providing the operator with a discretionary fund (typically ranging from $5,000 to $25,000 per year) that may be used for emergency items without advance approval by ownership. In some cases, owners tie the discretionary amount to a percentage (typically in the range of 25 to 35 basis points) of the hotel's gross revenue. Other owners take the view that providing operators with discretionary funds invites wasteful spending; these owners insist on approving any and all expenditures in advance. A middle ground is to give control over the discretionary monies to either the property management company's vice president of operations or the asset manager, providing a higher level of discipline in the process, yet still allowing flexibility and rapid decision-making.

Appendix 2 to this chapter shows a typical Unbudgeted Capital Justification Form that is initially prepared at the property level and ultimately signed by a high-ranking representative of the hotel operator before submission to the asset manager for spending approval.

Near-Term CapEx Planning

The most common form of near-term CapEx planning is derived from the CapEx plan prepared by the hotel's management team. The plan is typically developed using a "ground-up" approach whereby the operator looks at the property's physical condition and assesses guest satisfaction, improved brand maintenance-score opportunities, and weaknesses that reduce the property's competitiveness. This review is used to develop a three- to five-year plan for capital projects and a budget of their associated costs. Items in this plan are often ranked so that ownership can determine the projects that are critical to the survival of the building (e.g., replacing a deteriorating roof) versus those the property management team would like to have but that are not necessarily critical (e.g., expanded meeting space). Once

Exhibit 4 Operator-Generated Five-Year CapEx Plan

Project/Area	Year 1	Year 2	Year 3	Year 4	Year 5
Capital Expenditure Needs					
Exterior/Grounds	$ 12,000	$ —	$ 30,000	$ 50,000	$ 82,000
Guestrooms	280,000	100,000	605,000	445,000	408,000
Corridors	—	—	—	450,000	50,000
Public Areas	75,000	90,000	500,000	25,000	40,000
General/Mechanical	—	75,000	275,000	45,000	70,000
Systems	8,000	15,000	—	85,000	25,000
Total Expenditures	**$ 375,000**	**$ 280,000**	**$ 1,410,000**	**$ 1,100,000**	**$ 675,000**
Reserve Funding Levels					
Current Year Funding	$ 760,000	$ 783,000	$ 806,000	$ 830,000	$ 855,000
Plus: Prior Yr Carryover	—	$ 385,000	$ 888,000	$ 384,000	$ 114,000
Total Funds Available	**$ 760,000**	**$ 1,168,000**	**$ 1,794,000**	**$ 1,214,000**	**$ 969,000**
Less: Expenditures	$ 375,000	$ 280,000	$ 1,410,000	$ 1,100,000	$ 675,000
End-of-Year Fund Balance	$ 385,000	$ 888,000	$ 384,000	$ 114,000	$ 294,000

completed, this near-term plan provides a blueprint for future CapEx planning and provides ownership with a good grasp of future capital requirements.

The aggregate dollar amounts required under the plan for each year are weighed against the projected funds available from the property's replacement or FF&E (furniture, fixtures, and equipment) reserve fund to assess if adequate monies will be available. In cases where the reserve fund is determined to be inadequate to address the operator's requested capital expenditures, ownership needs to determine whether to (1) defer or eliminate non-essential items to conserve funds or (2) infuse additional capital into the project to complete all the requested projects. Exhibit 4 presents an example of an operator-generated five-year CapEx plan with corresponding estimates of capital-reserve funding levels. As this hypothetical plan demonstrates, the property has three years (Years 1, 2, and 5) where reserve funding levels exceed the anticipated expenditures, and two years (Years 3 and 4) where large expenditures come due, partially depleting the accumulated funds. In this example, the reserve remains adequate to fund all anticipated capital expenditures and reaches the end of the five-year projection period with a $294,000 surplus that would carry over into Year 6.

The principal challenges the asset manager faces when evaluating an operator-generated CapEx Plan are the following:

- The process often begins with an assessment of "How much money is there to spend?" and the plan is then constructed around that level of funding, rather than beginning the process with a thorough assessment of the property's true capital needs.
- The use of a five-year horizon provides no hint of the capital needs in Years 6 and beyond. It is therefore impossible to forecast whether the $294,000 surplus

at the end of Year 5 is adequate for the future needs of the property. For example, if Year 6 will be a year for a major renovation, there could be a significant shortfall that ownership should be aware of when assessing the plan.

- The system provides no incentive—and actually is a disincentive—for operators to be thorough in their analysis of capital needs or to address the replacement of expensive mechanical items or major repairs. By drawing attention to a major expenditure that ownership would otherwise not be aware of, the operator reduces the funds available for other items or risks throwing the reserve "into the red." Thus, items like carpet replacement and restaurant refurbishment are always included in operator-generated plans, but less visible yet equally essential items like replacing a chiller, roof repairs, or plumbing and electrical updates are often excluded, leaving ownership to fund those items on an unbudgeted basis when the repairs are needed.
- The system requires operators to be adept at cost estimating for their requested expenditures, placing a burden on managers who may not have adequate experience or corporate resources to develop accurate estimates and creating an opportunity for human error to render the five-year plan dangerously misleading.
- If the operator is given discretion over the timing of items within the five-year period of the plan, the opportunity exists for the operator to accelerate "pet projects" and defer projects that may be more important for the overall well-being of the property.
- A common approach that is employed when operators "fit" capital expenditure needs to the availability of funds is to undertake partial renovations—for example, renovating a portion of a property's guestrooms in one year and deferring the remainder until more funds are available. Although acceptable on a limited basis, this tactic can ultimately result in a property that has dramatically inconsistent quality levels, thereby diluting the overall impact on the guests. This approach often results in more money being spent in total because economies of scale are compromised when work is accomplished piecemeal or over a protracted period of time.

In short, although the five-year capital plan is a valuable resource and an important planning tool for ownership, if performed without the benefit of a corresponding long-term plan, it lacks the analytical muscle needed to maintain discipline in the CapEx process. This is particularly important in cases where the operator is not motivated to undertake mechanical system projects (e.g., plumbing or electrical repairs and updates) because they do not improve short-term operating performance—and management fees—or when the property's general manager has a short-term mentality, planning perhaps to relocate to another property before deferred items manifest themselves as major problems.

Long-Term CapEx Planning

The objective of planning for the full range of a hotel's CapEx requirements can best be achieved by the creation of a long-term planning model that uses the expected useful life of each capital expenditure item to anticipate aggregate annual capital requirements over the property's life cycle. By collecting and analyzing the appropriate data, the asset manager can anticipate the replacement of each major physical component of a property based upon its age, physical condition, and anticipated useful life. This analysis provides ownership with a clear picture of the level of theoretical annual expenditures necessary to maintain the property adequately, while also establishing a framework around which the operator can plan annual capital requests.

One modification to the capital planning model required to make it more useful to ownership is the effective age adjustment, which allows the asset manager to modify the estimated replacement date for an item to reflect either a premature or delayed expenditure. The basis of this technique is found in real estate appraisal methodology, which employs effective age adjustments to derive an estimate of accumulated economic depreciation as part of the cost approach to valuation. The definitive text on real estate appraisal, *The Appraisal of Real Estate*, published by the Appraisal Institute, defines effective age as "the age indicated by the condition and utility of a structure." The same text continues:

> [Effective age] is based on an appraiser's judgment and interpretation of market perceptions. Even in the same market, similar buildings do not necessarily depreciate at the same rate. The maintenance standards of owners or occupants can influence the pace of building depreciation. If one building is better maintained than other buildings in its market area, the effective age of that building may be less than its actual age. If a building is poorly maintained, its effective age may be greater than its actual age. If a building has received typical maintenance, its effective age and actual age may be the same.[1]

Applying the effective age adjustment to capital expenditure items reflects the reality that items are typically not replaced according to a schedule but according to when they fail, become damaged or worn, or when competitive conditions dictate.

Exhibit 5 presents a sample CapEx planning model for a 300-key full-service hotel, and Exhibit 6 provides a forecast of expenditures for the same hotel. The example hotel is approximately six years old and has already received numerous replacements and effective age adjustments, as shown in Exhibit 5. In Exhibit 6, the data from Exhibit 5 are extended into the future, anticipating the likely year that each item will be replaced and its cost. The model can be extended into the future indefinitely; however, the most common application is to look from 20 to 30 years into the future to identify the periods in which major capital investments will be required.

As the model presented in Exhibits 5 and 6 demonstrates, the typical lodging property has extreme fluctuations in required capital expenditures if items are replaced according to a disciplined capital plan. Low-expenditure years, chiefly the early post-construction period or immediately following major renovations, are followed by years with very high relative expenditure levels. This necessitates a high degree of frugality during the early years in order to escrow adequate funds to meet future capital requirements.

Exhibit 5 Capital Expenditure Planning Model

Property: Standard Full-Svc Hotel **Rooms: 300** **Current Yr: 2003**
Opening Date: Jan-97

Area/Item	Life Expectancy	Cost	Extended Cost	Year Installed	Chrono. Age(yrs)	Effective Age (yrs)	Yrs Remaining
Guestrooms							
Drapes, valances	12yrs	$ 750/rm	$ 225,000	1997	6	6	6
Shears	6yrs	$ 135/rm	$ 40,500	2002	1	1	5
Bedspeads	6yrs	$ 315/rm	$ 94,500	2002	1	1	5
Carpet & padding	6yrs	$ 825/rm	$ 247,500	2002	1	1	5
Bed sets	10yrs	$ 544/rm	$ 163,200	1997	6	6	4
Hard case goods	12yrs	$2,200/rm	$ 660,000	1997	6	6	6
Bathrooms							
Vinyl, towel racks	12yrs	$ 380/rm	$ 114,000	1997	6	6	6
Tile	12yrs	$ 550/rm	$ 165,000	1997	6	6	6
Vanity bath lighting	12yrs	$ 180/rm	$ 54,000	1997	6	6	6
Fixtures	15yrs	$ 635/rm	$ 190,500	1997	6	6	9
Corridors							
Carpet	6yrs	$ 440/rm	$ 132,000	2002	1	1	5
Vinyl	8yrs	$ 245/rm	$ 73,500	2002	1	1	7
Lighting/ceiling tile	10yrs	$ 100/rm	$ 30,000	1997	6	6	4
Ice machines	10yrs	$4,000ea	$ 32,000	1997	6	6	4
General Areas							
Parking—reseal/restripe	5yrs	$ 20,000	$ 20,000	2001	2	2	3
Pool deck—resurface	6yrs	$ 15,000	$ 15,000	2001	2	1	5
Pool furniture, equip.	5yrs	$ 12,000	$ 12,000	2001	2	4	1
Exterior painting	5yrs	$ 225/rm	$ 67,500	1997	6	5	0
Laundry washers (3)	12yrs	$ 11,000	$ 33,000	1997	6	6	6
Laundry dryers (4)	12yrs	$ 6,000	$ 24,000	1997	6	6	6
Landscaping (major)	5yrs	$ 75,000	$ 75,000	2001	2	2	3
Building Systems							
Roof	20yrs	$180,000	$ 180,000	1997	6	6	14
Franchise signage	20yrs	$125,000	$ 125,000	1997	6	6	14
Elevator—refurbish cab	15yrs	$ 25,000	$ 75,000	1997	6	6	9
Exercise room—equip, vinyl, carpet, tv	6yrs	$ 40,000	$ 40,000	1997	6	6	0
HVAC—cntl pkg units	8yrs	$103,500	$ 103,500	1997	6	6	2

Note: The above list is not comprehensive, but illustrative. A number of categories and individual items are omitted due to space constraints.

As suggested above, the model serves as a starting point for—and a countervailing balance against—the five-year CapEx plan prepared by property management. By sharing the long-range plan with the operator before submission of the near-term plan, the asset manager informs the operator of the theoretical timetable

Exhibit 6 Long-Range Forecast* of Capital Expenditures (in $000s)

Area/Item	2004	2005	2006	2007	2008	2009	2010	2011	2012	2013
Guestrooms										
Drapes, valances						$ 225				
Shears					$ 41					
Bedspeads					$ 95					
Carpet & padding					$248					
Bed sets						$ 90				
Hard case goods	$285						$285			
Bathrooms										
Vinyl, towel racks						$ 114				
Tile						$ 165				
Vanity bath lighting						$ 54				
Fixtures									$191	
Corridors										
Carpet					$132					
Vinyl							$ 74			
Lighting/ceiling tile				$ 30						
Ice machines				$ 32						
General Areas										
Parking—reseal/restripe			$ 20					$ 20		
Pool deck—resurface					$ 15					
Pool furniture, equip.	$ 12					$ 12				
Exterior painting	$ 68					$ 68				
Laundry washers (3)						$ 33				
Laundry dryers (4)						$ 24				
Landscaping (major)										
Building Systems										
Roof										
Franchise signage										
Elevator—refurbish cab									$ 75	
Exercise room—equip, vinyl, carpet, tv	$ 40						$ 40			
HVAC—cntl package units		$104								$104
Total—All Items	$432	$399	$ 49	$351	$586	$2,043	$486	$ 57	$470	$297
Total—Inflated at CPI	$443	$419	$ 53	$386	$660	$2,349	$572	$ 69	$583	$372
CapEx as % Projected Revenues	4.0%	3.7%	0.5%	3.3%	5.4%	18.9%	4.5%	0.5%	4.3%	2.7%

* Only the initial ten years of the long-range forecast are illustrated.

for replacement of the major capital items, thus alerting the operator to the items that will receive particular scrutiny from ownership for being ahead of schedule and those for which the operator will be credited for extending their useful lives. Years requiring exceptional levels of expenditures (Year 12 [2009], for example) can then be noted well in advance and prepared for, even if the required expenditure falls outside the horizon of the operator's five-year plan.

Exhibit 7 Annual Projected CapEx Spending As a Percentage of Total Revenues

Yr 1	0.3%	Yr 11	0.3%	Yr 21	1.3%
Yr 2	0.3%	Yr 12	28.0%	Yr 22	0.4%
Yr 3	0.3%	Yr 13	0.3%	Yr 23	0.4%
Yr 4	0.3%	Yr 14	1.3%	Yr 24	30.0%
Yr 5	1.7%	Yr 15	5.0%	Yr 25	1.7%
Yr 6	9.4%	Yr 16	3.8%	Yr 26	0.4%
Yr 7	1.3%	Yr 17	0.4%	Yr 27	0.4%
Yr 8	3.9%	Yr 18	8.9%	Yr 28	1.3%
Yr 9	0.3%	Yr 19	0.4%	Yr 29	0.4%
Yr 10	4.9%	Yr 20	7.8%	Yr 30	14.9%
Avg: Years 1-10:	**2.3%**	**Years 11-20:**	**5.6%**	**Years 21-30:**	**5.1%**

Exhibit 8 Projected FF&E Reserve Fund Balance (in $000s)

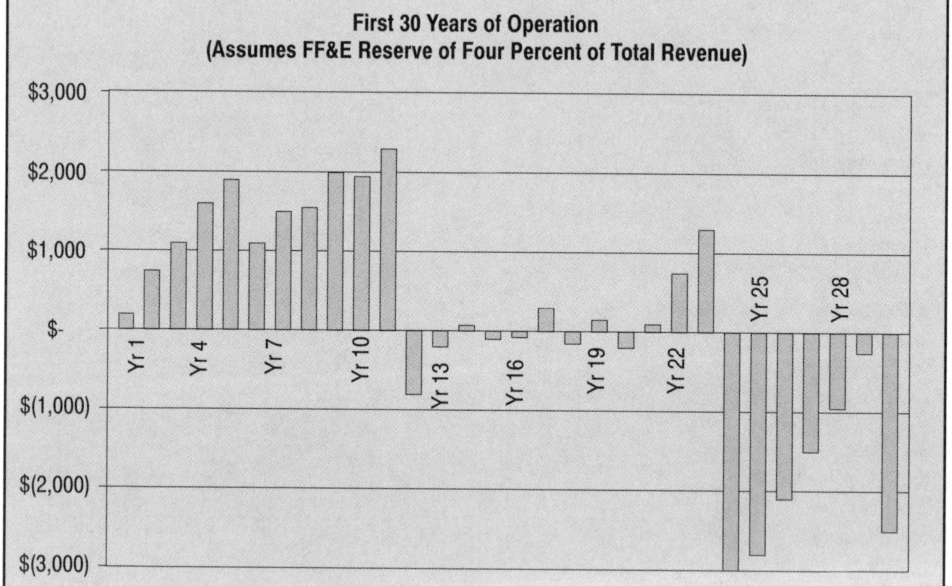

Another useful application of the CapEx planning model is to gauge the adequacy of the FF&E reserve's funding levels over the useful life of the hotel. As Exhibits 7 and 8 illustrate, comparing the annual capital expenditure requirements for the hotel illustrated in Exhibits 5 and 6 to the projected funds available from the FF&E reserve shows dramatic levels of surplus funding during the first decade of operations, followed by a decade of relative parity between funding and capital needs. The third decade of operations, however, shows dramatic deficiencies in the FF&E reserve's adequacy to cover capital expenditure needs.

As Exhibit 8 illustrates, this property's FF&E reserve fund is anticipated to accumulate a surplus of over $2 million by Year 11, but this surplus will be completely depleted in Year 12, when a number of routine items will need to be funded. Moreover, by Years 24–30, the FF&E reserve will be consistently underfunded, requiring a substantial permanent infusion of capital by ownership in Year 24.

The use of a capital planning model allows ownership to escrow an appropriate amount of money during the appropriate time period (subject, however, to requirements that may be imposed by a lender or franchisor), tying up neither too little nor too much capital, given the owner's investment objectives and the property's capital needs. The model provides ownership with a clear indication of when major financial contributions above and beyond the FF&E reserve funding levels will be required, permitting ownership to plan its refinancing or disposition strategies around the information. The model also helps the operator to appreciate the long-term challenges ownership will face in funding the property's upkeep, and this awareness helps maintain a higher level of discipline and frugality during the intervening years.

Owners who do not engage in long-term capital planning or are not adequately counseled by an asset manager run the risk of falling victim to three common mistakes:

- Allowing property management to undertake unnecessary projects or to use the reserve fund inappropriately to pay for improvements. The common mentality of hotel operators is to say to themselves each year: "We have *'x'* percent of total revenues to spend, what do we want to do with it?" During the intervening years between major expenditures, when anticipated CapEx spending should be minimal, this results in frivolous projects being undertaken or investments for improvements that may be cost-justified but should not be funded from the FF&E reserve. As a result, during the first years of operation, very few hotels actually accumulate the surpluses in their FF&E reserve accounts suggested by the plan presented in Exhibit 8, leading inevitably to greater deficits and out-of-pocket expenditures in the later years.
- Being misled into a false sense of security that funding levels are adequate for the long term based upon surpluses in the initial years. This overconfidence has led to the common practice of negotiated "ramped-up" reserve funding levels in the initial years of operations, whereby initial contributions to the reserve fund are one percent of revenue in Year 1, two percent in Year 2, three percent in Year 3, and four percent in subsequent years. Although the concept of reducing funding levels when expense levels are minimal is a step toward more efficient use of owner's capital, it is a dangerous maneuver if it is not accompanied by a corresponding ramp-up to *even higher* funding levels in the later years.
- Being taken by surprise when major refurbishment or replacement projects come due and the reserve fund is inadequate to cover the required expenditures. Shortfalls will eventually occur in most, if not all, FF&E reserve funds.

Reducing the amount of money accrued during the low-expenditure years, inappropriately spending FF&E reserves for capital projects that are not replacement or refurbishment-related, and not increasing the funding levels during the high-expenditure years will dramatically increase these eventual shortfalls. Having been misled by low CapEx requirements in the initial years of operations and having already deployed those surplus funds elsewhere, owners may not be prepared financially for the greater needs in later years.

Using the CapEx Planning Model as a Management Tool

In addition to serving as a planning tool that permits a property's owner and lender(s) to underwrite the investment appropriately and prepare for future CapEx requirements, the capital planning model can be used as the framework for assessing the effectiveness of a property's purchasing, maintenance, and preventive maintenance programs. This can be accomplished by adding a model that tracks not only the chronological age of each component of the hotel but also assigns an effective age to the item. The introduction of an effective age assessment allows comparison between how the item is actually aging and how a benchmark item in that category ages.

To allow the model to be a more effective working document rather than a theoretical tool, the assumptions need to be updated regularly to reflect the fact that capital items are not always replaced at the end of their estimated useful lives. Guestroom air conditioning units, for example, may provide more than the average 12 years of useful service if well-maintained; conversely, units that are not maintained properly may require replacement after only a few years. Similarly, ownership may decide not to replace the entire inventory of a particular item at the same year, opting to replace a portion initially and then attempting to prolong the useful lives of the remaining items for another couple of years.

The capital planning model presented in this chapter simplifies many of the line items and aggregates items of similar life expectancies. In practical application, line items are often split into multiple generations, reflecting partial replacements or allowing for the segregation of items that are on different cycles.

To keep the model current, the property must be inspected at least annually for the purpose of monitoring the condition of each item and gauging the effectiveness of the property's preventive maintenance programs. If a capital item is being properly maintained, it may be projected that the item will outlive its anticipated useful life. When this situation is determined to be the case, the asset's effective age is adjusted downward to reflect a deferred replacement date. Similarly, if an asset is determined to be aging prematurely, either due to inadequate maintenance or poor manufacturing or construction quality, it can be assigned an effective age greater than its chronological age, advancing its anticipated replacement date.

The excerpt from a larger table presented in Exhibit 9 illustrates the effective age adjustment for guestroom case goods that have been well-maintained and are anticipated to outlast their theoretical useful lives. The effect of the assessment is to defer the anticipated replacement date of the case goods by two years, from 2006 to

Exhibit 9 Effective Age Adjustments to CapEx Life-Cycle and Replacement Schedules

Area/Item	Life Expec.	Year Installed	Physical Condition	Chrono. Age	Effective Age	Years Remaining
Case Goods	12 yr	1994	Above Avg	9 yr	7 yr	5 yr

2008. The financial impact on ownership of this deferral is a decrease in the annual cost of the case goods from $500 per room annually ($6,000/12) to $429 per room annually ($6,000/14). Multiplied by 300 guestrooms, this amounts to a cost savings to ownership of over $21,300 per year over the revised expected life of the case goods.

Additionally, the effectiveness of the property's maintenance efforts can be better assessed because of the model's effective age adjustment. In the preceding example, the financial impact of keeping the guestroom case goods in above-average condition equates to a $21,300 annual cost savings to ownership. The property's management and maintenance staff can be motivated, either monetarily or through verbal recognition, to "keep up the good work." Conversely, premature aging of the case goods would result in an increase in cost to ownership and may be an indicator that the preventive maintenance program is inadequate for that item and must be revisited or better executed.

The exercise of making effective age adjustments and the interpretation of the adjustments may trigger a number of actions on the part of the asset manager. An above-average condition of the guestrooms, guest baths, and corridors would suggest that the property's housekeeping and room maintenance programs are effective. However, an unfavorable assessment of the restaurant and roof areas might prompt an additional inquiry into the maintenance efforts in those areas, as well as a review of the quality of items originally purchased. Likewise, if similar assets or areas are determined to be below average over multiple properties in a particular city or region, or within the entire portfolio, then ownership can identify opportunities for improvement within the relevant engineering or purchasing functions or can make needed improvements in corporate training programs for maintenance personnel. Over the long term, these assessments and investigations make both operators and asset managers much more effective in their fundamental task of managing the owner's financial investments in hotel properties.

Conclusion

An effective asset manager must understand the investment life cycle of hotels and recommend the most beneficial investment strategy to ownership, whether the owner's investment horizon is short term or long term. A critical aspect of fulfilling this duty is recognizing and anticipating the property's capital expenditure requirements and ensuring that CapEx dollars are spent wisely. By creating a series of management tools that impose discipline and foresight on the CapEx process, the asset manager enables ownership to optimize its return on investment, avoid the pitfalls and surprises that can occur along the way, and enjoy a higher comfort level that its assets are being adequately husbanded. In addition, a CapEx budgeting-and-approval process that provides clear goals and objectives has a greater likelihood of gaining "buy-in" from operators, creating a higher degree of alignment between the owner's and the operator's interests and reducing the friction that often occurs between the two.

Endnotes

1. Twelfth Edition Textbook Committee, *The Appraisal of Real Estate*, 12th ed. (Chicago: The Appraisal Institute, 2001), p. 385.

Appendix 1

REQUEST FOR CAPEX BUDGET OVERAGE

(Include separate justification for each item)

Property: ______________________________ Date: ________________

Job: ________________

Description of Project:
(Brand, Model, Size, Scope, etc. Attach brochure, literature if available.)

Timetable for Completion:

Anticipated Start Date: ________________

Anticipated Completion Date: ________________

Total Cost of Item: A. ________________
(attach bids/proposals)

BUDGET CONTROL:

Amount authorized in budget for this year: B. ________________

Less previous expenditures/commitments: C. ________________

Amount remaining in budget (B − C = D) D. ________________

Net Over/Under (A − D = Net) ________________

Requested by: ______________________________ Date: ________________

APPROVALS:

Mets Manager: ______________________________ Date: ________________

VP Regional: ______________________________ Date: ________________

VP Engineering: ______________________________ Date: ________________

Ownership Approval: ______________________________ Date: ________________

Authorized Period: From ____________ to ____________

Expenditures must be completed and invoices submitted within this time period.

Appendix 2

UNBUDGETED CAPITAL JUSTIFICATION FORM

(Include separate justification for each item)

Property: ______________________ Date Submitted: ________________

Description of Project:
(Brand, model, size, score, etc. Attach brochure, literature if available.)

Total Cost of Project or Equipment

Each __________ × Quantity ____________ Cost ______________

(15% for Freight & Tax) Tax & Freight _________

Total Cost __________

System Related: Y/N (If yes, VP of Accounting/Systems signature Required)

Justification:

(Check one ___Profit Improvement___ Profit Maintenance___Franchise Reqirement)

Age of Asset: ____________________ Account Category ______________

Indicate impact on operations from this expenditure. If profit maintenance, include condition of items being replaced. If profit improvement, detail estimates of additional revenues or cost savings and provide support.

Requested by: __________________________________ Date: __________

APPROVALS:

Dir Engineering: ________________________________ Date: __________

General Manager: ________________________________ Date: __________

RVP Operations ________________________________ Date: __________

Asset Manager: ________________________________ Date: __________

12

The Hotel Asset Manager's Guide to Information Technology

By Daniel J. Connolly and Rick Swig

Daniel J. Connolly, Ph.D.*, is an assistant professor of information technology and electronic commerce at the University of Denver's Daniels College of Business with a dual appointment in the School of Hotel, Restaurant, and Tourism Management and in the Department of Information Technology and Electronic Commerce. His teaching, research, and consulting are in the areas of information technology strategy and electronic business.*

Dr. Connolly serves as vice president of the Hospitality Information Technology Association (HITA) and is a founding member of the Hotel Technology Next Generation (HTNG) initiative. Before joining academia, Dr. Connolly worked for eight years at Marriott International's corporate headquarters in the area of information systems. In addition, he has consulted with numerous organizations in the hospitality, health care, and technology sectors, and has more than ten years of experience in hotel and restaurant operations. The author or co-author of numerous publications, he routinely presents his work at industry and professional conferences and symposiums around the world.

Before joining the faculty at the University of Denver, Dr. Connolly served on the faculties of Cornell University, Michigan State University, Virginia Polytechnic Institute and State University, and Concord College, where he taught graduate and undergraduate courses in information technology, strategic management, finance, and hospitality administration. He earned his Ph.D. from Virginia Polytechnic Institute and State University, his MBA from American University, and his B.S. from Cornell University.

Rick Swig *operates RSBA & Associates, which was founded in 1986. Since that time, Mr. Swig has provided advisory services to major hotel operating companies, as well as owners of individual hotels and portfolios. Along with his asset management and consultancy work associated with RSBA & Associates, he has also been an investor in hotels since 1989, including the Harvest Inn in Napa Valley, California, and the Hotel Pacific in Monterey, California. His background also includes a career with Fairmont Hotels, where he rose to Vice President and Managing Director of the Fairmont Hotel Management Company.*

The primary activities of RSBA & Associates include hotel operations reviews, asset strategy development, general operational troubleshooting, and asset management. Engagements have included work on hotels featuring business and leisure services in both urban and resort locations. The firm has a special expertise in reservations services and systems.

Swig is a member of the Hospitality Asset Managers Association (HAMA) and the International Society of Hospitality Consultants (ISHC), of which he is past Chairman. He currently serves as Vice Chairman of the Board of Directors of the San Francisco Convention and Visitors Bureau. Mr. Swig also serves on the advisory committees of the University of San Francisco Hospitality Management Program, The Collins School of Hospitality Management at California State Polytechnic University, Pomona, and City College of San Francisco. He is a graduate of Stanford University.

Changing Technology Paradigm:

> *Hotel marketing and operations continue to grow more complex. Equally complex systems and communications technology have become essential to manage effectively the enterprise and the flow of critical guest and operational data. However, the current fragmented vendor market requires hotel staff to spend too much scarce time and expertise to understand, acquire, and manage this technology, while financial resources to implement and maintain it are increasingly restricted. Fewer but more comprehensive systems need to become available on a service-model (non-capital) basis from fewer but more significant vendors. Greater awareness of the relative value of the various systems would also lead to better-informed and funded investment decisions on acquiring and supporting them.*

THE ABOVE EXCERPT IS TAKEN from the "Top Ten Issues and Challenges in the Hospitality Industry for 2003," at this writing the most recent installment of a list compiled annually by the International Society of Hospitality Consultants (ISHC). Like recurring New Year's resolutions, some variant of the same challenge is likely to make its way onto future lists as well.

The resolve to tackle the thorny issue of information technology, or IT for short, is not unlike our resolve to shed pounds, exercise more regularly, or save more for retirement: the objective is noble, but there are innumerable behavioral responses that interfere, not the least of which is the rueful reflection that we've failed in the past. Our purpose in the present chapter is to explore frankly the issues that make it difficult for asset managers to confront IT decisions, while arguing nevertheless that a systematic, proactive approach to IT decision-making is a necessity. Our approach is not to provide an inventory of currently available technology and systems—for these, alas, will change before this chapter is printed—but to provide asset managers with a methodology for analyzing IT.

The specific goals of this chapter are (1) to highlight the importance of IT as a core competency for asset managers; (2) to increase awareness of some of the key IT-related issues and decisions facing asset managers; and (3) to develop a structured, disciplined approach to IT decision-making, thus equipping asset managers with key questions to ask, whether at the property level or in their interactions with hotel operators and brands. As suggested above, our emphasis throughout the following pages will be on technology as a strategic enabler of commerce. Accordingly, we will emphasize business considerations, processes, and tools—not the technical elements of technology.

A Core Competency, but Bad Karma

IT is an important and necessary resource for any hotel firm. It is quickly reshaping all aspects of the business, from procurement to distribution. Over the years, its role has changed from a back office, support function—an overhead item—to a strategic function that drives business opportunities, bringing about sweeping changes in the industry with respect to fundamental day-to-day transactions, competitive differentiation, and cost structure. As such, IT must be taken into consideration when making virtually all business decisions.

Unfortunately, IT is one of the least understood aspects of the lodging business and one of the issues that causes consternation at all levels, from ownership through property management to operations. The reasons for this are fourfold. First, there is the pace of change. Second, there are the escalating costs of IT. Third, there is the difficulty of building a business case to justify investment in IT. Finally, there is the too-frequent syndrome where an IT application is purchased (or developed) and installed but full implementation is never realized. These fundamental factors equate to discomfort and increased risk for hoteliers. As a result, there is a natural tendency to avoid IT. Regrettably, the profession can no longer indulge this understandable reticence, but instead must confront the issues surrounding IT and IT decision-making.

Pace of Change

For the asset manager, technology's rapid pace of change poses planning problems not encountered for other types of assets, tangible and intangible, under his or her control. For most furniture, fixtures, and equipment (FF&E) and similar personalty, the planning horizon is five years, and there are historical trends to forecast obsolescence. In contrast, new technology—whether software or hardware—evolves so fast that its acquisition (or development) and implementation are constantly out of phase with normal reinvestment patterns, upsetting even the best of foresight and planning.

Moreover, hospitality industry vendors have evidenced an inability to keep abreast of rapidly changing technology. As a result, there is a significant history of IT innovations rolled out before they were fully ready for use in the lodging industry. These failures were of two kinds. Frequently, hoteliers discovered limitations on functionality as applications proved inadequate to the task, or unforeseen operational glitches arose from the implementation of technology. Second, many vendors "bet the farm" on a generation of technology that proved less durable than anticipated. This, especially for thinly capitalized vendors, hampered their ability to stay in business and support the applications sold to the lodging industry. Not surprisingly, asset managers and their owners, who provided the venture capital for these experiments, are reluctant to incur fresh risk for IT investments if previous outlays provided negative returns.

Exhibit 1 The Tumult of E-Commerce

The noticeably busy—even chaotic—graphic above presents a mere sampling of some of the latest buzz words expected to impact the hospitality business. The IT world's regrettable love of acronyms and technical terms does not assist the uninitiated. Help is at hand, however, if these terms are unfamiliar. Go to such resources as Whatis.com (http://whatis.techtarget.com) and Webopedia (http://www.webopedia.com) to gain a quick level of fluency in a given topic through simple definitions and hyperlinks to useful, more detailed sources of information.

Finally, the very pace of change has been revolutionary, not evolutionary. (See Exhibit 1 for a list of just a few of the most recent developments in IT.) As a result, hotel operators especially have been surpassed by events and must reach beyond their core competencies. Property-level hotel managers have been in the business of "selling sleep" and providing customer service appropriate to the quality level of their individual hotel properties. Hoteliers have never envisioned technology or distribution-channel management as one of their core competencies. Clearly this is an aspect of the contemporary hotel business model that must evolve.

Asset managers must take the lead in bringing about change, questioning their operators and hotel brands to ensure that appropriate research and development activities are constantly underway. This monitoring of operators and brands must not be confrontational, but rather must represent a collaborative partnership. It is important to understand that this is new territory for all parties. It is also important to understand that even with the most collaborative efforts and appropriate vision, asset managers and their owners, operators, and brands will continue to encounter very real financial, logistical, and marketing hurdles that will make advancing along the technology-improvement curve an arduous journey.

Costs

At both the individual property level and at the corporate level in hotel companies, IT ranks among the top capital expenses of the firm. As competitive forces require even more ambitious deployment of technology, it will continue to become more capital intensive. Therefore, it is reasonable to suggest that every manager must assume responsibility for IT and its implementation as part of his or her job duties.

Yet, however important IT might be to the future of hospitality firms, the very nature of the investment makes it difficult to justify. The benefits of technology are often intangible, making them difficult to quantify or, in some instances, even to articulate. The number and complexity of technology choices overwhelm managers and exceed their purview. The pace of technological advances is increasing, on one hand forcing down the price of existing options, but also bringing new capabilities whose useful lives decline ever more precipitously.

Of course, merely making choices among competing technologies and applications is only one of the challenges facing the asset manager evaluating an investment in IT. An asset manager contemplating any investment must consider *alternative* uses of ownership's capital. When the alternatives include cosmetic property enhancements to stay competitive, additional marketing expenditures to build market share, or legally mandated improvements, the perceived riskiness of technology militates against its selection over more commonplace investments. The asset manager, as a representative of ownership, is charged with maximizing the investment return from an asset. Only capital expenditures that maintain or improve the asset's competitive position are consonant with this fundamental charge to the asset manager. When brand compliance forces technology improvements on asset managers and their owners, these expenditures never seem timely from either an investment or an implementation standpoint.

In the face of competing investment opportunities and IT's rapid pace of change, it is not surprising that asset managers and their owners have temporized, reasoning that it is more advantageous to wait until both the technology and its costs stabilize before making a decision and committing the firm's limited resources. Given the conditions of the economy since 2001 and the outlook for the lodging industry, this approach has great appeal, since it allows hotel firms to preserve precious capital and proceed cautiously in a time of great uncertainty. Although survival may dictate the deferral of some capital investments until the economy rebounds, asset managers must realize that a "do nothing" strategy is only effective if all competitors are similarly paralyzed.

Consider, for example, the lodging industry's response to the Internet and the online marketing of hotel rooms. In this instance, a "do nothing" approach has proved disastrous. Yes, the pace of change was dramatic, but hoteliers' lack of understanding of the opportunities and threats posed by these changes in technology were compounded by their inability or unwillingness to act. As a result, the entire distribution process is being redefined, and hoteliers have realized belatedly that they have lost control of one of their most strategic functions to third-party intermediaries.

The marketplace and competitive landscape will continue to change. Customer needs and demands will continue to increase, and technology will continue to advance. Delaying all action risks placing hotel companies, which are already behind where they need to be, in a position of disadvantage as they lose competitiveness. Consequently, it may never be possible to catch up, which is an extremely risky proposition. Instead, a more balanced approach of conservation and investment is required. With technology vendors being forced to discount and with some competitors at a standstill, asset managers have a great opportunity—the ability to change affordably their competitive advantage and positioning, forcing others to respond and catch up.

The Difficulty of Making a Business Case for IT

For the foreseeable future, all indicators suggest that the hotel industry will become more dependent on technology and that IT will become an integral part of all aspects of the business. As the lodging industry becomes more sophisticated and complex to operate, new skill sets, knowledge, and discipline will be required to succeed. It is important to note, however, that IT in and of itself is seldom the source of competitive advantage, since it can be easily acquired and copied. Rather, it is how IT is implemented and used within a firm that leads to competitive advantage.

The asset manager occupies a boundary-spanning position that requires an interdisciplinary focus to most business decisions and problems. IT knowledge is just one of many requisite skills to be an effective asset manager. Although all asset managers will undoubtedly accept the proposition that they must have some command of IT, the field is understandably daunting. New technologies and applications cover a wide swath of disciplines, including energy management, physical plant maintenance, monitoring of mechanical systems, inventory control, labor control, human resources management, accounting, sales and catering management, guest history and customer relations management, point of sale, reservations, distribution-channel management, property management, and telecommunications. Moreover, asset managers must not only understand what systems are available and their capabilities, they must also weigh the potential for these systems to fit into a property's or a company's financial and operational framework.

It is important for an asset manager to have some grounding in the technical aspects of technology—such as, for example, understanding what a database is, hardware and software security, and the infrastructure required to run a property's or a firm's applications. However, it is more important for the asset manager to understand the business of technology—what technology can and cannot do, when to apply it and when not to, and the impacts (both positive and negative) to the business. Exhibit 2 presents some of the pertinent business-related questions asset managers might pose as they contemplate various investments in technology. The asset manager's decisions must be centered on business value and how IT can be applied to drive revenues, reduce costs, improve customer service, increase

Exhibit 2 To Invest or Not—Key Questions to Ask

- Can IT create barriers to entry, keeping out potential new competitors? If so, how?
- Can IT create switching costs that lock in customers and make it difficult or undesirable for them to seek out alternative services or products?
- Can IT help the firm understand its customers better, use this information to provide unique experiences and customer service, and build lasting relationships that lead to loyalty?
- Can IT be used to lower the firm's cost structure, streamline operations, or create economies of scale?
- Can IT be used to create new business opportunities and revenue streams?
- Can IT be used to differentiate the firm's products and service offerings? If so, how?
- Can IT be used to improve or ensure the consistency of product and service quality?
- Can IT be used to build better alliances or strategic partnerships, helping the firm gain access to new markets or access to resources and skills it does not currently have?
- Can IT be used to gain an edge in dealing with suppliers or enable greater negotiating leverage?
- Can IT change the nature of competition and the dynamics within the industry, shifting them in the firm's favor?
- Can IT help the firm sustain its competitive advantage in the marketplace?
- Can IT better equip employees to be more productive and capable, perhaps by providing information to them or providing faster access to information to help them do their jobs better and outperform the competition?
- Is IT aligned with the strategic objectives of the firm?
- How can IT be better used to help the firm achieve its strategies?

customer loyalty, attract and retain competent employees, etc. IT is not a panacea, but a competitive method—one of many that asset managers may select from to play in the marketplace.

Mastery of IT and its impact on the hotel business represents an opportunity for hotel asset managers to excel, providing value to the owners they serve and improving the decision-making processes in hospitality firms. Knowing how to evaluate technology and balancing immediate revenue-producing opportunities with long-term revenue streams is crucial, as is recognizing opportunities to champion versus projects to reject. It is also important to know how to fund IT projects and manage capital reserves that can be used to support and replace technology as needs warrant.

Finally, a hotel asset manager is involved in a number of contract issues relating to IT. To represent ownership properly, an asset manager must understand the terms of these contracts—from the fundamentals of who is to provide and pay for what to the more sensitive and complex issues, such as system ownership and, above all, data ownership and use.

Effective Implementation

An asset manager must also prepare the organization and its employees to achieve maximum value from the implementation of IT projects. Whatever the objectives of an IT project—from driving revenues to operational improvement to enhanced customer satisfaction—achieving the desired results will depend on the operator's ability to use the technology. An outdated property management system, for example, may have greater value than the latest application because at least management and line employees know how to use the technology. Because of time constraints, lack of focus, and inadequate training, new technologies are often wasted when operators are unable to implement them. As with so many other aspects of his interaction with property management personnel, the asset manager must assume the role of coach, focusing management and line employees on the efficiencies necessary to build value.

Approaches to IT Investment Decisions

Loveman[1] suggests that because business executives are unable to measure IT costs and benefits effectively, they cannot make informed decisions regarding information technology resources and investments—leading, in turn, to misallocated resources and ineffective or unrealized benefits. Unfortunately, the benefits of IT are not always obvious or certain, take years to realize, and are sometimes elusive and plagued by hidden costs, as suggested by the great productivity paradox of hotel industry technology identified by David, Grabski, and Kasavana nearly a decade ago.[2]

In the earlier years of hotel IT, it was relatively simple to quantify and value the contributions resulting from IT applications because a transaction-oriented paradigm that focused almost exclusively on internal efficiencies and productivity gains[3] was used. The analyses conducted were based on simple cost-benefit economics, with the emphasis on transaction-related cost reductions and labor savings. If the savings exceeded the costs, the decision was a "go." Today, however, many IT applications are much more strategic in nature, and much of their value is intangible or more difficult to quantify.

Obviously, the difficulty of knowing the magnitude and timing of the benefits of IT investments is fundamentally at odds with the discounted cash flow (DCF) models that are the asset manager's stock-in-trade to demonstrate that expenditures add value. Moreover, taking the longer-term, strategic view of an expenditure holds little appeal if ownership is a public company driven by quarterly earnings reports or if the objective of ownership, whether public or private, is to maximize short-term operating results and trade the asset. As a result, the asset manager must often contend with a conflict between the owner's vision for a lodging asset and the incumbent operational and marketing needs of a hotel property.

Because technology pervades a firm's value chain,[4] it is difficult—if not impossible—to measure benefits derived from the technology, attribute benefits directly to the technology, or establish causal relationships. Moreover, the study of the impact of IT on firm performance is a difficult and complicated task due to the many confounding variables involved (e.g., organizational structure and organizational processes) and the many sources of extraneous variance.[5] As an industry, we lack effective tools and techniques to address these problems properly. Thus, for the asset manager it is a difficult environment in which to effect change. But as suggested previously, if asset managers, brands, and hotel operators work in the spirit of collaboration rather that confrontation, effective IT initiatives can move forward. When these initiatives are on solid ground, asset managers must then take responsibility for stimulating owners to support the implementation of technology improvements.

In light of the difficulties of building a business case for IT investment, it is not surprising that, when competing for resources and capital, IT often loses out to more tangible and visible projects. For example, one hotel IT executive of a leading international hotel chain reported at an industry workshop how he competed for and lost funding for an IT project to a physical facility upgrade. Senior executives favored marble in guest bathrooms over the IT initiative because the former was viewed as having an immediate and direct impact on the brand's guests. While one cannot defy this logic, it is representative of the emphasis placed on tangibility and the short-term mentality of industry leaders. It is this short-term thinking that fails to capture the long-term strategic potential of IT applications and plagues the development and advancement of IT throughout the industry.

The industry must embrace—and the asset manager must champion—the concept that technology initiatives are more than business developments; they are vehicles for cultural change. The dilemma, however, is that the process of cultural change triggers conflicts between the owner's more global pursuits and the needs of the individual operating unit. Asset managers are potentially in the line of fire between opposing sides. They have a fiduciary responsibility and inherent loyalty to ownership, but they are also aware that the long-term performance and value of an asset may be improved through apparently speculative investment in technology.

Applying the Co-Alignment Principle to IT Decision-Making

Setting priorities and creating investment strategies for IT are difficult processes. Since few formal methodologies exist, these processes are as much art as science, causing many firms to struggle and fail.[6] Financial theory suggests measuring financial returns on a risk and time-adjusted basis;[7] in most cases, firms rely on financial measures such as return on investment (ROI), net present value (NPV), and internal rate of return (IRR). However, more often than not, the financial rationalization fails to capture the complete picture in terms of customer satisfaction, service, quality, employee satisfaction, productivity, or strategic positioning.[8] The principle of co-alignment, depicted in Exhibit 3, offers the asset manager a rigorous

Exhibit 3 The Co-Alignment Principle

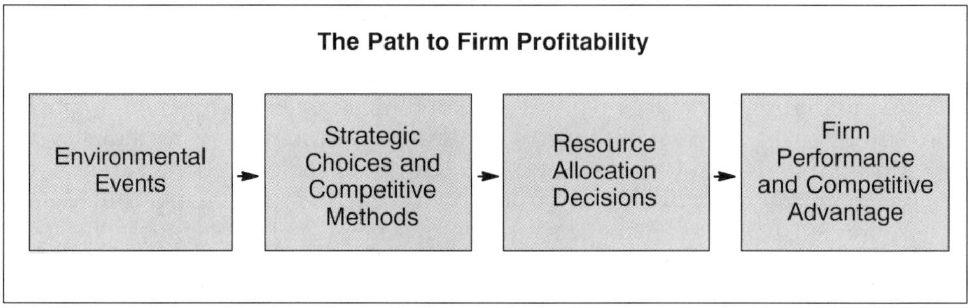

approach to IT decision-making that complements standard financial analyses and assists in making a business case for investments in technology.

Simply stated, the co-alignment principle suggests that if a firm understands the environmental events affecting its business and shaping the future of its industry, plans and develops its strategies so as to exploit these environmental opportunities and minimize any threats, and appropriately allocates and aligns its resources (e.g., people, capital, technology) through *consistent* investment to create product and service offerings, it will outperform industry players and achieve competitive advantage.[9] A well-developed strategy will recognize the opportunities and threats in a firm's external environment and provide an action plan for dealing with them, helping the firm navigate effectively the external forces, position it for the future, and maximize shareholder value, which is usually defined in terms of cash flow per share. Thus, all decisions—or resource allocations—and actions of the firm and its employees should be consistent with this strategy, either enabling it or delivering on it.

Obviously, the co-alignment principle also applies to the alignment of business strategy and IT strategy. These are inseparable and must be developed concurrently. It also implies the alignment of IT, processes, and people. Throughout a firm, the use of IT should reflect that firm's strategic plan. This principle should provide asset managers with a litmus test for all key business decisions, especially those involving IT. Simple questions to ask include: "Is the project aligned with the firm's strategy and long-term goals?" or "How will it help the firm to achieve these?" In short, IT should be an integral part of every business decision, not an afterthought.

The process of achieving this strategic alignment between business strategy and IT strategy is neither simple nor straightforward due to multiple, often conflicting stakeholder perspectives and the lead time and technical expertise typically required to develop and implement IT solutions.[10] Moreover, environmental uncertainty and industry fragmentation, both in terms of hotel ownership and in the IT vendor community, have complicated matters, making it difficult to achieve this alignment. Brand strategy can periodically conflict with a property's strategy or capabilities, particularly from a capital standpoint. Additionally, the lack of suitable technology product offerings sometimes requires hotels to select less-than-optimal solutions to meet even basic business requirements. Finally, the lack of an IT capital reserve can preclude a hotel from fully implementing its strategies.

It falls to the asset manager to recognize these challenges and take action to mitigate them by defining and articulating well-crafted strategies, finding common ground with the governing brand, and setting aside sufficient funds to build an IT replacement reserve. To realize one's strategic goals, one must exercise disciplineing, acting responsibly and in a manner that will produce the desired strategic outcomes.

Criteria for Selecting IT Projects

Why should an asset manager care what criteria are used to select or reject IT projects? Bacon[11] and Farbey *et al*[12] postulate that the criteria used in evaluating and making IT investment decisions are important because they determine which projects are accepted and the level of funding and resources they receive. Moreover, they become instrumental in determining and measuring the overall success and effectiveness of the decisions. The assumption is that the criteria used will ensure that only the *right* projects are accepted, while all others are rejected. These authors suggest the following significant implications regarding the criteria used:

1. The criteria used (or omitted) and the manner in which the criteria selected are used affect the opportunities and projects that are funded or rejected and the pace at which they are adopted.
2. The criteria provide justification and set expectations within the firm for the performance of the application, system, or technology.
3. The criteria provide a basis for comparison and a way to prioritize multiple projects competing for a finite set of resources.
4. The criteria affect how a firm attempts to maximize return on investment and implement any ensuing cost-benefit analysis.
5. The criteria affect how a firm balances multiple stakeholder requirements and needs.
6. The criteria provide a set of measures so a firm can monitor and control a project and judge its degree of success.
7. Evaluation and subsequent measurement and comparison with actual achievements or impact provide a basis for learning that can be factored into future evaluation processes.

More often than not, decisions related to IT tend to be made on an ad hoc basis because of the difficulties in evaluating IT investment decisions and judging their strategic benefits in advance of implementation.[13] In many firms, formal justification procedures simply do not exist, or where they do exist, they are not always followed or enforced. Instead, a project champion is left to determine the approach(es) deemed appropriate and sufficient to gain project approval and funding.[14] Similarly, in setting overall IT budgets, firms tend to use simple approaches, such as developing guidelines based on existing budgets (some percentage of the current year's budget, which is often determined through a series of negotiations between senior executives and IT management) or benchmarking IT expenditures with those of competitors so as to maintain competitive parity. Needless to say, these approaches demonstrate little rigor and may lead to inappropriate or ineffective investment decisions, especially when resources must be allocated to multiple, contending projects and involve large sums of capital.

Allocating Resources

The co-alignment model stresses the importance of consistently allocating firm resources in accordance with the firm's strategy. A useful process and appropriate variables to consider to aid hotel asset managers in their efforts to determine how best to allocate ownership's limited resources are illustrated in Exhibit 4. The process can be just as important as the criteria used because it provides a disciplined, rigorous approach to the analysis of IT investments.

The first step in the process is to identify a need or opportunity for the firm. All decisions must begin with a problem-awareness phase, where the problem to be solved or the need to be met is identified and agreed upon by members of the firm. These needs or opportunities stem from environmental events, competitive threats, and customer, employee, and business needs.

The second step in the decision-making process is problem analysis. During this stage, a hotel firm analyzes the problem at hand; develops a set of functional, technical, and organizational criteria that must be met; determines the sources of input and the participants on the analysis team; and defines and selects the appropriate evaluative tools, techniques, and processes that will be used.

The third stage, the analysis of alternatives, applies the tools, criteria, and processes specified in the preceding step. The evaluation and decision criteria play an important role in the selection of investments or projects and the subsequent allocation of resources.[15] During this phase, each alternative is considered in relation to a hotel firm's strategic priorities and core competencies and compared to the firm's critical success factors, decision criteria, and past history with respect to the technology or application under consideration. The fit between the technology and its application are also assessed. Projected costs, benefits, and risk are analyzed and studied within a defined context of time, namely the firm's planning horizon and the specific timing of the analysis. Finally, an often-overlooked consideration that should be reviewed as part of a detailed risk assessment is an analysis of the opportunity costs. In particular, the costs of forgoing a decision and doing nothing should be considered in addition to the costs of accepting a project.

Lastly, step four yields the selection of choices and the actual resource allocations. Selections and resource allocations are ultimately made by the appropriate decision-makers in the organization based upon their level of authority, the domain(s) affected by the decision, and input provided by the evaluation team. After the selection has been made, it is then necessary to monitor and evaluate the appropriateness and effectiveness of the decision to ensure that a firm's resources are deployed in the most productive manner possible to maximize firm value. The expectation is that a firm will track the benefits realized from its IT and the overall

Exhibit 4 Resource Allocations

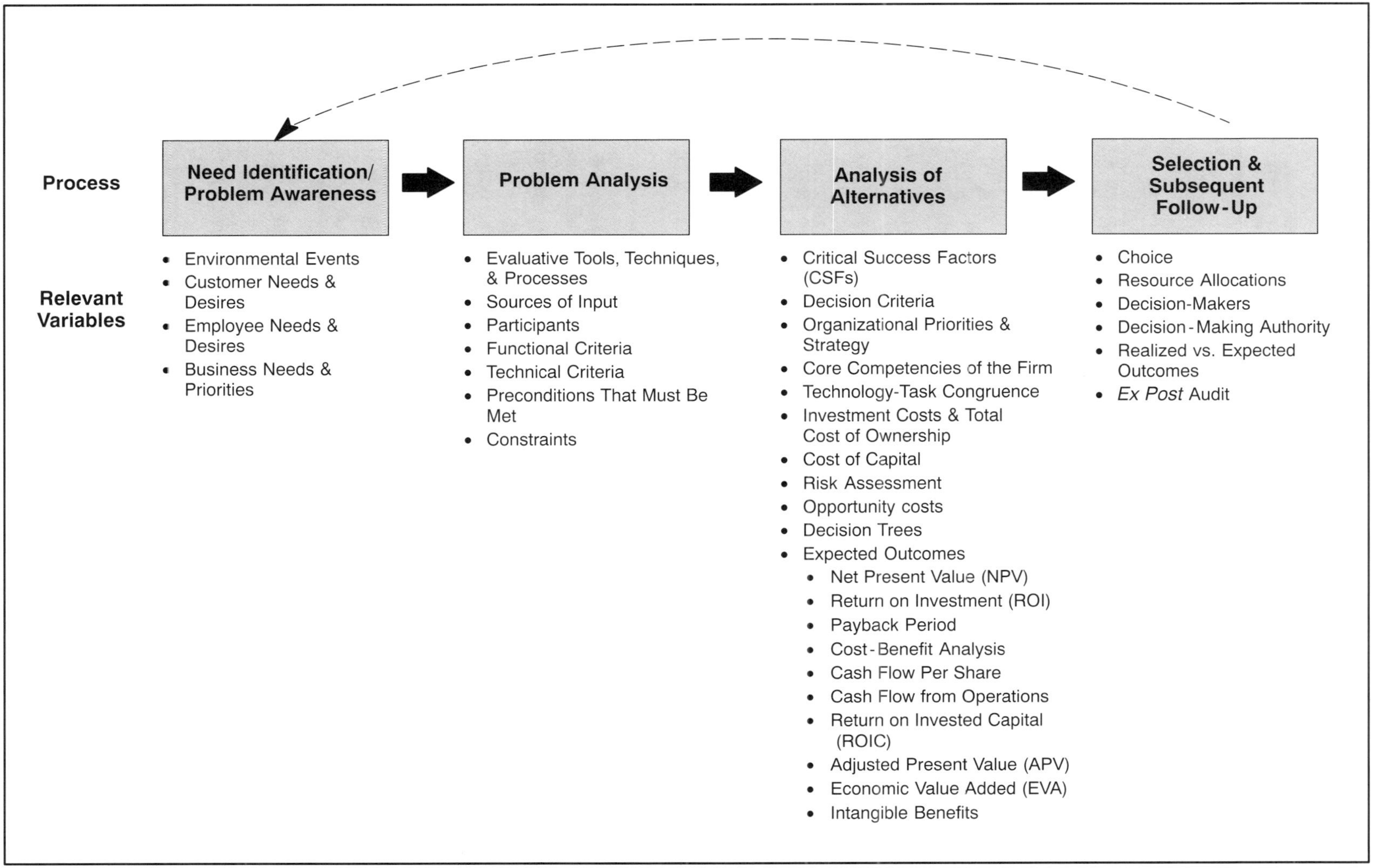

Exhibit 5 Proposed Business Case Structure and Content

1. Executive summary
2. Problem/opportunity statement
3. Project definition and scope
4. Needs analysis and alignment to company strategies and priorities
5. Competitor activity assessment and industry trends analysis
6. Project budget and funding request
7. Key assumptions
8. Cost-benefit analysis, including financial analysis, cash flows, and NPV
9. Risk assessment
10. Alternatives considered
11. Opportunity costs of forgoing a decision
12. Recommendations
13. Project work plan and time line
14. Signatures of approval
15. Appendices (as needed)

impact of its decisions on the firm. This analysis is necessary to track how close a firm's realized strategy came to its intended strategy[16] and how wide the gap is between expected benefits and actual benefits.[17]

This *ex post* evaluation process provides a meaningful source of feedback for process improvement and organizational learning. If necessary, management intervention occurs and adjustments are made as deemed appropriate. In some cases, this may require abandonment and sending the project team back to the drawing board. In other situations, the actions taken will be less drastic and essentially involve tweaking the strategy and the deployment of firm resources. As indicated by the arrow between the last step and the first step, the process is considered cyclical, since a firm will constantly be on the lookout for new opportunities, problems, and organizational needs.

Preparing Business Cases

For each request for capital resources, a detailed business case should be prepared to articulate the business rationale for the proposed investment. To win the desired funding and executive support for opportunities they champion, hotel asset managers must be adept at creating compelling business cases. Similarly, they must be astute when evaluating the business cases made (or not made) when property managers and others within the organization propose expenditures, ensuring the firm is making sound decisions that add value. A proposed structure and content of a business case are defined in Exhibit 5.

Assessing Risk

Because the hotel industry has a less than reassuring track record when it comes to IT and because of the high costs and extensive scopes often found in hotel IT projects, most hotel executives view IT investment decisions as highly risky. To compensate for this, they typically impose intense scrutiny, assess risk premiums, and hold IT projects to higher standards of accountability than they do for other projects in the firm.

Although the definitions of risk are many and broad, there are three common dimensions—project risk, technical risk, and business risk—that are almost always considered. These three risk factors all contribute to a project's success or failure, in terms of a project being on time, within budget, and having the defined functionality.

Project risk pertains to issues of project size, reach, complexity, and schedule. These usually involve project delays, "scope creep," cost overruns, and projects that fail to meet their defined objectives or provide the agreed upon functionality. Risks such as these can be mitigated through disciplined project management, the establishment of frequent project milestones, open communications, well-formed customer relationships, and an effective change management process.

Technical risk addresses issues related to the underlying technology employed in the project, its proven track record (or lack thereof), and system downtime. Technical risk includes a technology's life cycle, stability, reliability, portability, scalability, etc. By employing reliable technologies with proven track records, by hiring skilled staff with expertise in the chosen technologies, and by building in system redundancy wherever possible, these risks can be reduced.

Business risk refers to impact on the business, financial, or other aspects of the enterprise (e.g., reputation) due to system outages or failures. Business risk also includes the firm's ability to recover its investment and realize the expected benefits from the implementation of the IT system or application. Finally, it considers flexibility and the firm's ability to adapt to a changing marketplace. These are typically measured in financial terms or in terms of customer service. Business risk can be addressed in part by strong project management, detailed budget tracking, back-up policies and procedures, contingency plans, and the purchase of insurance.

A firm's IT should be treated as any financial investment portfolio; that is, as a collection of assets that, when managed well, will generate suitable returns on investment.[18] Just as with any financial portfolio, the asset manager must balance the short- and long-term needs of various stakeholders as well as risk and return, while maintaining appropriate levels of investment to achieve ownership's objectives.

Measuring IT's Contributions to the Firm

There is consensus in the literature that no single metric can adequately capture the contributions of IT. Assessing the impact of IT should not rely on a single metric, but instead must look at a composite of measures. Multiple techniques are almost

Exhibit 6 IT Project Selection and Investment Criteria

Category	Measure
Financial Criteria	
Discounted Cash Flow	1. Net Present Value 2. Internal Rate of Return 3. Profitability Index
Other Financial	4. Average/Accounting Rate of Return 5. Payback Method 6. Budgetary Constraint
Management Criteria	7. Support Explicit Business Objectives 8. Support Implicit Business Objectives 9. Response to Competitive Systems 10. Support Management Decision-Making 11. Probability of Achieving Benefits 12. Legal/Government Requirements
Development Criteria	13. Technical/System Requirements 14. Introduce/Learn New Technology 15. Probability of Project Completion

Source: C. James Bacon, "The Use of Decision Criteria in Selecting Information Systems," *MIS Quarterly*, Vol. 16, No. 3 (1992): 338.

always preferred to a single measure because of the richness that can be captured. As depicted in Exhibit 6, Bacon[19] provides a multi-measure framework based on financial, management, and development criteria.

A somewhat contrarian approach to the multi-measure framework favored by so many commentators is advocated by Weill, Olson, and Broadbent.[20] Based on a series of studies across multiple industries, the three researchers conclude that not all IT investment decisions are alike but rather can be defined by five basic categories: strategic, informational, transactional, infrastructural, and threshold. The authors suggest that firms apply a contingency theory approach to decision-making, where the type of investment and the context of the investment determine the criteria to be used in evaluating that investment. As illustrated in Exhibit 7, they posit that there is generally one prevailing measure for each category.

Conclusion

This chapter has focused on the area of IT to provide a set of tools and considerations that will help asset managers better understand, evaluate, and derive value from IT. Investment decisions for IT are typically complex problems involving a

Exhibit 7 A Simplified Approach to IT Investment Analysis

Investment Category	Description	Prevailing Measure(s)
Strategic IT	IT decisions designed to alter a firm's products and services or change the way a firm competes in its industry to create competitive advantage and build market share; the overall objective is to drive sales.	Revenue and market share growth rates to capture long-term goals related to competitive advantage.
Informational IT	IT geared toward the development of a firm's information and communications infrastructure to provide better information in the hands of a firm's decision-makers for managing and controlling the business.	Return on assets to measure medium-term goals for improved decision-making and firm performance.
Transactional IT	IT that supports the firm's operations and typically involves repetitive transactions; the primary foci are cost reduction, productivity, efficiencies, and labor savings.	Indirect labor to capture reductions in labor resulting from the use of IT; productivity and efficiency metrics.
Infrastructural IT	IT that provides the foundation and support infrastructure necessary for shared information technology services and capabilities. The evaluation criteria are typically based on the investment's utilitarian attributes.	Focus tends to emphasize the IT infrastructure's utility, cost savings, and/or [strategic] enabling capabilities. Traditional accounting measures (e.g., NPV, IRR, and payback) are used and often coupled with subjective evaluations.
Threshold IT	IT investment required to compete in a given industry, without which a firm cannot survive; the investment is mandatory or a competitive necessity.	No measure is suggested since the investment is required for a firm to enter, compete, or remain in a marketplace; the investment should be treated as a sunk cost.

Sources: Peter Weill and Margrethe H. Olson, "Managing Investment in Information Technology: Mini Case Examples and Implications," *MIS Quarterly*, Vol. 3, No. 1 (1989): 13–15; Peter Weill, "The Information Technology Payoff: Implications for Investment Appraisal," *Australian Accounting Review* (1991): 4–5; and Peter Weill and Marianne Broadbent, *Leveraging the New Infrastructure: How Market Leaders Capitalize on Information Technology* (Boston: Harvard Business School Press, 1998).

great deal of ambiguity and intangible aspects. They are not straightforward textbook problems, and each project is unique, due to a different set of variables. Thus, IT project evaluation is no simple feat.

IT investment decisions must be carefully weighed in terms of economic and strategic significance to a hotel company. Every attempt should be made to quantify the impact of IT and the financial benefits, and procedures should be established and used to ensure objective evaluation, screening, benefit tracking, and rigor for all relevant variables—quantitative and qualitative.[21] There are no hard-and-fast rules or methodologies that apply to the evaluation of investments in technology. The technology domain is fast moving; conclusions reached today regarding the best methods of analysis run the risk of becoming obsolete as readily as the technology whose acquisition they support. However, asset managers confronted with the difficulty of quantifying the tangible benefits of IT projects can mitigate some of this frustration and uncertainty by employing the approaches discussed in this chapter, including especially the co-alignment principle. If the principle is applied thoughtfully, asset managers will gain confidence that they are consistently allocating resources in accordance with the firm's strategy, thus adding value over the long term.

Endnotes

1. Gary Loveman, "Cash Drain, No Gain," *Computerworld,* November 25, 1991, pp. 69–70, 72.
2. Julie Smith David, Severin Grabski, and Michael Kasavana, "The Productivity Paradox of Hotel-Industry Technology," *Cornell Hotel and Restaurant Administration Quarterly,* Vol. 37, No. 2 (1996): 64–70.
3. Don Tapscott and Art Caston, *Paradigm Shift: The New Promise of Information Technology* (New York: McGraw-Hill, 1993).
4. Michael E. Porter, *Competitive Advantage: Creating and Sustaining Superior Performance* (New York: The Free Press, 1985).
5. See: (a) Carol Hildebrand, "The Nature of Excellence," *CIO (Online),* http://www.cio.com/archive/080197_overview_content.html

   (b) Loveman.

   (c) J. Yannis Bakos, "Dependent Variables for the Study of Firm and Industry-level Impacts of Information Technology," *Proceedings of the Eighth International Conference on Information Systems* (Pittsburgh, Penn., 1987), pp. 10–23.

   (d) Balaji S. Chakravarthy, "Measuring Strategic Performance," *Strategic Management Journal,* Vol. 7 (1986): 437–458.

   (e) William R. King, "Evaluating Strategic Planning Systems," *Strategic Management Journal,* Vol. 4 (1983): 263–277.
6. Miryam Williamson, "Weighing the Nos and Cons," *CIO (Online),* http://www.cio.com/archive/041597_need_content.html
7. Gary Hamel and C. K Prahalad, "Corporate Imagination and Expeditionary Marketing," *Harvard Business Review,* July–August 1991, pp. 81–92.
8. See: (a) Williamson.

(b) Anandhi Bharadwaj and Benn R. Konsynski, "Capturing the Intangibles," *Information Week,* September 22, 1997, pp. 71–73, 75.

9. M. D. Olsen, J. J. West, and E. C. Tse, *Strategic Management in the Hospitality Industry* 2nd ed. (New York: John Wiley & Sons, 1998).

10. Peter Weill and Marianne Broadbent, *Leveraging the New Infrastructure: How Market Leaders Capitalize on Information Technology* (Boston: Harvard Business School Press, 1998).

11. C. James Bacon, "The Use of Decision Criteria in Selecting Information Systems" *MIS Quarterly,* Vol. 16, No. 3 (1992): 335–354.

12. B. Farbey, F. Land, and D. Targett, "Evaluating Investments in IT," *Journal of Information Technology,* Vol. 7 (1992): 109–122.

13. See: (a) Y. L. Antonucci and J. J. Tucker, III, "Responding to Earnings-Related Pressure to Reduce IT Operating and Capital Expenditures," *Information Strategy: The Executive's Journal* (Spring 1998): 6–14.

    (b) E. K. Clemons and B. W. Weber, "Strategic Information Technology Investments: Guidelines for Decision Making," *Journal of Management Information Systems,* Vol. 7, No. 2 (1990): 9–28.

    (c) J. Diebold, "Criteria for Information Technology Investment," *International Journal of Technology Management,* Vol.2, No.5/6 (1987): 583–595.

    (d) Farbey *et al.*

14. Farbey *et al.*

15. See: (a) Bacon.

    (b) Farbey *et al.*

16. Henry Mintzberg, "Patterns in Strategy Formulation," *Management Science,* Vol. 24, No. 9 (1978): 934–948.

17. See: (a) Farbey *et. al.*

    (b) Peter Weill, "The Information Technology Payoff: Implications for Investment Appraisal," *Australian Accounting Review* (1991): 2–11.

18. See: (a) Weill and Broadbent.

    (b) Weill.

    (c) Peter Weill and Margrethe H. Olson, "Managing Investment in Information Technology: Mini Case Examples and Implications," *MIS Quarterly,* Vol. 13, No. 1 (1989): 3–18.

19. Bacon.

20. See: Weill and Olson; Weill; and Weill and Broadbent.

21. Bacon.

13

Quantitative Risk Analysis for Hotel Investors

By Ross Woods

Ross Woods *is Vice President, Hotel Investments with Prudential Real Estate Investors (PREI). He oversees the asset management of a $400 million portfolio of 18 institutional-quality hotels held in both commingled, open-ended separate accounts and single-client accounts. In addition, his responsibilities include the design and implementation of hotel investment strategies, sourcing and negotiating potential acquisitions, management and franchise selection and contract negotiation, due-diligence reviews, and underwriting new acquisitions.*

Before joining PREI, Mr. Woods was a Director of Horwath Asia Pacific, based in Brisbane, Australia. He has over 25 years of experience in hotel investment strategy, investment analysis, real estate transactions, and asset management and has extensively used cutting-edge quantitative decision and risk analysis techniques to maximize returns relative to risks in the acquisition, development, financing, management, and disposition of hotel real estate assets. His current research interests include the strategic implications of hotel real estate cycles on investment decision-making in the lodging industry.

He is a member of the Hospitality Asset Managers Association (HAMA) and the New York Hospitality Council. He has lectured at universities throughout the Asia Pacific region and more recently at New York University. He has a Bachelor of Natural Resources from the University of New England, Australia.

HOTEL ASSET MANAGEMENT IS the process of adding value to a hotel investment during the ownership life cycle using various return maximization and risk minimization strategies in accordance with the investor's objectives. As a consequence, the risk-return tradeoff is one of the most important relationships for the asset manager to understand.

Although both risk and return are acknowledged, our thinking and training emphasize the rate of return. But if the variables affecting the risk-return relationship are more explicitly identified, quantified, and evaluated, more accurate projections can be made of the risk of a hotel investment. The analysis of return necessitates the analysis of risk. The two are inseparable and, as a result, it is essential that investors evaluate both when making investment decisions.

Despite the importance of risk to the success of most hotel investment decisions, it is undoubtedly one of the most difficult of the decision variables to define and quantify. Measures of industry risk remain more subjective and heuristic than objective and quantifiable. Traditional risk-adjustment techniques such as payback period, risk-adjusted discount rates, and risk-adjusted cash flows can be criticized as inadequate because they fail to quantify risk or separate it from the investor's subjective biases and perceptions. More recent techniques, such as sensitivity analysis and best case/worst case analysis, have also been criticized as crude forms of risk analysis because they fail to quantify risk adequately or take into account the probabilities associated with possible outcomes.

This chapter discusses the importance of risk analysis in the hotel investment arena and examines the characteristics of risk. Different types of risk analysis used in the hotel sector are discussed, commencing with traditional methods and concluding with more modern and sophisticated risk analysis techniques, such as Monte Carlo simulations. While the analysis of risk is a valuable tool to assist the asset manager during all stages of the ownership life cycle of a hotel, it is especially important in the acquisition phase, as the risk profile of an investment is largely determined at this critical juncture. The case study presented examines the use of the different risk analysis techniques in the underwriting of a potential hotel investment.

The Importance of Risk Analysis

It is human nature to burden the concept of risk with a negative connotation. But risk simply means that the exact outcome or return is uncertain. Identifying, quantifying, and evaluating risk reduces the opportunity for cognitive errors commonly made in investment decisions. These errors, as outlined by Borge,[1] include estimating error, overconfidence, optimism, complacency, and overcompensation. Assuming a normal distribution can also lead to less-than-optimal decisions.

The decision-making process is sharpened if the investor is armed with more insightful data about the risk profile of a hotel investment. The investor is then positioned to outmaneuver competitors by taking on calculated, reasonable risk rather than assuming unidentified and unnecessary risks. Investors cannot know what the future holds, but they need to be able to make informed, realistic, and justifiable decisions in the face of uncertainty.

Risk must be measured and quantified before it can be correctly integrated into an investment analysis and used to estimate the risk-return tradeoff, the cornerstone of all investment decisions. Only then can asset managers communicate the risk-return relationship to investors, enabling them to make truly informed decisions. As noted by Lord Kelvin, "When you can measure what you are speaking about, and express it in numbers, you know something about it; but when you cannot measure it, when you cannot express it in numbers, your knowledge is of a meager and unsatisfactory kind."[2] Through greater expertise in risk analysis, the hotel investor can arrange the acquisition, operation, and exit from a hotel investment so that returns are increased relative to risks. In a marketplace characterized by a heterogeneous hotel product and relative inefficiencies, better-than-average returns are available to better-than-average hotel investment decision-makers. Buyers who derive the most realistic risk profile for a hotel will have the highest probability of success in hotel investing.

Definition and Nature of Risk

Risk is the uncertainty associated with possible future outcomes. In the context of this chapter, risk is defined as the *chance* or *probability*[3] that the investor will not receive the expected or required rate of return on a hotel investment. The fact that risk inherently involves chance or probability leads directly to a need to describe and deal with uncertainty.

The concept of risk is fundamental to any form of investment analysis in the real estate industry. Indeed, Jaffe and Sirmans contend that, "The real basis of investment analysis is the identification, measurement, and assessment of risk and the ways the investor can deal with risk. This activity is called risk analysis."[4]

Characteristics of Risk

Risk can be categorized as either objective or subjective. If the probabilities are well known and agreed upon, the risk can be termed objective, even though the outcome is uncertain. An example would be an actuarial risk, such as the risk of a fire in a particular type of hotel. Describing the probability that new competitive rooms will be added in a marketplace in three years is more difficult, and represents a subjective risk. Given the same information, one investor may think the odds of additional rooms are 30 percent, while another investor may think the odds are 65 percent. Neither is wrong. Describing a subjective risk is open-ended in the sense that an investor's assessment could be altered using new information or after further study.

Most risks are subjective, and this has important implications for anyone analyzing risk or making hotel investment decisions based on quantitative risk analysis. Moreover, deciding that a scenario is risky requires personal judgment, even for objective risks. Individual investors differ in the amount of risk they are willing to accept. A range of considerations, including wealth, pre-existing risk exposure, cultural background, and subtle psychological factors, influence an individual's risk preferences. Few investors, therefore, have a common attitude toward risk, and this helps to explain the wide variation in required risk-adjusted rates of return observed in the hotel sector.

Another major characteristic relates to the fundamental relationship between risk and return. If a hotel investor wants a higher return, the investor must generally accept more risk. The extra return for a given level of risk is the "risk premium" that is necessary to induce investors to invest their money in a hotel whose cash flows are less certain. The risk premium is also defined as that part of the investment's total return that reflects the level of risk over and above the risk-free rate of return. The risk-free rate is the rate of return that an investor could obtain from a guaranteed investment, such as a U.S. government-backed treasury security.

The analysis of return necessitates the analysis of risk. Both must be quantified before tradeoffs between risk and return can be analyzed. A good hotel investment is one from which the investor expects a high rate of return relative to the level of perceived risk. Clearly, every hotel investor would be interested in investments with a weak—and therefore favorable—relationship between the expected rate of return and the expected level of risk. Over the long run, risk and return are closely

Exhibit 1 Risk-Return Comparison: Hotels vs. Apartments, Retail, Office, and Industrial Real Estate

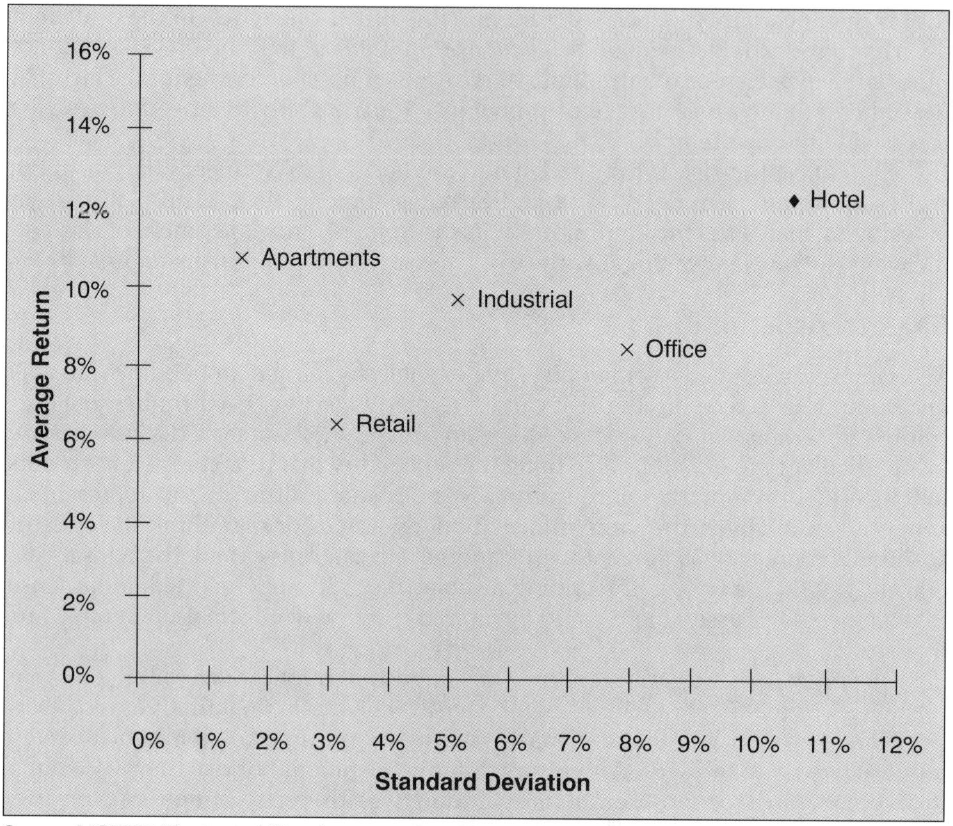

Source: NCREIF (Ten-year rolling four-quarter returns, 1993–2002.)

related; however, in the short run, imbalances often occur, thus enabling astute investors to capitalize on the imperfections or inefficiencies in the marketplace. The relationship between risk and return is borne out in practice by examining the historical returns and risk associated with investments in different property types.

The Risk and Return Relationship

Since 1978, the National Council of Real Estate Investment Fiduciaries (NCREIF) has provided investment performance data[5] on private commercial real estate throughout the United States. The historical relationship between rates of return and risk for different types of real estate asset classes for the ten-year period 1993–2002 is illustrated in Exhibit 1. Hotels represent the asset class with the highest return, and hotels also exhibit the highest risk, as measured by the standard deviation of their returns. A full discussion of the standard deviation and its usefulness as a measure of the dispersion of outcomes is presented later in this chapter, but it is sufficient to note here that a higher standard deviation equates to a wider range of returns, and we would thus term hotels more "volatile" than the other real estate asset classes presented in Exhibit 1. This greater volatility arises in part from hotels' extremely short effective lease terms. The relatively long lease terms for most other property types make cash flows, and therefore investment performance, considerably less volatile. The graph in Exhibit 1 supports the relationship between risk and return: investors receive higher returns for bearing greater risk, with hotel properties representing the high end of the risk-return spectrum.

Measures of Variability

Over the ten-year period from 1993 through 2002, hotels in the NCREIF database generated returns averaging 12.59 percent over rolling four-quarter periods. This compares with 11.11 percent for apartments and 10.12 percent for industrial properties. Does this mean that hotels should be selected over apartment and industrial buildings? Not necessarily. Recall that properties that provide a higher return are normally riskier relative to investments with somewhat lower returns. Risks associated with a particular type of asset serve to induce variability in a property return.

Statistically, 68 percent of the time hotel investors earned returns within one standard deviation of the hotels' average return of 12.59 percent. Since the standard deviation for hotel returns during the period was 10.76 percent, 68 percent of the time investors achieved returns between 1.83 percent and 23.35 percent. A much smaller 12 percent of the hotel returns were negative, compared with four percent for industrial properties. All of the apartment returns were positive over the period.

As shown in Exhibit 2, although the average returns for hotels were higher than both apartments and industrial properties, the range of returns for hotels is greater than for the other property types. The "narrowness" in the range of outcomes for the apartment and industrial classes relative to the outcomes for hotel properties indicates there is lower variance in returns. Lower variance in returns is associated with lower risk. Therefore, by using a statistical measure of variance, such as the standard deviation, risk can be measured for any property type.

The risks associated with hotel investments are more complex than for other types of real estate because the investment is both an operating business and a real estate investment. The less certain an investor is regarding the prospects for a hotel investment, the greater is the perception of risk in making that investment. The more risk associated with a specific investment, the higher the return required to compensate the investor for the uncertainty of the outcome. Risk and expected return are directly related to each other, but they are not always perfectly correlated. The objective is to increase return and reduce risk. If the correlation is weakened, the investor knows that in some cases high rates of return are possible with lesser amounts of risk. To capitalize on these opportunities, it is imperative that the investor be able to quantify risk in measurable terms. The primary task of the asset manager in such circumstances is to identify and evaluate the major factors contributing to expected risk and return, thereby enabling the implementation of specific value-added strategies.

Exhibit 2 Distribution for Apartment, Industrial, and Hotel Annual Returns: 1993–2002

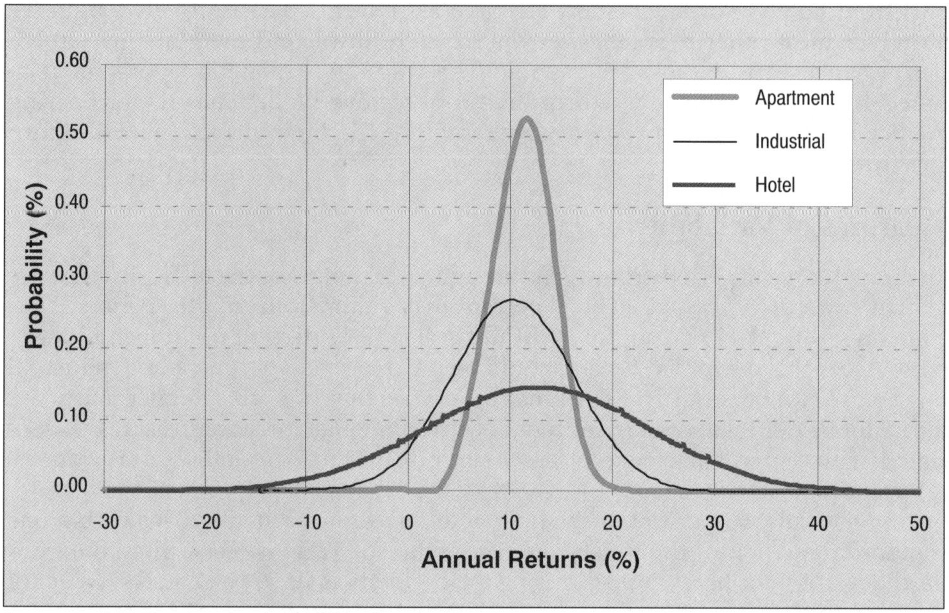

Source: NCREIF and author's calculations

Exhibit 3 Risk, Return, and Correlation Statistics

	Apartment	Industrial	Office	Retail	Hotel	Total
Average Return	11.11%	10.12%	8.79%	7.13%	12.59%	8.82%
Standard Deviation	2.70%	5.78%	8.02%	3.41%	10.76%	5.07%
Correlation w/ Hotel	0.51	0.60	0.64	0.12	1.00	0.55

Source: NCREIF (Ten-year rolling four-quarter returns, 1993–2002.)

Although the emphasis in the present chapter is on measuring the risk of individual lodging assets, it is interesting to note that the same set of NCREIF data demonstrates that hotel investments may offer diversification advantages. As shown in Exhibit 3, hotel sector returns correlate only moderately with apartment and retail returns, suggesting that hotel property investments offer important diversification benefits in portfolios with a heavy concentration of apartment and retail properties.

Types of Risk

The risks associated with hotel investments are usually categorized into business and financial risks. However, many investors further divide risk into other categories such as liquidity risk, purchasing power risk, insurable risk, management risk, interest-rate risk, legislative risk, and so on.[6] Regardless of the system of categorization employed, the investor must first recognize the need for risk analysis and then seek to identify the different outcomes that may occur. Using the information gathered, the investor makes an assessment of the risks and their impact on the expected rate of return by providing an estimate of the magnitudes of the uncertain outcomes and their probabilities. It is important to recognize the need for formal risk analysis and then to classify risk in the early stages of the investment decision-making process.

Business Risk. Business risk is the probability that the hotel investor will not receive the expected or required rate of return on the hotel investment. It is therefore related to unexpected changes in such variables as room occupancy, average daily rate (ADR), departmental and undistributed operating expenses, annual capital expenditures, renovation or refurbishment costs, and market value. Clearly, these business variables can be further disaggregated to identify more precisely the sources of potential risk. For example, room occupancy can be disaggregated into future supply and demand trends, and demand can be broken down into transient, group, contract business, etc. Business risk stems not only from circumstances attributable to the economic environment surrounding the hotel but also from factors internal to the hotel's operation. Management inefficiencies may cause operating expenses to exceed expectations, for example, or may result in an inordinately low occupancy rate. High staff turnover and poorly executed marketing strategies may lead to lower operating income. Any of these events, all internal to the investment, will cause net operating income to fall below the forecast.

Financial Risk. Financial risk is defined as the possibility of not achieving the required rate of return on equity as a result of the hotel's obligation to meet the fixed financial requirements created by debt financing. The variability of possible returns to equity investors is amplified by the use of financial leverage. Increased variability represents additional risk due to the financing decision, and so is part of the financial risk associated with the hotel investment.

Financial risk can be further classified as either internal or external. Internal financial risk relates to the hotel's ability to meet debt service, while external financial risk relates to the investor's ability to raise sufficient funds at a cost that is less than the return from the assets financed by the borrowed capital.

It is advantageous to understand the common categories of risk even though the classification of risk in the hotel industry is not as exact or as sophisticated as it is in other fields of economic activity. By examining different forms of risks, a complex risk environment can be compartmentalized into smaller and more manageable parts, thereby assisting in quantifying the risk associated with a hotel investment. Above all, it is important to know how business risks and financial risks combine to create the aggregate risk profile of a hotel.

Risk Analysis Techniques

In a broad sense, risk analysis is any method—qualitative or quantitative—for assessing the potential impact of risk on investment decisions. Financial risk ratios, such as the debt-service-coverage ratio and the loan-to-value ratio, provide some information about the risk profile of a hotel. While such ratios have become increasingly common and popular for evaluating a hotel's risk profile, they do not provide data about the possible deviations from the most probable values used in the analysis. A full risk analysis provides data on (1) the magnitude of potential deviations that can occur under different business and financial circumstances and (2) the probability associated with each of these deviations.

None of the risk ratios currently being used by the majority of investors to evaluate hotel investments provides this type of data. Most market and financial models used in hotel investment analysis are deterministic; that is, a specific value for each input variable is used. Risk analysis models are said to be probabilistic when the values of uncertain input variables are defined as ranges with associated probability distributions, rather than as single-point estimates.

A variety of techniques has been used to assist in making hotel investment decisions, but the most important is clearly discounted cash flow (DCF) analysis. While a DCF model explicitly considers changes in revenues, expenses, property value over time, equity buildup through loan amortization, transaction costs, expected holding period, and the time value of money, it does not adequately measure risk—the probability that the investor will not receive the expected rate of return on a hotel investment. The comment of Pellat is as apt today as it was in 1972 when he stated: "The contemporary models of real estate analysis all are grossly inadequate and are incapable of generating realistic estimates of the overall rate of return on a real estate investment and the risk of that investment."[7]

A number of methods have been used that allow for the inclusion of the uncertainty dimension as part of the process of hotel investment analysis. As shown in Exhibit 4, these risk analysis techniques may be classified into two categories: intuitive and analytical. Intuitive techniques rely not on detailed analysis of the uncertainties surrounding rates of return, but rather on simple rules of thumb or heuristics. Most are essentially judgmental, relying on a subjective rather than a quantitative assessment of uncertainty. By contrast, analytical techniques involve quantification of the uncertainties surrounding the expected rate of return. Ideally, when returns are uncertain, the investor should quantify the uncertainty and then calculate a risk-adjusted measure of investment return.

It should be noted that risk analysis can be separated into two kinds: individual hotel risk and portfolio risk. Analysis of hotel-specific risk, which is the primary concern of this chapter, evaluates a single hotel and implicitly assumes that the risk coupled with it can be considered independently of the uncertainty in other hotels or other property types. The study of portfolio risk, conversely, notes the interrelations of various hotel investments or other property types. The overall risk profile of a portfolio of diversified hotels with different cyclical characteristics may be significantly less than the average of the individual hotel risks because the counter-cyclical return patterns of some of the hotels in the portfolio have a stabilizing effect. Portfolio risk is briefly addressed later in the chapter, but since asset managers tend to assess risk at the property rather than the portfolio level, the emphasis in the present chapter is on reviewing and evaluating risk analysis techniques for individual lodging assets. Before the more common risk analysis

Exhibit 4 Risk Analysis Techniques

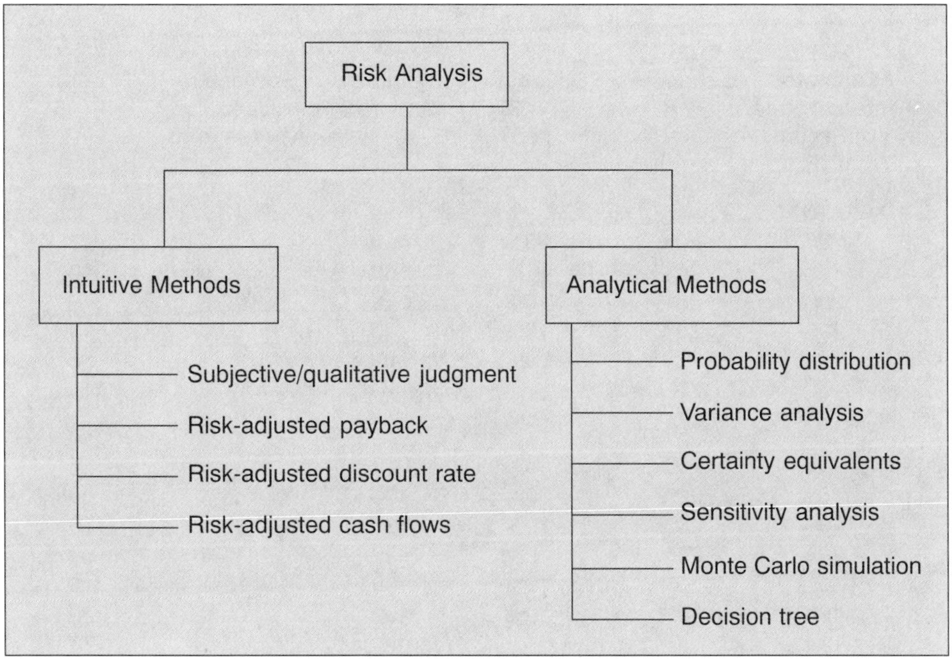

techniques are discussed, let us examine variance, a standard measure of risk introduced earlier, in greater detail using an example.

Measuring Variance and Risk

Determining the statistical variance in returns is a very simple procedure, as demonstrated for Hotels A, B, and C in Exhibit 5. Taking the square root of the variances of 90, 173, and 305 provides the standard deviations of 9.5 percent, 13.1 percent, and 17.5 percent, respectively, for Hotels A, B and C. What does the variance mean? What does the standard deviation mean?

Looking first to the measure of variance, we find that the variation about the mean return for Hotel B of 173 is far greater than Hotel A's, which is only 90, despite the fact that both have the same expected return of 20 percent. This measure of dispersion tells us that the actual return for Hotel A, when compared to Hotel B's return, is more likely to be closer to its expected return of 20 percent. Hence, if variability in returns is a good indicator of risk, then Hotel B is clearly the riskier of the two investments.

If the return distributions for the two hotels expecting a 20 percent internal rate of return (IRR) are normal (i.e., distributed symmetrically in the classic bell curve), the standard deviation of returns for each investment also provides valuable information. The standard deviation defines a specific range over which the actual return for each investment will fall in relation to its expected return. For example, 68 percent of the time Hotel A's actual return will fall within plus or

Exhibit 5 Variance Analysis for Hotels A, B, and C

(1) Estimated Internal Rate of Return (IRR)	(2) Expected IRR	(3) Deviation (1) - (2)	(4) Deviation Squared	(5) Subjective Probability Assessment	(6) Product (4) x (5)
		Hotel A			
0%	20%	-20%	400	10%	40
10%	20%	-10%	100	40%	40
20%	20%	0%	0	40%	0
30%	20%	10%	100	10%	10
			Variance		**90**
			Standard deviation		**9.5%**
		Hotel B			
-10%	20%	-30%	900	5%	45
0%	20%	-20%	400	15%	60
10%	20%	-10%	100	30%	30
20%	20%	0%	0	30%	0
30%	20%	10%	100	15%	15
40%	20%	20%	400	5%	20
			Variance		**173**
			Standard deviation		**13.1%**
		Hotel C			
-20%	25%	-45%	2025	2.5%	51
-10%	25%	-35%	1225	5%	61
0%	25%	-25%	625	10%	63
10%	25%	-15%	225	15%	34
20%	25%	-5%	25	35%	9
30%	25%	5%	25	15%	4
40%	25%	15%	225	10%	23
50%	25%	25%	625	5%	31
60%	25%	35%	1225	2.5%	31
			Variance		**305**
			Standard deviation		**17.5%**

minus one standard deviation of its expected return of 20 percent. Stated alternatively, there is 68 percent probability that the return on Hotel A will fall between 10.5 and 29.5 percent. We can expect its actual return to fall within plus or minus two standard deviations from its expected return approximately 95.5 percent of the time and plus or minus three standard deviations from its expected return approximately 99.7 percent of the time. In contrast, 68 percent of the time the actual return for Hotel B will fall in a much wider range of plus or minus one standard deviation from its expected return of 20 percent, or in a range of 33.1 percent to 6.9 percent.

Not only does this type of analysis provide the investor with a more quantitative measure of potential variance as a proxy for risk, it also provides the basis to develop a measure of risk per unit of expected return. Dividing the standard deviation of the returns by the expected mean return yields a statistic called the coefficient of variation. In the case of Hotel A, the coefficient of variation is 9.5/20 = **0.47**; for Hotel B it is 13.1/20 = **0.65**; and in the case of Hotel C, it is 17.5/25 = **0.70**.

Hotel A clearly has less risk per unit of expected return. Does this mean that Hotel A should be chosen over the other two hotels? If the choice is between Hotel A and Hotel B, the answer is yes because the expected return for both hotels is 20 percent, but there is less risk per unit of return in Hotel A.

If the choice is between Hotel A and Hotel C, the preferred investment is less clear, although many investors are likely to favor Hotel A over C. Unless the coefficient of variation for Hotel C were at least equal to the coefficient computed for Hotel A, there would be a tendency for many investors to select the investment with the lower coefficient of variation. However, as noted earlier, not all investors view risk the same way. For some more aggressive investors, the incremental risk of Hotel C may represent an appropriate tradeoff, given C's higher expected return. On the other hand, more risk-averse investors who feared Hotel C's greater probability of losses would reject it, preferring Hotel A despite its lower expected return.

If we assume an investor requiring an IRR of ten percent is evaluating Hotels A, B, and C, that investor would summarize the risk-return profiles of the three hotels using the probability distributions presented in Exhibit 6. Hotel A has only a 14.6 percent probability of returning less than the investor's required ten percent hurdle rate, whereas Hotels B and C have a 22.3 and a 19.5 percent chance, respectively. Clearly, if the investor is concerned by the downside risk, Hotels B and C are riskier than Hotel A, because there is a higher probability of not achieving the required ten percent IRR. Taking a worst-case approach, the investor might also assess the risk of achieving a negative return from the three hotels. There is less than a two percent chance that Hotel A will yield a negative IRR, while in the case of Hotels B and C there is a 6.4 percent and 7.6 percent chance, respectively. This type of analysis, which permits the investor to evaluate expected investment returns and risk together, is at the core of the probabilistic modeling explored further through the use of a case study.

Case Study: Lodging Industry Risk Analysis Techniques

The following case study is used to illustrate the risk analysis techniques described in the remainder of the chapter. An investor plans to acquire the 210-room Prospect Hotel. The asking price for the full-service property is $26 million. For the sake of simplicity, we will assume an all-equity purchase. After purchasing the hotel, the investor plans to spend $3 million to renovate the property. Based on the projected supply of and demand for hotel rooms in the competitive marketplace and the investor's experience with similar renovations, RevPAR is projected to grow by 14.3 percent in the second year and 10.0 percent in the third year, as illustrated in the pro forma in Exhibit 7. Closing costs are projected at $475,000 and operating

Exhibit 6 Distribution of Projected IRRs for Hotels A, B, and C

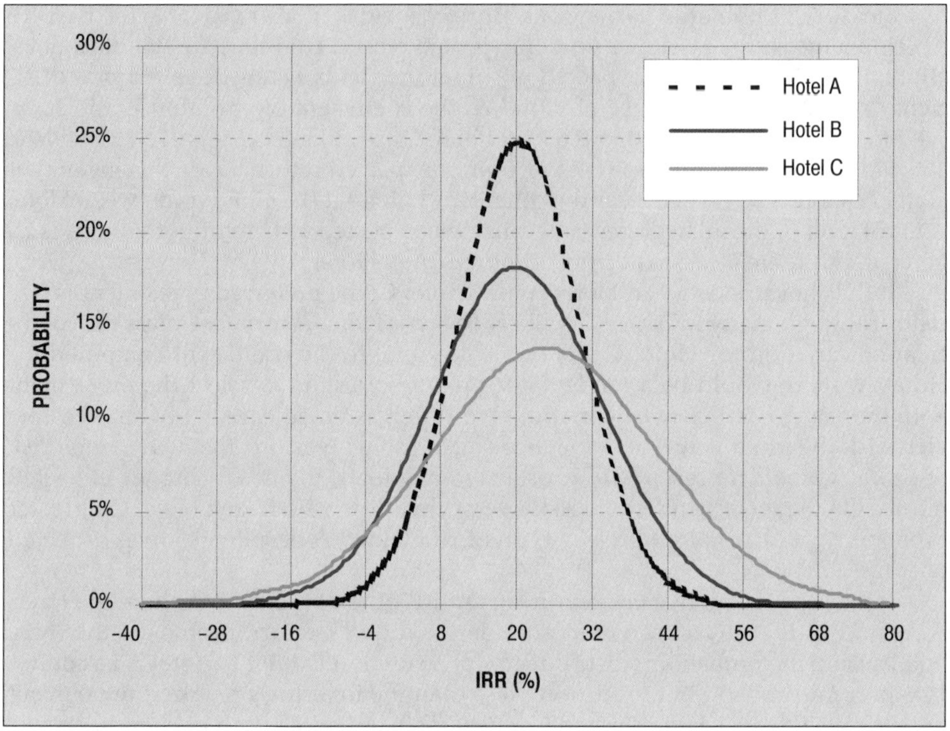

capital is estimated at $158,000. The base-case scenario for the hotel projects a 14.1 percent IRR from the total investment.

Risk-Adjusted Discount Rate

The risk-adjusted discount rate approach attempts to account for risk by adding a premium to the risk-free rate. Most hotel investors deal with risk by using a risk-adjusted discount rate. They hope that the interest rate they use to discount a property's cash flows is appropriate to its likely volatility or risk exposure.

The fundamental problem with using a risk-adjusted rate is finding the appropriate discount rate to use. The rate may be implicit in the market price of a comparable hotel, but finding the appropriate comparable discount rate is incredibly difficult because it is the rate that the market should apply to *equally* risky cash flows. Unfortunately, this rate is unobservable. Moreover, the comparable is priced in an imperfect market, which means that the rate may reflect excess returns as well as risk. Using a comparable's return without quantifying the risks associated with the comparable's cash flow is fraught with problems and is likely to lead to less-than-optimal investment decisions. Despite its shortcomings, this technique is perhaps one of the most common methods used to account for the perceived risk of hotel investments.

Exhibit 7 Prospect Hotel Five-Year Pro Forma Operating Results

Year	2003		2004		2005		2006		2007	
Number of Rooms	210		210		210		210		210	
Rooms Available	76,650		76,650		76,650		76,650		76,650	
Rooms Occupied	49,056		52,889		55,955		55,955		53,655	
% of Occupancy	64.0%		69.0%		73.0%		73.0%		70.0%	
Average Daily Rate	$130.72		$138.57		$144.11		$149.87		$152.12	
%Change ADR	0.0%		6.0%		4.0%		4.0%		1.5%	
REVPAR	$83.66		$95.61		$105.20		$109.41		$106.48	
%Change RevPAR	0.7%	%	14.3%	%	10.0%	%	4.0%	%	-2.7%	%
REVENUE										
Rooms	6,413	69.8%	7,329	66.1%	8,064	66.5%	8,386	66.8%	8,162	66.5%
Food and Beverage Total	2,570	28.0%	3,553	32.0%	3,842	31.7%	3,955	31.5%	3,924	32.0%
Telephone	108	1.2%	105	0.9%	100	0.8%	90	0.7%	77	0.6%
Minor Operating Dept.	92	1.0%	104	0.9%	112	0.9%	115	0.9%	113	0.9%
Rent & Other	0	0.0%	0	0.0%	0	0.0%	0	0.0%	0	0.0%
Total	9,182	100.0%	11,091	100.0%	12,118	100.0%	12,546	100.0%	12,276	100.0%
DEPARTMENTAL PROFITS										
Rooms	4,830	75.3%	5,673	77.4%	6,267	77.7%	6,541	78.0%	6,362	77.9%
Food and Beverage Total	975	38.0%	1,351	38.0%	1,461	38.0%	1,504	38.0%	1,492	38.0%
Telephone	37	34.0%	34	32.1%	29	29.4%	22	24.1%	12	16.1%
Minor Operating Dept.	84	91.3%	95	91.3%	103	91.3%	105	91.3%	103	91.3%
Rent & Other	0	----	0	----	0	----	0	----	0	----
GROSS INCOME	5,926	64.5%	7,153	64.5%	7,860	64.9%	8,172	65.1%	7,970	64.9%
UNDISTRIBUTED OPERATING EXPENSES										
Administrative and General	585	6.4%	597	5.4%	610	5.0%	625	5.0%	641	5.2%
Credit Card Commissions	208	2.3%	252	2.3%	275	2.3%	285	2.3%	279	2.3%
Marketing	697	7.6%	662	6.0%	697	5.7%	718	5.7%	721	5.9%
Franchise Fee	257	2.8%	403	3.6%	443	3.7%	545	4.3%	531	4.3%
Management Fee	275	3.0%	333	3.0%	364	3.0%	376	3.0%	368	3.0%
Property Operations & Maintenance	360	3.9%	429	3.9%	463	3.8%	470	3.7%	482	3.9%
Energy	356	3.9%	371	3.3%	386	3.2%	398	3.2%	407	3.3%
Total	2,739	29.8%	3,047	27.5%	3,238	26.7%	3,417	27.2%	3,428	27.9%
HOUSE PROFIT	3,187	34.7%	4,106	37.0%	4,622	38.1%	4,755	37.9%	4,542	37.0%
FIXED EXPENSES										
Property Taxes	294	3.2%	299	2.7%	306	2.5%	314	2.5%	322	2.6%
Insurance	93	1.0%	95	0.9%	97	0.8%	99	0.8%	102	0.8%
Business License	29	0.3%	29	0.3%	30	0.2%	31	0.2%	32	0.3%
Fixed 2	0	0.0%	0	0.0%	0	0.0%	0	0.0%	0	0.0%
Fixed 3	0	0.0%	0	0.0%	0	0.0%	0	0.0%	0	0.0%
Reserve for Replacement	367	4.0%	444	4.0%	485	4.0%	502	4.0%	491	4.0%
Total	783	8.5%	867	7.8%	918	7.6%	946	7.5%	946	7.7%
NET OPERATING INCOME	2,405	26.2%	3,239	29.2%	3,704	30.6%	3,809	30.4%	3,596	29.3%

Based on our hypothetical investor's perception of the risk associated with the Prospect Hotel and information gleaned from comparable sales, our investor deems that a risk-adjusted discount rate of 16 percent on equity is required. As a consequence, the investor determines that the maximum price he or she can pay for the hotel is $24 million. The investor who rejects the purchase of the Prospect Hotel may have overestimated the likely risks associated with the hotel and may have been too timid about taking reasonable risks that offered reasonable rewards.

Risk-Adjusted Cash Flows

The risk-adjusted cash flows approach deals with risk by reducing a property's forecasted cash flows to some "acceptable" level by increasing projected expenses, reducing projected revenues, or both. If the investor accepts the hotel as a good investment under these circumstances, the investor is tempted to make the purchase because the analysis assumes bad outcomes in every case. Simply using an acceptable level of cash flow tells us nothing about the distribution of possible levels of cash flow; nor does it tell the investor the probability of the acceptable level occurring. Most hotel investors are more likely to adjust the required rate of return than they are to adjust the forecasted cash flows, although some are known to adjust downward the stabilized occupancy and ADR of a property.

To achieve our hypothetical investor's minimum acceptable level of net operating income, occupancy is reduced by five percentage points throughout the projection period, with all other variables remaining the same. Based on the resultant risk-adjusted cash flows, the property returns an IRR of 10.4 percent.

Best Case/Worst Case Analysis

Sometimes called the optimistic-average-pessimistic method, best case/worst case analysis is one of the most commonly used risk analysis techniques in the hotel investment arena. This approach uses spreadsheets to calculate the rate of return using the most likely values as the base-case scenario. However, the resulting scenario gives us no information about how far away the actual return might be from the expected or most likely return. In an attempt to overcome this shortcoming, the investor calculates the rates of return using the most optimistic values (best case) and the most pessimistic values (worst case) for the major risk variables. A best case/worst case analysis for the Prospect Hotel, specifying five risk variables, is presented in Exhibit 8. As can be seen from the exhibit, the best case projects a 17.8 percent return, while the assumptions of the worst-case scenario yield a return of 7.0 percent.

This approach can be criticized on three accounts. First, it does not provide the distribution of possible returns within the range of best case to worst case. The analyst undertaking the analysis usually provides an equidistant best case and worst case result by assuming that the major risk variables are normally distributed, which is rarely the case. Second, the analysis does not identify the probability of either scenario occurring. Third, it is likely to underestimate the total uncertainty due to over-confidence in estimating narrowness of the best case/worst case range—an all too common occurrence in hotel investment analysis.

Exhibit 8 Prospect Summary of Best Case Worst Case Assumptions and Resulting IRRs

Variable	Worst Case	Best Case
Terminal Cap Rate	11%	10%
Renovation Costs	$3.5 Million	$2.8 Million
Occupancy Rate	Drop by 5 percentage points 2003-2007	Increase by 2 percentage points 2003-2007
ADR	Increase by 3% after 2003	Increase by 4% from 2004
Reserve for FFE	Expensed at 5% per year	Expensed at 3% per year
IRR%	7.0%	17.8%

Exhibit 9 Prospect Hotel: Summary of Sensitivity Analysis Variables and Resulting IRRs

VARIABLE	YEAR			
	2004	2005	2006	2007
Occupancy **IRR% 11.6%**	64.7%	65%	66%	67%
ADR Growth **IRR% 12.6%**	3%	3%	3%	3%
Terminal Cap Rate		10% 11%	**IRR: 14.9%** **IRR: 13.4%**	
Renovation Budget		$2.8 million $3.5 million	**IRR: 14.3** **IRR:13.7%**	

Typically, the best case/worst case scenario involves arbitrarily reducing both occupancy and ADR. Rarely are other variables factored into the calculations. The widespread use of the personal computer and electronic spreadsheets in the early 1980s enabled the analyst to move beyond best case/worst case analysis, undertaking sensitivity analysis.

Sensitivity Analysis

"What if?" or sensitivity analysis is the most commonly used risk analysis technique. It reveals the relative sensitivity of returns to different variables by changing one or more of the values for the uncertain variables. For example, how would a lower occupancy rate in the first two years affect the IRR? Assumptions that are typically examined in a sensitivity analysis include growth in RevPAR, stabilized occupancy and ADR, labor expenses, capital expenditures, and the terminal capitalization rate. The table in Exhibit 9 illustrates the final results of a sensitivity analysis for the Prospect Hotel. Among the most important determinants of the investor's IRR were the terminal capitalization rate, the expected occupancy level, the growth rate in ADR, and the cost of the renovation. The table demonstrates the effect of changes in these four variables on the projected IRR.

Although this type of analysis is frequently used in hotel investment decision-making, it has three important limitations. First, if the values selected for the major risk variables are based on the investor's judgment, the resulting returns are likely to be biased. Second, hundreds or thousands of what-if scenarios might be required to create a valid representation of the investment's potential performance. Faced with this problem, most investors simplify the approach and rely on intuition and past experience, which invariably introduces biases. The third problem with sensitivity analysis is that it does not provide the investor with the tangible results needed to justify an investment decision because it does not estimate the distribution of cash flows or investment returns in a formal enough way.

The techniques discussed above all share a serious shortcoming: they do not explicitly quantify risk. They all rely on subjective impressions of risk and the perceptions of the investor. A risk analysis simulation overcomes these shortfalls.

Monte Carlo Simulation

Monte Carlo[8] simulation is a powerful and comprehensive risk analysis technique suitable to the inherent complexity of hotel investments and the range of risk factors likely to affect an investor's return. The technique "attempts to imitate the various ways that all the variables which influence the investor's rate of return could combine as the complex future unfolds."[9] Monte Carlo simulation was developed in the early 1960s; one of its first proponents was David Hertz, whose classic article[10] in the *Harvard Business Review* did much to bring the technique to a wider audience.

Essentially, Monte Carlo simulation involves the use of both probability distributions and random numbers to estimate, with the aid of a computer, a distribution of possible IRRs rather than a single IRR. Starting from a conventional market and financial model, probability distributions for all of the major risk factors are used instead of point estimates. These might include such factors as market-segment growth rates, refurbishment costs, and future changes in supply. Thus, a factor whose value was quite uncertain—for example, a market-segment growth rate—would be modeled by means of a dispersed probability distribution, while a more predictable factor would be modeled by a less dispersed probability distribution. Using a computer, the simulation is generated by drawing a random observation from each probability distribution. The observations are combined to provide a projected net cash flow for each year in the life of the hotel investment. The process is repeated a large number of times to build up not a single IRR, but a distribution of IRRs. The dispersion, or spread of the IRR distribution, reflects the level of uncertainty surrounding the cash flows.

Monte Carlo simulation estimates the probability as well as the magnitude of potential outcomes, thus providing a complete risk analysis. The technique overcomes the limitations of both sensitivity analysis and best case/worst case

Exhibit 10 Probability Distributions Used in Monte Carlo Simulation for Prospect Hotel

Risk Variable	Type of Probability Distribution	Comment
Occupancy (2003-2006)	Normal	
Stabilized Occupancy	Uniform	Minimum 66% Maximum 74%
ADR (2003-2006)	Normal	
Stabilized ADR	Uniform	Minimum $144 Maximum $160
Capital Expenditure	Uniform	Minimum 2% Maximum 6%
Renovation	Triangular	Minimum $2.6 M Most Likely $3 M Maximum $3.6 M
Terminal Cap Rate	Uniform	Minimum 9.75% Maximum 11.25%
Food Sales Per Occupied Room	Normal	Mean $55.13 Standard deviation $5
Room Attendants' Hourly Wage Rate	Normal	Mean $8 Standard deviation $1

analysis. For this reason, Monte Carlo simulation should be the preferred risk analysis technique for hotel investment decisions, since it provides the best possible information on the risk-return profile of a lodging investment. Its use is facilitated by the use of inexpensive add-in programs available for popular spreadsheet packages, such as Microsoft's Excel. Two popular and affordable Monte Carlo spreadsheet add-ins are @RISK and Crystal Ball.[11] Both programs provide the capability of adding distributions to a spreadsheet model and generating Monte Carlo simulations.

Monte Carlo Simulation Illustrated

To illustrate how Monte Carlo simulation can be implemented with relative ease in a spreadsheet, data from the Prospect Hotel case study are used. The initial step is to develop probability distribution functions instead of point estimates for the uncertain variables. Historical or empirical data have been used to derive the probability distributions for all of the risk factors except the cost of renovations. The probability distributions used in the analysis are described in Exhibit 10.

In addition to the normal or bell-shaped distribution, there are many types of probability distributions, each describing a range of possible values and the

Exhibit 11 Prospect Hotel: Comparison of Food Sales Per Occupied Room and Normal Distribution

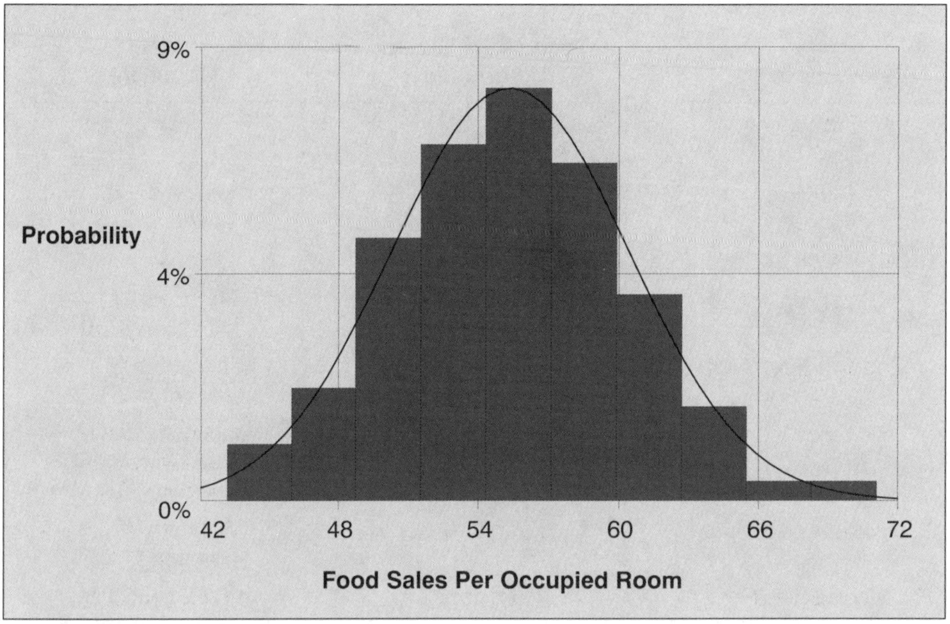

likelihood of their occurrence. As shown in Exhibit 11, the food-sales-per-occupied-room variable for the Prospect Hotel is best described by a normal distribution with a mean of $55.13 and a standard deviation $5.00, meaning that 68 percent of the time food sales per occupied room have been between $50.13 and $60.13.

All types of distributions use a set of arguments to specify a range of actual values and a distribution of probabilities. The simplest non-normal functions are those such as triangular or uniform, which take arguments specifying the minimum, most likely, and maximum possible value for the uncertain input. A uniform distribution requires the analyst to specify the variable's minimum and maximum values. A triangular distribution is often used when actual data are absent. The triangular distribution requires the analyst to specify three points—the minimum, most likely, and maximum values. The probability of occurrence of the minimum and maximum values is zero. The direction of the skew of the triangular distribution is set by the magnitude of the most likely value relative to the minimum and maximum.

The triangular distribution is used to model the uncertainty surrounding the renovation. The most likely renovation cost is $3 million. As shown in Exhibit 10, based on the experience of previous renovations and the uncertainty of local material and labor costs, the minimum renovation cost is set at $2.6 million and the maximum is set at $3.6 million.

The next step is to simulate the possible outcomes based on the distributions of the variables as specified by the analyst and presented in Exhibit 10. The selection of values from the probability distributions is called sampling, and each

Exhibit 12 Distribution of IRRs for the Prospect Hotel

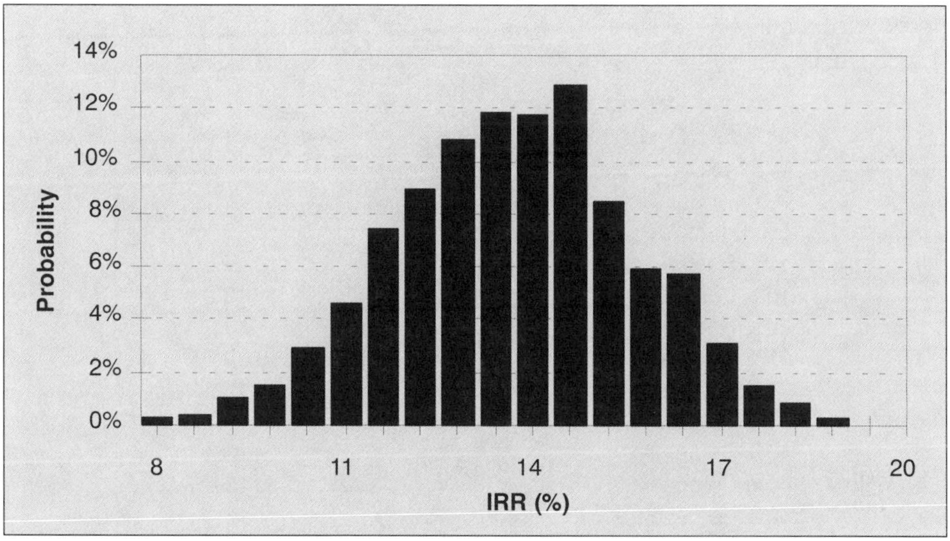

recalculation of the model is called an iteration. For the purpose of this example, one set of simulated results was generated by running one thousand iterations. For each iteration, the computer uses a unique combination of variables randomly chosen from the pre-specified distributions. The model uses multiple sets of random selections to determine the Prospect Hotel's probable rates of return, which are displayed in the probability distribution depicted in Exhibit 12. The histogram, or relative frequency distribution, is a graphic display of the uncertainty inherent in the projected IRRs. The height of each bar represents the probability that the outcome will occur in the range of values occupied by the bar.

In addition to the graphic presentation of the probable rates of return, Monte Carlo simulation software programs typically generate various statistics in tabular form. As shown in Exhibit 13, the statistics for the distribution of the Prospect Hotel's probable IRRs show a minimum value of 7.4 percent, a maximum value of 19.5 percent, and a mean of 14 percent, which is similar to the point estimates derived using traditional approaches to risk analysis. Also presented are other statistics that give additional information about the distribution, including the standard deviation and the most frequently observed value for the IRR, or the mode. Finally, the percentile values are displayed. A percentile value indicates the percentage of the generated results that are less than or equal to the associated value. For example, the 35th percentile value for the IRR, 13.2 percent, means that 35 percent of all outcomes will be less than or equal to 13.2 percent. Conversely, 65 percent of all results will be greater than 13.2 percent. The analysis clearly illustrates the risk-return profile of the hotel and enables the investor to evaluate the expected returns and the risks of the investment.

Most of the add-in programs allow sophisticated analysis of both input distributions and output values. The two most commonly used are sensitivity analyses and scenarios.

Exhibit 13 Distribution Statistics for the Prospect Hotel's IRR

Minimum	7.4%
Maximum	19.5%
Mean	14.0%
Standard Deviation	1.9%
Variance	0.04%
Mode	14.1%
5% Percentile	10.9%
10% Percentile	11.6%
15% Percentile	12.0%
20% Percentile	12.3%
25% Percentile	12.6%
30% Percentile	12.9%
35% Percentile	13.2%
40% Percentile	13.4%
45% Percentile	13.7%
50% Percentile	13.9%
55% Percentile	14.2%
60% Percentile	14.5%
65% Percentile	14.8%
70% Percentile	15.0%
75% Percentile	15.4%
80% Percentile	15.7%
85% Percentile	16.2%
90% Percentile	16.6%
95% Percentile	17.2%

Sensitivity analysis identifies those input variables that have the most impact on the model's output. The results of the sensitivity analysis are displayed as a "tornado" chart (see Exhibit 14), with the longer bars at the top representing the most significant input variables. The sensitivity analysis enables the investor to focus on the more significant risks, saving the time and money that might be expended on the analysis of less important factors.

Note in Exhibit 14 that the input stabilized occupancy is the most important variable in determining the simulation's resultant IRRs. (The sensitivity analysis ranked all the variables that had an impact on IRR, but only the most significant are depicted in Exhibit 14.) The relationship between the input variable and the simulation results is defined by calculating the correlation coefficient for the input variable. Coefficients range from + 1, indicating a perfectly positive correlation, to –1, indicating a perfectly negative correlation. A correlation coefficient of zero indicates the variable is uncorrelated with the model's results. The correlation coefficient for stabilized occupancy is 0.55, indicating that as stabilized occupancy increases, the Prospect Hotel's IRR will improve.

Exhibit 14 Sensitivity of Case Study IRR to Major Risk Variables

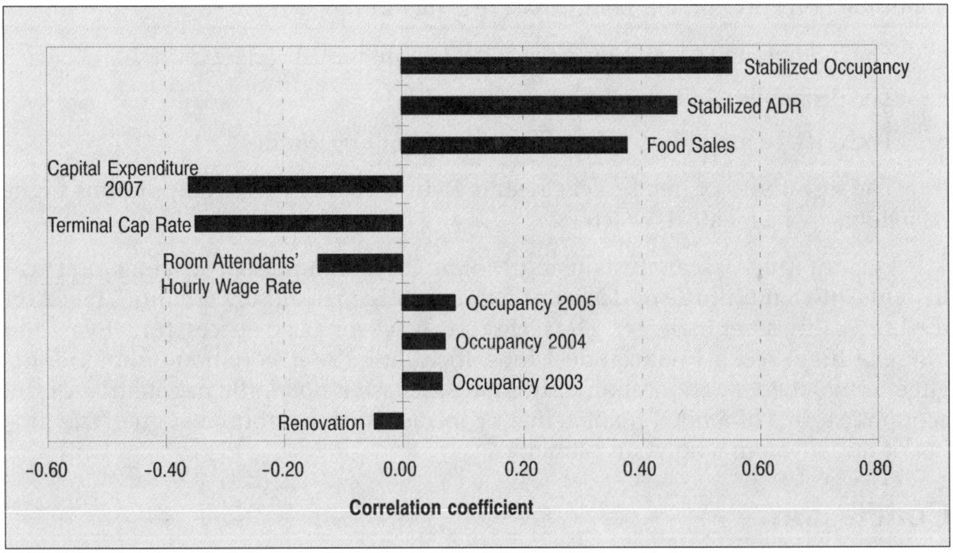

Exhibit 15 Prospect Hotel: Combination of Input Variables to Achieve a 16 Percent IRR

Variable	Percentile	Actual
Stabilized Occupancy	75.2%	72.0%
Stabilized ADR	77.8%	$156.57
Capital Expenditure 2007	29.1%	3.2%
Terminal Cap Rate	24.3%	10.1%
Food Sales	70.1%	$57.95

Scenario analysis determines the input variables that contribute most significantly to achieving the model's results. For example, the investor may use Monte Carlo simulation software to determine the most important variables contributing to an IRR greater than 16 percent for the Prospect Hotel. As shown in Exhibit 15, to realize an IRR of 16 percent, the property needs to achieve a stabilized occupancy of at least 72 percent, a stabilized ADR of at least $156.57, and food sales per occupied room of $57.95. Further, the property may reinvest no more than 3.2 percent of total revenue in capital expenditures and be sold to yield a terminal capitalization rate no higher than 10.1 percent. Although other variables may have *some* impact on the Prospect Hotel's IRR, the analysis identifies the most significant factors that drive the IRR to the 16 percent threshold or higher. Armed with this type of information, the hotel investor is able to focus on the variables identified by the scenario analysis, making "go/no go" investment decisions with confidence that he or she is concentrating on an evaluation of the most pertinent risk factors.

In summary, Monte Carlo simulations provide considerable information about the hotel investment being analyzed, including:

- The likely range of outcomes the investor can realistically expect.
- The probability of exceeding a target result.
- The relative magnitude of various sources of uncertainty.
- The sensitivity of the model's results to uncertainty in each input, thus highlighting the major risk factors.

Quantitative risk analysis using Monte Carlo simulation provides practical insights into a multitude of decision-making problems and uncertainties faced by the hospitality asset manager. The technique has been used successfully in a wide range of hotel-sector financial decisions, including the negotiation of hotel mortgage terms, the valuation of an option to purchase a hotel, the negotiation of the economic terms of a hotel management contract, and the optimization of the timing of the exit from a hotel investment.

Conclusion

Risk is a concept that hotel investors, operators, and lenders associate strongly with the hotel industry. There are many different property types and market segments within the hotel sector, each with its own risk and return characteristics, and each with its own operational characteristics that directly affect the performance of the underlying real estate. For investors who can tolerate the higher volatility of the hotel sector, the best approach to mitigating the many challenges of investing in hotels is to have a focused strategy. The investor's strategy should clearly define not only the expected returns but also the means by which they will be achieved and the potential risk exposure that will be incurred over the investment period. Once these parameters have been defined, quantifiable risk measures can be developed to identify an asset's risk-return tradeoffs. The key to successful investing in the hotel industry is to understand — and, where possible, to reduce — the level of uncertainty about future cash flows. The first and most important step in this process is to identify and quantify the risks associated with the investment. In this way, investors can improve the odds of achieving their return objectives.

Endnotes

1. Dan Borge, *The Book of Risk* (New York: Wiley, 2001), pp. 86–99.
2. William Thomson, Lord Kelvin, *Popular Lectures and Addresses* (London and New York: Macmillan, 1891–1894).
3. *Probability* is defined as *the relative likelihood that a specified event will occur.* Based on experience and other factors, judgments have been made about the foreseeable future. Various possibilities are identified and their relative probabilities are assessed. Therefore, probability, the relative frequency of an expected occurrence, is linked to risk, the identification of events that are unlikely to occur, in the framework of risk analysis.

   Ranges of probability can be determined by at least four methods:

- First, observation and analysis of past events may indicate patterns or measures of relative frequency.
- Second, probability may be determined through controlled experiment and observation, which is the method applied in scientific experiments. In real estate applications, survey research methods may be employed.
- Third, theoretical distributions may be used to establish probability. For example, an investor may infer that the rates of return on a particular type of investment will fall within a given range because of a theoretical relationship between these rates and rates of return in other capital markets.
- Fourth, probability ranges can be based on subjective judgment. When ranges of probability are determined in this way, they should be tested, and all judgments should be evaluated.

4. Austin J. Jaffe and C. F. Sirmans, *Fundamentals of Real Estate Investment*, 2nd ed. (Upper Saddle River, N.J.: Prentice-Hall, 1989), p. 310.
5. NCREIF provides the longest historical record of hotel investment returns, although the sample of properties is quite small, consisting of fewer than ten properties during the early 1980s and from 20 to 30 properties for most of the 1990s. For the charts and tables in this section, rolling four-quarter returns are used to reduce the effect of property-appraisal timing differences on return correlations and standard deviations. NCREIF properties must be revalued at least once a year.
6. A somewhat different approach to risk classification is taken by other authors. See, for example, Allen J. Ostroff and Allen Toman, "Hotel Investment and Risk Analysis," in *Hotel Investments: Issues and Perspectives* (East Lansing, Mich.: Educational Institute of the American Hotel & Motel Association, 1995), pp. 41–52, and Lori E. Raleigh, "Asset Management," in *Hotel Investments: Issues and Perspectives*, 2nd ed. (Lansing, Mich.: Educational Institute of the American Hotel & Motel Association, 1999), pp. 102–103.
7. P. G. K. Pellat, "The Analysis of Real Estate Investments Under Uncertainty," *Journal of Finance*, Vol. 27, No. 2 (1972): 459.
8. The mathematics behind Monte Carlo originated from the Manhattan Project to build the atomic bomb during World War II. The work is largely credited to Stanislaw Ulam, an Austrian-born mathematician, along with computer pioneer John von Neumann. The simulations offered a way of arriving at approximate solutions to troubling problems associated with random neutron diffusion in nuclear material. Ulam named the method "Monte Carlo" after a relative fond of sneaking off to Monaco's casinos.
9. Stephen A. Pyhrr, "A Computer Simulation Model to Measure the Risk in Real Estate Investment," *American Real Estate and Urban Economics Journal*, Vol. 1, No. 1 (1973). 48–78.
10. David B. Hertz, "Risk Analysis in Capital Investment," *Harvard Business Review*, Vol. 42, No. 1 (1964): 95–106.
11. Palisade Corporation (http://www.palisade.com), Newfield, New York, publishes @RISK. Decisioneering, Inc. (http://www.decisioneering.com), Denver, Colorado, publishes Crystal Ball.